ASIAN PEACE

Human Security and Global Governance

Series Editor: Majid Tehranian

Published and forthcoming:

ASIAN PEACE

Security and Governance in the Asia-Pacific Region

Edited by

Majid Tehranian

I.B.Tauris *Publishers*
LONDON • NEW YORK

in association with
The Toda Institute for Global Peace and Policy Research

Published in 1999 by I.B.Tauris & Co Ltd
Victoria House, Bloomsbury Square, London, WC1B 4DZ
175 Fifth Avenue, New York NY 10010
Website:http://www.ibtauris.com
In association with the Toda Institute for Global Peace and Policy Research

In the United States and Canada distributed by St. Martin's Press
175 Fifth Avenue, New York NY 10010

ISBN: 1 86064 469 4

A full CIP record for this book is available from the British Library
A full CIP record for this book is available from the Library of Congress

Library of Congress catalog card: available

Typeset in Baskerville 11/12pt by The Midlands Book Typesetting Co, Loughborough, Leicestershire
Printed and bound in Great Britain by WBC Ltd, Bridgend

Contents

In Fond Memory of

Mahbub ul-Haq (193? – 1998)
A Pioneer in Human Development Studies

and

T. V. Sathyamurthy (1929 – 1999)
A Leader in Development Studies

Contributors

Dayle Bethel is dean and professor of education and anthropology at the International University Learning Center in Kyoto, Japan. His special interest is the role of education in the formation of persons and societies. He has written widely on these subjects, including *Compulsory Schooling and Human Learning: The Moral Failure of Public Education in America and Japan* (1994). Professor Bethel introduced the life and work of Tsunesaburo Makiguchi, a Japanese educator, to the English-speaking world in *Makiguchi, the Value Creator* (1973). This volume and his *Education for Creative Living* (1989), an edited volume of Makiguchi's educational writings, have been translated into several languages. In addition to his writings, Dr. Bethel has been an active participant in movements for holistic educational alternatives, both in Japan and in the United States.

Joseph Camilleri is professor of politics at La Trobe University, Melbourne, where he teaches international relations. He has written widely on foreign policy, international relations theory, and Australia's relations with the rest of the world, including *Civilizations in Crisis: Human Prospects in a Changing World* (1976), *Chinese Foreign Policy: The Maoist Era and Its Aftermath* (1980), *The Australian–New Zealand–U.S. Alliance: Regional Security in the Nuclear Age* (1987), *The End of Sovereignty? Politics in a Shrinking and Fragmented World* (1992), and the recently co-edited *The State in Transition: Re-imagining Political Space* (1995). Professor Camilleri is active on issues of security, disarmament, and arms control and has testified before several government committees. He has traveled extensively and has participated in many national and international conferences on issues of security, disarmament, human rights and political economy. He is a well-known commentator on international affairs. He chairs the editorial committee of the scholarly journal *Pacific Review: Peace, Security and Global Change* and is currently directing a four-year research project, Emerging Asia-Pacific Multilateralism.

Rohan Gunaratna, British Chevening Scholar, Department of International Relations University of St. Andrews, Scotland, United Kingdom, held fellowships in war and peace issues at the universities of Maryland, Notre Dame, and Illinois from 1994 to 1996. He is a council member of the Asia Pacific Peace Research Association, Tokyo; a member of the Regional Centre for Strategic Studies, Colombo; and a visiting fellow of the Institute of Strategic Studies, Islamabad. He served as a consultant to the UN Centre for Disarmament Affairs, USAID, the World Bank, and the United States Institute of Peace. He is a contributor to the *World Terrorism Encyclopedia*, U.S., and *Jane's Global Security Assessments*, U.K. He is the author of six books, including *Sri Lanka's Ethnic Crisis and National Security*.

Wenrong Qian is executive deputy director of the Xinhua Center for World Affairs Studies in Beijing, China. He served as vice-president of Nanjing Mechanical Institute from 1952 to 1964. From 1964 to 1992, he served as editor, correspondent of Xinhua News Agency, managing editor of the regional bureau for the Middle East of Xinhua News Agency in Cairo, and director of the Xinhua News Agency United Nations bureau in New York. He has held his present post since late 1992. He is also a member of the CSCAP China Committee and a council member of the United Nations Association of the People's Republic of China.

Fred W. Riggs is professor emeritus of political science at the University of Hawaii. He has been a visiting scholar at the Institute for Social Studies at the Hague, Massachusetts Institute of Technology, the University of the Philippines, the National Official Training Institute in Korea, City University of New York, and Yale University. He is a past director of the Social Science Research Institute; Arthur F. Bentley Professor of Government, Indiana University; and assistant to the director of the Public Administration Clearing House. He is active in numerous professional societies and is a frequent contributor to journals. Among his recent publications are "Turmoil Among Nations, A Conceptual Essay: Ethnonationalism, Authoritarianism, Anarchy and Democracy" (1996), "Migration and Ethnonationalism" (1996), "Onomatics and Terminology" (1996), and "Para-Modernism and Bureau Power: An Essay Honoring Dwight Waldo" (1996). Professor Riggs received the Dwight Waldo award for lifetime achievements in public administration in 1991. The king of Thailand conferred upon him the Order of the White Elephant in 1986, and he was the first non-Asian to be honored by the Eastern Regional Organization for Public Administration, at the ERORA Conference, Seoul, Korea, 1983.

Florangel Rosario-Braid is the president and executive dean of the Asian Institute of Journalism and chair of the Communication Committee of the UNESCO National Commission of the Philippines. She is a frequent contributor of articles on communication, alternative education, and development issues for professional journals and national dailies and has conducted research on communication, culture, and development. Among her publications are *Communication Strategies for Productivity Improvement; The Philippines at the Crossroads: Some Visions for the Nation; Development Issues: Constitutional Response; Communication and Society;* and *Social Responsibility in Communication Media.* As a member of the 1986 Constitutional Commission, Dr. Rosario-Braid authored provisions on communication, nonformal education, cooperatives, science and technology, and nongovernmental organizations. She is a former senior researcher at the East-West Communication Institute and has taught graduate courses at the University of Hawaii and the University of the Philippines. Dr. Rosario-Braid holds master's and doctoral degrees from Syracuse University. She is a recipient of the Service Award from the College of Education of the University of the Philippines, the Alumni Outstanding Professor Award in Mass Communication, and Women of Distinction Award for Communication.

Amin Saikal is the director of the Center for Middle Eastern and Central Asian Studies and professor of political science at Australian National University, where he teaches and writes about the politics, history, political economy and international relations of the Middle East and Central Asia. He has been a visiting fellow at Princeton University, Cambridge University, and the Institute of Development Studies (University of Sussex), as well as a Rockefeller Foundation Fellow in international relations (1983–1988). He is the author of numerous works on the Middle East, Central Asia, and Russia. His recent work includes "Iran's Foreign Policy 1921–1979" in the *Cambridge History of Iran,* Vol. 7 (1991); (co-author) *Regime Change in Afghanistan: Foreign Intervention and the Politics of Legitimacy* (1991); (co-editor) *Russia in Search of its Future* (1995); (co-editor) *The Middle East: Prospects for Settlement and Stability?* (1995); (editor) *Turkey: A Bridge between East and West* (1996); (co-author) *Security and Security Building in the Indian Ocean Region* (Canberra Papers on Strategy and Defense No. 116 Canberra: Strategic and Defense Studies Center, ANU); and (co-editor) *Lebanon Beyond 2000* (1997).

Johan Saravanamuttu, B. Soc. Sc. (Singapore), M.A. Ph.D. (UBC)
Professor Saravanamuttu is Professor of Political Science at the Universiti Sains Malaysia in Penang where he served as Dean of the School of Social Sciences from 1994–1996. His published works include the first major study of Malaysia's foreign policy (1993). He has also published numerous articles on issues pertaining to regional security, foreign investment, the role of major powers, the Cambodian peace process and the rise of middle class as a factor in politics in journals such as Contemporary Southeast Asia, Journal of Contemporary Asia, Sojourn, Security Dialogue, Interdisciplinary Peace Research, Journal of Oriental Studies and Asian Journal of Political Science and has conducted major researches on questions such as the Cambodian conflict, ASEAN political economy, Japan–Malaysia relations and on ethnic relations and growth of civil society in Malaysia. In 1997, he held the Chair in ASEAN and International Studies in 1997 at the Centre for International Studies, University of Toronto.

Most recent publication: "The Southeast Asian Development Phenomenon Revisited: From Flying Geese to Lame Ducks?", Pacifica Review, Vol.10, No. 2, June 1998, pp, 111–125.

Chaiwat Satha-Anand is the founder and director of the Peace Information Center, Foundation for Democracy and Development Studies and president of the Social Science Association of Thailand. He is also a former vice-rector of Thammasat University, where he now teaches courses on political philosophy and nonviolence. He is a former convenor of the Nonviolence Commission, International Peace Research Association. Professor Satha-Anand is the author of ten books, published both in Thailand and abroad. His most recent publications include *Thailand's Military Budget 1982–1991* (1996, in Thai), *Peace Theory/Cultural Means* (1996, in Thai), and *The Nonviolent Crescent* (1996). He is currently working on a monograph titled *State and Nonviolence*, commissioned by the Thai National Security Council.

T. V. Sathyamurthy (1929-1998) taught politics since 1961. After brief assignments at Indiana University, the University of Singapore, the University of Makerere, and Strathclyde University (1961–1968), he joined the staff of the University of York in England. Professor Sathyamurthy held appointments as special consultant to the director-general of UNESCO (Paris), as professional fellow in politics and sociology at the Christian Michelsens Institute (Bergen), and as visiting professor of politics at universities and institutes in Africa, Latin America, and Asia. He contributed many scholarly articles of general interest. He brought together a four-volume study of Indian politics under the general title *Social Change and Political Discourse in India: Structures of Power, Movements of Resistance* (1994–1996).

Majid Tehranian is professor of international communication at the University of Hawaii and director of the Toda Institute for Global Peace and Policy Research. A political economist by education, he received his bachelor's degree from Dartmouth College and master's and doctoral degrees from Harvard University. He has taught at Oxford, Harvard, Tufts, and Tehran universities. He is a former director of the Iran Communication and Development Institute (Tehran), Communication Research and Planning at UNESCO (Paris), the Matsunaga Institute for Peace at the University of Hawaii (Honolulu), and a trustee of the International Institute of Communications (London). His publications include more than 10 books and numerous articles in scholarly journals, translated into many languages. Tehranian is a global nomad banished to paradise, where he surfs the Net and the Pacific. He can be reached at majid@hawaii.edu.

Teng Teng is the vice-president of the Chinese Academy of Sciences and a member of the standing committee of the National People's Congress of the People's Republic of China. He served as vice-chairman of the executive board of UNESCO from 1989 to 1993. From 1988 to 1992, he was vice-minister of the State Education Commission. He served as vice-president of the Chinese Academy of Sciences and president of Science and Technology University of China from 1986 to 1987. Professor Teng graduated in 1951 from Tsing Hua University, where he served as assistant and lecturer. He began his career as a visiting scholar at Leningrad Technological Institute from 1957 to 1959, then returned to Tsing Hua University, rising from assistant professor to professor, dean of the graduate school, and deputy president.

Haunani-Kay Trask is an indigenous nationalist, political organizer, and poet. She is professor of Hawaiian studies and former director of the Center for Hawaiian Studies at the University of Hawaii. Professor Trask has written three books, including a volume of poetry titled *Light in the Crevice Never Seen*, as well as numerous political essays, including *From a Native Daughter: Colonialism and Sovereignty in Hawaii*. Professor Trask co-produced the award-winning documentary *Act of War: The Overthrow of the Hawaiian Nation* (1993). As a member of Ka Lahui Hawaii, a pro-sovereignty initiative in Hawaii, Professor Trask has represented her nation at the United Nations in Geneva and at various gatherings throughout the Pacific and the Americas.

Preface

This volume is the second in a series of books emerging out of a collaborative international project on Human Security and Global Governance (HUGG). Since 1996, the Toda Institute for Global Peace and Policy Research, in collaboration with other peace and policy research institutes, has engaged a growing number of peace scholars, policymakers, and community leaders in this project. In search of new solutions to the old and emerging problems of human insecurity, the project particularly focuses on those areas most neglected by the international community.

The objectives of the project are fourfold:

1. To focus on how the international community is managing or mismanaging human security problems.
2. To empower the voices that are largely conspicuous by their absence in the international discourse on security and governance.
3. To employ a dialogical method at small international conferences during which representatives from different cultural and epistemic communities can engage each other in a frank and creative problem-solving mode.
4. To promote resolution of protracted conflicts while drawing attention to the root causes of violence in international and domestic life.

Each volume stands on its own while together the series offers students of international affairs a deeper understanding of the role of global governance in enhancing or constraining human security and international peace. The first volume reviewed the past discourses and practices in human security and global governance while identifying the main challenges ahead. This second volume focuses on problems of peace, human security, and governance in the Asia-Pacific region. Volume 3 takes up the problems of nuclear disarmament, the most challenging security problem that the world has faced since the nuclear bombing of Hiroshima and Nagasaki. Future volumes will focus on food and governance in Africa, globalization, employment and quality of life, migration and cultural security, peace and security in West Asia, and democratizing global governance. The project will conclude its first phase with a conference in the year 2000 on Dialogue of Civilizations: A New Peace Agenda for a New Millennium.

In keeping with the Toda Institute's motto, "Dialogue of Civilizations for World Citizenship," the purpose of the HUGG Project is to foster an intercivilizational dialogue on the global governance of human security problems facing the world in the 21st century. Like other conceptual categories such as culture, ethnicity, or nationality, "civilization" is admittedly a fuzzy concept, but we have found it a useful metaphor for approaching the current normative conflicts in the world.

However, a dialogue of civilizations on "human security" and "global governance" raises perplexing questions. The two concepts stand at micro and macro polarities. Whereas human security is concerned with culturally constructed individual welfare conditions, global governance focuses on the more generalized rules of international regimes. To juxtapose these two concepts into a single sweep may be considered too thematically ambitious and methodologically impossible. However, it is a sign of our own era of globalization that the HUGG Project has received considerable scholarly collaboration. Threats to basic human security such as proliferation of weapons of mass destruction, famines, ethnic cleansing, and human-rights violations have already prompted United Nations interventions, albeit awkwardly and haphazardly. It is timely therefore to ask the question: How can the international community intervene responsibly in situations where basic human rights are violated or threats to international peace and security are blatant?

This question cannot be answered in the abstract, but it raises fundamental questions about the conflicts between national sovereignty and global responsibility. It also conjures up fears about undemocratic and unaccountable governance, both domestic and international. Global governance is not global government. Conspicuous by its absence, global government suggests a centralized political system of rule making, rule enforcement, and rule adjudication. By contrast, global governance implies a far more complex, explicit or implicit, evolving system of interlocking unilateral, bilateral, and multilateral body of rules and laws that only partially govern the world. These rules have been primarily focused on matters of international peace and security. But globalization of the world economy and society is increasingly demonstrating the inadequacy of such an approach. It calls for broader considerations of security to include such human rights as political, socioeconomic, cultural, communication, and environmental security. We are at a critical juncture in human history in which the forces of globalization can tip us toward either more humane forms of governance or growing global gaps and ghettoes that will turn the world into islands of riches in oceans of structural poverty, resentment, and violence.

As the world embarks upon a new century, the issues of Human Security and Global Governance are gaining even greater importance and urgency. The topic has focused on the institute's research program on a single most important issue while allowing it the flexibility to broaden and deepen its research program into several different aspects of human security by collaborating with a diversity of peace and policy institutes around the world. Moreover, the Institute's decision to focus on *process* as much as on *outcome* has committed it to the dialogical methods of peace research, education, and action. It has accented the truth of the Gandhian wisdom that there is no way to peace; peace is *the* way. *Satyagraha* (truth seeking through sustained dialogue) is the method.

The Contribution of this Volume

The present volume of essays by a group of distinguished Asia-Pacific peace scholars provides guideposts for the path to regional cooperation, peace, development, and security. It particularly concentrates on regionalization and its linkages with global processes. In chapter 1, Fred Riggs furnishes a historically grounded balance sheet of the costs and benefits of modernity that puts Asian modernization in a larger context. In chapter 2, the late T. V. Sathyamurthy provides an overview of the changing patterns of world and regional politics. He traces these patterns from First, Second, and Third World dynamics of the Cold War era to a far more complex layering of global society in which different regions and social classes are assigned a new unequal role. In chapter 3, Joseph Camilleri focuses on the same set of issues and demonstrates the linkages between globalism and regionalism in the fast-growing Asia-Pacific region as well as the nexus between security and economy. The bad-news–good-news messages of the two lead articles are further amplified by Teng Teng in chapter 4, on problems of environment, equity, and sustainable development, more specifically with respect to the Asia-Pacific region. The following two chapters, by Wenrong Qian and Johan Saravanamuttu, review the APEC and ASEAN models of regional organization for cooperation and development. Each model has its own unique features. As the most successful Asian model of regional organization, ASEAN has provided for mutual security and prosperity of its members. However, APEC has not yet lived long enough to demonstrate what value it has in a vast, heterogeneous, and fast-growing region facing serious conflicts and security problems in the years to come. Chapter 7, by Rohan Guranaratna focuses on the regional conflicts and peacemaking in South Asia. Similarly, Chapters 8 and 9, by Amin Saikal and Florangel Rosario-Braid, provide regional reviews of protracted conflicts and peacemaking efforts in Southwest Asia and the Philippines. Chapter 10, by Haunani-Kay Trask, is a passionate plea on behalf of indigenous peoples of the world who have lost their sovereignty and security under colonialism and neocolonialism. The last two chapters, by Dayle Bethel and Chaiwat Satha-Anand, provide unique perspectives on the Asian philosophical and methodological approaches to peace and security. As reviewed by Bethel, Makiguchi's philosophy of human peace and security provides a road to ecological harmony, democratic education, and political participation. Satha-Anand goes to the central issue by identifying the states as the main sources of domestic and international violence and proposes methods for teaching them nonviolence.

Acknowledgments

This volume is dedicated to the fond memory of two cherished friends and colleagues who were close collaborators with the Toda Institute and its HUGG Project. Mahbub ul-Haq and T. V. Sathyamurthy were both born in the Indian subcontinent before it was torn by religious and political rancor. By the time of their passing in 1998, they were both acknowledged world citizens and pioneering scholars in human security, development, and peace studies.

The publication of this volume would have been impossible without the unfailing support of Daisaku Ikeda, the Institute founder, and Einosuke Akiya, the chairman of the Board of Directors. My colleagues at the Toda Institute, the Board of Directors, and the staff in Tokyo and Honolulu have worked hard beyond the call of duty through thick and thin to bring the project to fruition. They have faithfully provided the logistical support for the international conferences out of which the Toda Institute Book Series is emerging. Without the hard and dedicated work of Misaichi Ueda, Tomosaburo Hirano, Hiromu Yamaguchi, Koichi Taniguchi, Satoko Takahashi, Hauʻoli Busby, Hiroshi Morita, and Aiko Nakao, the Toda Institute would not have been able to conduct its program. Michael E. Macmillan assisted me in the editing of the first two volumes, for which I am grateful. Sincere thanks also are due to the contributors to this volume, who have demonstrated a lifetime of commitment to a just world without wars. The first step on that long and bumpy road is to change the dominant global discourse that often confuses national strength with armament and political domination. If the Toda Institute Book Series contributes to that process, we will be also deeply grateful to our thoughtfully critical readers and reviewers who spread the word.

Majid Tehranian
Honolulu, Hawaii
January 24, 1999

Introduction

Majid Tehranian

The Asia-Pacific region is a vast one stretching all the way from the North and South American West Coast to the Asian landmass. Although a proper definition of Asia should include West and Central Asia, known from Western perspectives as the Near or Middle East, for reasons of economy this volume stretches its coverage only to southwest Asia.

The complexity of this vast region can be best appreciated by a quick reference to the size of its territory and population as well as its political and cultural diversity. The Pacific is the largest ocean, and Asia is the largest and most populated continent in the world. Together, the two cover more than half of the globe's surface and population. In economic diversity, the region includes some of the highest and lowest per capita incomes in the world (United States and Nepal), some of the fastest and slowest growing countries (China and Myanmar), and some of the largest and tiniest economies (United States and Nauru). In political diversity, the region includes old-style communist dictatorships (North Korea), new-style market communism (China and Vietnam), democratic capitalist countries (United States, Canada, Australia, and New Zealand), authoritarian capitalist countries (Singapore and Indonesia), and democratizing capitalist countries (Taiwan, Malaysia, Thailand, and the Philippines). In cultural diversity, few other regions can match the Asia-Pacific in the number of languages, religions, ethnicities, and nationalities. The region also includes seven of the most populous countries in the world (China, India, United States, Indonesia, Russia, Pakistan, and Bangladesh) while containing some of the most sparsely populated island nations in the Pacific.

Regional Imaginaries

In the light of such great diversities, is it justified to speak of the Asia-Pacific as a region? From a postmodernist view, a "region" is conceived in the eye of the beholder. Such spatial configurations as empires, nation-states, and regional groupings are in part acts of political imagination that serve certain hegemonic interests at given times and places. However well founded this point is, it still leaves some material preconditions for regional integration unexamined. Nation-states or regional groupings are often unsuccessful unless there is strong economic, political, and cultural affinity and complementarity among their constituent parts. Witness the breakup of Pakistan into Pakistan and Bangladesh in 1971, due to their geographic, ethnic, and political divisions. The breakup of the Soviet empire in 1991 also suggests the difficulties of keeping widely dispersed and economically incompatible units together.

In a pioneering essay, *Political Community and the North Atlantic Area*, Karl Deutsch (1957) established some useful links between a "security-community" and "peaceful change" that are profoundly relevant to the future of the Asia-Pacific:

A SECURITY-COMMUNITY is a group of people which has become "integrated."

By INTEGRATION we mean the attainment, with a territory, of a "sense of community" and of institutions and practices strong enough and widespread enough to assure, for a long time, dependable expectations of "peaceful change" among its population.

By SENSE OF COMMUNITY we mean a belief on the part of individuals in a group that they have come to agreement on at least one point: that common social problems must and can be resolved by processes of "peaceful change."

By PEACEFUL CHANGE we mean the resolution of social problems, normally by institutionalized procedures, without resort to large-scale physical force.

Deutsch goes on to make another distinction between two types of security-communities: amalgamated and pluralistic:

By AMALGAMATION we mean the formal merger of two or more previously independent units into a single larger unit, with some type of common government after amalgamation. This common government may be unitary or federal. The United States today is an example of the amalgamated type. It became a single governmental unity by the formal merger of several formerly independent units. It has one supreme decision-making center.

The PLURALISTIC security-community, on the other hand, retains the legal independence of separate governments. The combined territory of the United States and Canada is an example of the pluralistic type. Its two separate governmental units form a security-community without being merged. It has two supreme decision-making centers. Where amalgamation occurs without integration, of course a security-community does not exist.

By Deutsch's yardstick, the grandiose claims of a Pacific Community should be considered with a grain of salt. Nevertheless, the Asia-Pacific region has in recent decades made great strides toward regional association, amalgamation, and integration. The region is an example of a pluralistic, amalgamated community. In light of the economic and political crisis of 1997–1998, however, this progress must be weighed against the enormous obstacles that the region still faces in order to become a true security-community.

	Non-Amalgamation	Amalgamation
Integration	Pluralistic Security-Community Example: United States-Canada Norway-Sweden	Amalgamated Security-Community Example: USA
	Integration/Threshold	
Non-Amalgamation	Non-Amalgamated Not Security-Community Example: US-USSR 1917–1989	Amalgamated But Not-Security-Community Example: Hapsburg Empire 1914

Mapping Asia-Pacific Regionalism

Regionalism in international affairs owes itself fundamentally to two main push and pull factors. On the one hand, regional organizations are expressions of a desire for economic, political, and cultural cooperation. On the other hand, they are defensive measures against perceived domination from the outside world. The history of the European Union illustrates this point. Western European countries came together under the visionary leadership of such figures as Jean Monet to build a common future but also to avoid past wars and to defend against the threats of domination from the Soviet Union and the United States.

The history of Asia-Pacific regionalism is no different. During the Cold War, the region was generally under the U.S. nuclear umbrella. Fear of Japanese or Chinese hegemony continues to motivate the less-powerful Asian states to want a U.S. military and economic presence in the region. During the Cold War, as part of the U.S. grand strategy of containment of the Sino-Soviet bloc, bilateral defense treaties with Japan and Taiwan and a multilateral treaty with the South East Asia Treaty Organization (SEATO) provided a cordon sanitaire around the communist bloc. The organization was formed in 1954 to respond to the French defeat in Vietnam. It consisted of Australia, France, Great Britain, New Zealand, Pakistan, the Philippines, Thailand, and the United States. As part of the grand containment strategy, SEATO linked up with ANZUS (Australia, New Zealand, and United States), Central Treaty Organization (CENTO), including Turkey, Iran, and Pakistan, and the North Atlantic Treaty Organization (NATO) in Europe. The war in Vietnam was both the outcome and end of this adversarial and competitive approach to regional and global security. The defeat of the United States in that war proved the futility of such an approach when allied countries were internally torn in civil wars for national liberation and social justice. ANZUS was a casualty of the U.S.–New Zealand conflicts over the presence of nuclear weapons on the visiting ships from the United States. SEATO was dissolved in 1977, as was CENTO after the Iranian Revolution of 1979.

In the meantime, a more indigenous approach to regional security was initiated by four different groups of Asia-Pacific countries, leading to the formation of the Colombo Plan, the South Pacific Forum, the South Asian Association for Regional Cooperation (SAARC), and the Association of South East Asian Nations (ASEAN). Founded in 1950 to promote the development of newly independent Asian member countries, the Colombo Plan has grown from a group of seven Commonwealth nations into an international organization of 24 countries. Although the Plan started initially for a period of six years, it was subsequently extended into a permanent organization. The Plan is multilateral in approach by identifying the common problems of its member states, but it is bilateral in addressing the needs through negotiations between a donor and a recipient country. Member countries are Afghanistan, Australia, Bangladesh, Bhutan, Burma, Cambodia, Fiji, India, Indonesia, Iran, Japan, South Korea, Laos, Malaysia, Maldives, Nepal, New Zealand, Pakistan, Papua New Guinea, Philippines, Singapore, Sri Lanka, Thailand, and the United States.

The South Pacific Forum was formed in 1971 among Australia, the Cook Islands,

Nauru, New Zealand, Tonga, and Western Samoa. The Federated States of Micronesia, Kiribati, Niue, Papua New Guinea, the Republic of Marshall Islands, Solomon Islands, Tuvalu, and Vanuatu joined later. Its achievements consist of the South Pacific Bureau of Economic Cooperation (1973), the South Pacific Regional Trade and Economic Cooperation Agreement (1980), the South Pacific Nuclear-Free Zone Treaty (1985), a Fisheries Treaty with the United States (1987), and a Convention on Fishery and Protection of Marine Resources (1978, 1986, 1989).

SAARC is a regional organization among the countries of the Indian subcontinent, including India, Pakistan, Bangladesh, Sri Lanka, Nepal, and Bhutan. Due to the continuing hostilities between the two main member states, India and Pakistan, the organization so far does not have much to show for itself.

By contrast, ASEAN has proved itself to be the most successful regional organization in Asia. Although it initially came about as a result of political tensions among its founders, it soon turned into a pluralistic and amalgamated security-community extending into social, economic, and cultural cooperation. Indonesia, Malaysia, the Philippines, Singapore, and Thailand formed the organization in 1967. Brunei joined in 1984 and Vietnam in 1995. Myanmar, Cambodia, Laos, and Papua New Guinea have had observer status, but in 1997, Myanmar and Laos were admitted into the ASEAN ranks. The main objectives of ASEAN are to accelerate economic growth, social progress, and cultural development in the region, to promote active collaboration and mutual assistance, to ensure the stability of Southeast Asia, and to maintain close cooperation with existing international regional organizations with similar aims. For the past three decades, the extraordinary rates of economic growth of the ASEAN countries have diffused political tensions among them while deepening their economic dependence on each other and global capitalism.

The end of the Cold War in 1989 and the demise of the Soviet Union in 1991 introduced a new era in world affairs characterized by shifts from national to global capitalism, from bipolarity to multipolarity, and from nationalism to regionalism. The trend from national to global capitalism, or pancapitalism, has been underway since the end of World War II. Transnational corporations (TNCs), mainly from North America and Europe followed by an increasing number of Asian partners, had already paved the way for a global economy. National economies that tried to stand aloof from the pancapitalist nexus of capital markets, technological know-how, and managerial control of patents, prices, raw materials, and consumer markets, have done so at their own risk. The collapse of the communist regimes in Eastern and Central Europe and their new market orientation in Asia signaled the triumph of globalism over nationalism. At the same time, the end of bipolarity introduced a new world political environment in which the United States as the single superpower could now lead the globalist forces toward their goal of a neoliberal regime of capitalist hegemony. Responding in part to the potential threats of a single hegemon, regional groupings also took on new life. The European Community quickly moved toward consolidation into a European Union with a common currency soon to follow. The former republics of the ex-Soviet Union organized themselves into the Commonwealth of Independent States (CIS). The newly independent states of Central Asia and Caucasus joined Iran, Turkey, and Pakistan in a revived regional organization named the Economic Cooperation Organization (ECO). The southern Latin American countries formed MERCOSUR. In recognition of the strong regionalist trends, the United States also moved to organize the North American Free Trade Area (NAFTA) with Canada and Mexico.

Asia was no less caught up in the regionalist impulse. There are a number of nongovernmental Asia-Pacific organizations that consist of academics, business people, and public figures. Among them, the Pacific Economic Cooperation Council somewhat parallels the membership of Asia-Pacific Economic Cooperation (APEC) and often cooperates with it to provide information, liaison, and policy recommendations. Under the leadership of Australia and Japan, the initial idea was to organize an exclusively East Asian and South Pacific regional organization to defend the region against possible domination by the European Union and the U.S.–Canada Free Trade Agreement (Langdon and Job 1997). Vociferous objections by the United States and Canada, however, led to the formation of a more inclusive and open regional association. Asia-Pacific Economic Cooperation was thus formed in 1989 to bring this vast region into an organization of regional cooperation. In 1995, APEC's 18 member economies had a combined gross domestic product of more than $13 trillion, approximately 55 percent of total world income and 46 percent of global trade. With the expected addition of Russia, Vietnam, and Peru, APEC will increase its share of those indices. But APEC so far excludes such other large and important Asian countries as India, Pakistan, and Bangladesh.

The politics of APEC are complex and likely to become more so in the future. The very name of the organization reflects conflict of interests. To avoid any formal organization, APEC was christened, as Australian Foreign Minister Gareth Evans has aptly put it, with "four adjectives in search of a noun." The most basic conflict within APEC is between the more developed (MDCs) and the less developed countries (LDCs). While the United States and its advanced allies have tried to establish a tighter organization with firm rules and objectives toward a more integrated regional economy, the LDCs wish to maintain APEC as a loose, consultative forum while keeping their options open with respect to objectives and deadlines. It was thus a great achievement to arrive at the dates of 2010 for the advanced states to reach the goal of complete liberalization and 2020 as the date for the LDCs to do so. But the collapse of the East Asian economies in 1997 has put those targets into considerable doubt.

From Miracle to Mirage

The ASEAN countries, along with other East Asian tigers (South Korea, Hong Kong, and Taiwan), have more or less followed a Japanese export-driven model of growth. This strategy has been based on state alliance with conglomerates (corporate groups known as *zaibatsu* in prewar Japan, *chaebol* in South Korea, and crony capitalism in the Philippines, Indonesia, Malaysia, and Thailand), capital liberalization, and heavy foreign borrowing combined with loosely regulated and often corrupt financial systems. For a while, this particular cocktail combined with the "Confucian ethics" of education, hard work, and need for achievement, produced what became known as the Asian Miracle.

In 1997, however, the bubble burst. The degree of the economic disaster befalling the Asian tigers cannot be fully appreciated through numbers alone. Nevertheless, the falling numbers are so dramatic that they tell much of the story. East Asia's three decades of growth averaged about 8 percent a year (or 5.5 percent per head). Never before had any economy in the world had sustained such rapid growth for so long. As *The Economist Survey* (March 7, 1998, p. 3) notes, "The four original 'tiger' economies (Hong Kong, Singapore, South Korea and Taiwan) had worked themselves up to developed-country status, and Indonesia, Malaysia and Thailand were catching up fast. There was much talk about an 'Asian century' ahead, when the region's economies would leap ahead of America's and Europe's."

However, having pegged their national currencies to the U.S. dollar, most of the East Asia economies experienced a rapid fall in 1997–1998. As *The Economist* (March 7, 1998, p. 6) explains,

> This proved to be a big mistake. Not only did it encourage foreign currency borrowing, but the pegged exchange rate also prevented central banks from raising interest rates to curb an explosion in domestic credit. Economies therefore overheated, sucking in more imports. Then the dollar started to rise, gaining 50% against the yen between 1995 and 1997 and pulling the Asian currencies with it. As producers became less competitive, export growth slumped and current-account deficits widened.

The fall in the Asian fortunes has been dramatic. As *The Economist Survey* (March 7, 1998, p. 3) reported:

> At its low point, the Indonesian rupiah was more than 80% down against the dollar, and the currencies of Thailand, South Korea, and Malaysia, and the Philippines have all dived by 35–50%. These countries' foreign-debt burdens have therefore swollen alarmingly in local-currency terms. The stockmarkets of all five countries have also seen losses of at least 60% in dollar terms since the start of 1997, and shares in Hong Kong and Singapore too have taken a severe beating. Despite the recovery in share prices this year, in total some $600 billion, the equivalent of two-fifths of the region's GDP, has been wiped off the stockmarkets' value.

Despite the similarity of the downward trends, there are huge differences in the problems and prospects of the East Asian economies. These differences may be attributed to the role of the state, foreign borrowing, and domestic banks in their economies. Hong Kong, Singapore, and Taiwan have had less state intervention, foreign borrowing, greater banking regulation, and consequently stronger currencies. By contrast, South Korea, Thailand, Malaysia, and Indonesia have seen greater state intervention, foreign borrowing, less regulated banks, and consequently more currency collapse. Having emerged in 1986 from a long period of crony capitalism under Marcos, the Philippines did not have a chance to experience the heady growth rates of the other East Asian states nor their collapse.

The Asian model of development as represented by Japan and other East Asian tigers has thus come under increasing scrutiny. Its strengths have long been celebrated, but its weaknesses are less known. The "Confucian ethics" of devotion to family, education, collective responsibility, hard work, and high rates of savings and investment have been considered a major factor in their success. But the incestuous relations between the state and business conglomerates (*zaibatsu,* enterprise groups, or *chaebol*) have now backfired. Developing an industrial policy and coordinating the economy toward low wages, high profits, great international competitiveness, and consequently high exports was considered the supreme virtue of the Asian model. The system performed well for a while, but as banks increasingly indulged in corrupt sweetheart deals, and foreign borrowing outstripped export earnings, financial collapse became unavoidable.

The role of global capital in this fiasco cannot be ignored. As Martin Wolf (1998) has argued, countries must never combine ill-regulated financial systems with capital liberalization. When the Asian tigers were growing fast, foreign banks and investors did not question the governments' corrupt practices, the banking systems' loose controls, or the inflated statistical figures. Seduced by fat profits, they went in and engaged in whatever it took to take part in the bonanza. Nor did the highly paid economists at the World Bank or International Monetary Fund (IMF) predict the crisis and ring the warning bells. The one exception, Paul Krugman (1994) of MIT, who questioned the prevailing myths, did so on grounds of economic laws of gravity rather than mismanagement. Rapid growth in the area, he argued, came about because of heavy investment and high employment rather than productivity gains. As in the case of the Soviet Union, he concluded such growth is not sustainable and will soon come to an end.

Is there, therefore, no bright future for the East Asian economies? Far from it. Sir Donald Tsang (1998), the financial secretary of Hong Kong, has argued that government bonds can free Asia's economy. When banks shrank and stock markets collapsed, overseas investors could not diversify into bonds, because a thriving Asian bond market did not exist. There are structural reasons for this. The international bond market requires government and corporate financial transparency, and that is not what the private and public sectors in Asia have been accustomed to. If the current crisis leads to structural reforms, including democratization and creation of domestic demand, Asia, with its vast resources and population, can continue its climb out of poverty. The strongest of the Asian economies (China, Hong Kong, Singapore, and Taiwan) are already on the right path. But nothing can replace market discipline and democratic accountability for long-term and sustainable economic growth, and those ingredients have for long been absent in some of the Asian economies. If the East Asian countries fail to undertake the necessary political and economic reforms, the current economic recession can last for a very long time. It may even threaten the world economy by exporting the Asian economic flu instead of Asian cheap goods.

How about the role of regional organizations in the current crisis? It is noteworthy that none of the Asian regional organizations has been visible in this crisis. The global economic institutions, the International Monetary Fund and the World Bank, have taken the lead in the rescue operations. This suggests that globalism is still a more powerful trend than regionalism, at least in Asia. There are rumblings of discontent among the Republicans in the U.S. Congress about the use of U.S. taxpayers' billions of dollars to pay off the bad debts of irresponsible Asian governments and corrupt private banks. But the reality of the situation dictates continuing rescue operations by the IMF and the World Bank. The Mexican financial collapse of 1995 is often cited by the Clinton Administration to justify its policies of aid to global capital. Following the IMF rescue operation, Mexico experienced only one year of recession before growth rebounded strongly. Some differences between the Mexican and Asian situations are, however, noteworthy (*The Economist Survey*, March 7, 1998, p. 8). In Mexico, foreign capital inflows were used to finance a consumer-spending spree; in East Asia they went into overinvestment, especially in property. Mexico thus did not face the sharp drop in asset-price deflation that East Asia is now facing. Second, the East Asian economies have a higher domestic debt than Mexico did in 1995. Third, NAFTA gave the Mexican economy a new lease of life at about the same time. Fourth, the Mexican government responded quickly to the IMF structural adjustment measures while the East Asian countries have shown reluctance.

The Future of Regionalism

In this context, greater regional cooperation could be a solution to the East Asian economic crisis. Unlike Mexico and its two neighbors to the north, however, East Asian economies are more competitive than complementary. We may identify at least five distinctly different sets of state interests in the Asia Pacific region. First, we have the advanced industrial states, including the United States, Canada, Australia, and New Zealand. These countries wish to see regional integration advance quickly without much protection for the infant industries of the Asian states. Second, Japan as an Asian pioneer of industrialization stands somewhat between the developed and developing world. With a per capita income of $24,000 in 1991, Japan is the only country in Asia that belongs to the rich countries' club, the Organization of Economic Cooperation and Development (OECD). Its interests are thus primarily global, but accounting for about 40 percent of the Asia-Pacific region's trade, it also has strong interests in regional integration. Third, we have the original four Asian tigers (South Korea, Taiwan, Singapore, and Honk Kong), whose relatively high per capita incomes and disciplined economies put them in a category apart. Fourth, the ASEAN nations have represented a distinct pressure group in regional politics establishing their own ASEAN Free Trade Area (AFTA). Finally, there is China, which now controls the fate of Hong Kong and competes effectively against all of the other developing countries in low wages and production costs.

In regional integration, such an incongruous group of countries compares rather unfavorably with the European Union's relative homogeneity of economic and cultural status. However, there are powerful common interests in political, military, and economic security that have brought the countries of the region together into an open and inclusive regional association with the objectives of promoting military security, political cooperation, trade and investment. Such is the regional venture of APEC. However, APEC, would have to be reinforced by other subregional organizations such as ASEAN to provide a more equal playing field for the smaller and less powerful countries in the region. If the Asian recession leads to a world depression followed by the collapse of pancapitalism and its system of global flows of capital, trade, and investment, a worst-case scenario could pitch fortress America against fortress Europe and fortress East Asia. To prevent such an outcome, the introduction and maintenance of the disciplines of the market as well as democracy are essential to global as well as regional peace, development, and security.

CHAPTER 1

The Malody of Modernity: Some Remedies

Fred W. Riggs

Frequent references to the "End of the Cold War" suggest that the fundamental problematic of the new world (dis)order arises from the collapse of the polarizing pressures of Soviet (communism) and American (capitalism/democracy). No doubt this is part of the story, but it is only part. A deeper historical perspective suggests that the last half-century of tension between the United States and Soviet Union was the final phase of a much deeper struggle between modern empires in which such fundamental issues as those raised by industrialization, democratization, and nationalism (the three main pillars of modernity) provided a focus.

What is unfolding before our eyes is a malady[1] caused by modernity, including the rise, conflicts, and collapse of all the modern empires. The gigantic struggle between the Russian and American superpowers, under the slogans of communism and capitalism, was merely the last phase of the interimperial conflict. In its wake a host of maladies attributable to modernity now manifest themselves throughout the world, most poignantly in the successor states of the great empires, but also in the homelands of these empires. The need for remedies to cope with these maladies is urgent and something will be said about them below, but the relevance and effectiveness of these remedies hinges on a more precise diagnosis than we can secure by making the end of the "Cold War" our starting point. A much deeper historical framework is needed.

The Rise of Modernity

A complete analysis requires a comprehensive look at world history going back several millennia, but a much simpler starting point for present purposes dates back only three or four centuries, perhaps to the Treaty of Westphalia (1648) as a convenient benchmark. Under the terms of that treaty, modern states can be said to have been born in Western Europe, which until then had been peripheral to the great civilizations of the world as they evolved in China, India, and Central and Southwestern Asia. New maritime links to those civilizations and the Americas, which had been opened by the great voyages of discovery that ended the 15th century, were exploited by ambitious kings and merchants relying on mercantilist arrangements and empowered by the enhanced weapons and manufactures produced by industrialization.

Uniquely in world history, three separate but interdependent modern processes unfolded during this period: industrialization, democratization, and nationalization. Some of the modern states that evolved out of these processes created a few vast empires that eventually conquered or marginalized all the great world civilizations as well as many smaller nations of the world. However, conflicts between these empires led to their mutual self-destruction and the loss of their conquests, but the dynamic forces of modernity (industrialism, nationalism, and democracy) had a universal appeal that transformed them into global processes that now also pervade the former colonies reborn as new states.

The collapse of the modern empires also means that we no longer need to fear gigantic interimperial wars such as those that marked the 20th century. However, a new kind of global anarchy and malaise has emerged. It needs to be understood as a late and disastrous phase of modernity. It cannot be understood as the "end of history," a struggle between "civilizations," a universalization of "anarchy," or a new "postmodern" age. Instead, it involves the bitter fruit of modernization, its paramodern consequences, its late-modern manifestations.

It clarifies nothing to speak of a "postmodern" era—the phrase merely begs the question of what will follow modernity. It explains more to see what we are experiencing now as a consequence of modernity, a syndrome rooted in its achievements, a malady to be explained and remedied, but not a stage to be transcended. We cannot simply jettison modernity—it has come to stay. But we need to recognize its untoward progeny, its tragic fruits, and its horrible effects.

The Paramodern

Of course, modernity also brought with it many triumphs of the human spirit, imagination, and enterprise of which we can be justly proud: I think of them as the orthomodern or positive aspects of modernity. From its inception, however, modernity has also created negative symptoms or reactions that we deplore. I refer to them as paramodern. *Para-* is a prefix that can identify the side effects, or harmful consequences, of something, as in paralysis or paradox. It is an error to think of these negative aspects of modernity as though they were merely the residues of premodernity. The nonmodern world lives vigorously today and admittedly has its own bitter harvests. Many ancient problems, however, have been compounded and reshaped by modernity. We cannot, therefore, solve contemporary puzzles by premodern means. Everything that happens in today's world is touched, perhaps contaminated, by the effects of modernity. We need to look fearlessly at all these problems because, as the saying goes, the answer is *us*. We are responsible and we must find the solutions.

The negative consequences of modernity have always accompanied the positive ones, but we have tended to ignore them. It has always been comforting to blame them on the past and to expect that modernity would overcome them. For many moderns, the secret of modernity was problem solving. Little did we think that our solutions might generate worse problems. How discomforting it is to find out that we are the ones responsible for most of the world's ills. They are primarily (though not exclusively) a result of our greatest achievements, and we cannot just brush them aside.

As the world begins a new millennium, it will increasingly confront disasters generated by modernity. Among these paramodern phenomena, the rise of ethnic nationalism is a salient and frightening force, often causing civil strife and genocide (in the name of "ethnic cleansing"). Drug addiction, criminal gangs, and official corruption are also increasing, together with authoritarianism, anarchy, and growing poverty. Ignorance increases with knowledge because the more there is to be known, the greater become the costs of not knowing. We yearn for peace and order and strive for increased security at the personal, local, and global levels. This is not a hopeless cause, but it challenges our best efforts to find viable solutions. By the time we finally realize that world wars caused by imperial rivalries are over, we will discover more pervasive and threatening causes of despair. It will be easy enough to slide into deepening despair as the crises of paramodernity deepen. How can we understand and solve the newly emergent problems of paramodernity?

We must certainly stop looking for villains to blame or for heroes who can rescue us, as in our Superman fantasies. Appealing as such children's stories may be, in the real world we cannot meaningfully dichotomize the world between friends and foes. The real problems we face are inexorably linked to our own greatest achievements. Only when we understand these linkages, their interactive cause/effect relationships, can we learn to intervene in cyclical processes so as to turn vicious circles into benign ones.

A good way to start, I think, is to look separately at each of the main pillars or processes of modernity—industrialism, democracy, and nationalism—and consider how they interact with each other and how each produces harmful effects. No doubt modernity has many other aspects, including all its intellectual and perceptual concomitants, including such values as individualism, secularism, acquisitiveness, curiosity, and community spirit. Unfortunately, I cannot discuss these matters here. They deserve separate attention and equal weight, but here I intend to focus on three basic modern processes. Their positive (orthomodern) consequences are well known and need little comment here, but their negative (paramodern) effects are rarely discussed. I shall focus on them here.

Industrialism

The three processes of modernity are interdependent and equally important. Like the three legs of a stool, each is as important as the others. Each stands alone, yet each is linked to the others. Each has its own history—its own causes and consequences—yet each depends upon the others for its successes. Although we cannot understand each process without taking the other two into account, we cannot start by looking at all three simultaneously. Each becomes easier to understand when it is considered independently and then linked with the others.

The easiest one to start with is industrialism. Fortunately, the main features of the Industrial Revolution are well known and have been frequently described. However, several points need to be emphasized here to pave the way for an understanding of the paramodern consequences of industrialism.

First, it is important to distinguish between industrialism and capitalism. Capitalism is much older than industrialism. There have been traders, merchants, and small city states governed by them for several thousand years. Politically, however, capitalists were always marginalized by kings and emperors, nobles and landowners, churches and priests. As "middle-men" they existed on the fringes of power, tolerated and even patronized by ruling groups who coveted the good things they could provide but never empowered enough to secure their property and to protect their inventions.

Industrialism, by contrast, requires security of investments, expensive factories, reliable sources of raw materials and inanimate energy, access to markets and large supplies of capital, trained and efficient managers and engineers, complex technologies that are very hard to invent and produce, long-distance facilities for transportation and communication. Capitalists could not create or maintain these infrastructures by themselves. They required the administrative and political support of states whose rulers were willing and able to guarantee them and also to regulate market institutions so as to prevent the self-destructive fires of capitalist competition that quickly destroy any uncontrolled open-market system.

State support for industrialization could be explained in part by the growing power of the bourgeoisie, especially because of their coordinated control over the growing revenues produced by industrialization. The power to tax is always counterbalanced by the power of taxpayers able to exact a price for their cooperation. Moreover, industrial exports could also finance the importation of highly valued pre-industrial products from the great civilizations of the world, an obvious benefit enjoyed by all the privileged classes whose support the industrialists required in order to achieve the industrial revolution.

No doubt, the Industrial Revolution was driven by the energy and inventiveness of capitalists without whose creativity and entrepreneurship it could never have occurred. Subsequently, however, industrialization anywhere could be managed by the state without reliance on capitalists. In countries where capitalists have lost their power—or never even developed as a power-holding class—citizens of all classes have acquired a taste for industrial products: trains, automobiles, airplanes, telephones, radio and television, computers, air conditioners, vacuum cleaners, and a host of everyday products from soap to cotton to thermos bottles. The products of industrialism can be made by state or private enterprises. Consequently, after industrialization has evolved, capitalism is no longer necessary, although, no doubt, it makes productivity easier to achieve.

The beneficial aspects of industrialization are continuously celebrated, but they have always been unequally distributed. The production and use of machine-made products belongs to the positive (orthomodern) aspect of modernity, but inequality and poverty exemplify the negative (paramodern) results. A sense of injustice and oppression, therefore, is a ubiquitous consequence of industrialization. It struck first in the European homelands, generating radical political movements and, eventually, single-party dictatorships and genocide on a large scale. As the great industrial powers expanded their empires, more and more victims of inequality appeared, ranging from the African slaves on American plantations who supplied cotton for the new factories to the contract laborers who mined for coal and iron and manned the rubber plantations and paper mills that provided raw materials and energy for increasingly voracious enterprises. Industrialism also produced sabotage, the anti-industrial protests of workers, symbolized by the delusions of alienated proletarians who tried to stop the machines by using their wooden shoes as weapons.

Delusions

The quest for independence, which liberated the imperial possessions at a time when the capacity of the empires to maintain effective control over these possessions had been undermined by interimperial warfare, was also fueled by delusions. A "cargo cult" mentality proliferated on the basis of expectations that, magically, independence would create industrial productivity: Giant planes would emerge from the sky loaded with goodies to be made freely available to everyone. Increasingly, the political elites in all the new states expected to enjoy the benefits of industrialization, even if they were unable to manage the enterprises or produce the goods required to provide them.

Unfortunately, most people reduce industrialism to capitalism as though having an unregulated open market powered by the greed for wealth of individual entrepreneurs would produce universal prosperity. Foreign capitalists thought that free trade and open markets would permit unlimited growth in all countries, and domestic capitalists claimed the right to exploit property without limits as the road to development for all. Historically, industrialization required a partnership between open-market institutions and the state—neither by itself could have brought about the industrial revolution. Subsequently, states can industrialize by themselves, but only within limits—eventually they will self-destruct. Capitalists working without state controls and infrastructure will surely destroy themselves. Industrialization really works, I think, only when a partnership prevails between the state and capitalism.

The Vortex

To see why this must be so, consider that everyone is gradually sucked into the vortex of industrialism. The poorest citizens find that they can no longer support themselves on a subsistence basis as they formerly could. Marketization has not only made them increasingly dependent on cheap manufactures they cannot afford to buy without abandoning subsistence production in order to produce cash crops or manufactured goods they cannot consume. When they fail to earn enough cash to pay for the goods they have learned to need, they may borrow money and put themselves into desperate straits as indebted peons. In pre-industrial contexts, peasants and serfs were no doubt poor and oppressed, but their sense of injustice was ameliorated by beliefs that blamed supernatural forces rather than human enemies. Their survival needs were met by subsistence production and they were scarcely aware of the inconspicuous luxury enjoyed by their oppressors, making their penury easier to bear.

By contrast, industrialization makes everyone aware of the conspicuous consumption available to rich people, who, they feel, have enriched themselves unjustly. Thus the orthomodern results of industrialization enhance the gratifications available to increasingly affluent upper classes around the world, while the paramodern consequences of industrialization add to the burdens and sense of injustice experienced by rapidly expanding lower classes. Although capitalists are often blamed by reformers as the enemy, the truth is that industrialism, whether under communist dictatorships or free-enterprise democracy, generates both inequities and hardships and also great benefits for humanity.

Industrialism has many more side effects linking positive and negative consequences that I cannot discuss here, but consider the following items:

- Industrialism has supported the growth of scientific knowledge that improved public health, increased life expectancy, and reduced infant mortality, while also accelerating the growth of human populations, creating a demographic explosion that has fearsome consequences for the whole world.
- The environmental degradation caused by industrialization reduces the productive capabilities of the earth and intensifies the miseries experienced not only by its poorest inhabitants but even by affluent people.
- The technology of lethal weapons produced by industrial processes has enhanced the security of some states and individuals, but it has also made warfare between states more deadly, empowered modern empires to conquer most of the world, made illegal gangs more pestilent, and strengthened ethnopolitical and revolutionary movements.
- Modern communications and transportation technologies have enhanced the quality of life for billions of people, but they have

also helped the enemies of states and communities to coordinate their activities and cause escalating disasters.

● Organizational and bureaucratic technologies not only permit modern states and nongovernmental organizations to operate more effectively, but they also enable antisocial groups to carry out their plots more efficiently.

The cumulative impact of these paramodern effects of industrialization strikes most ferociously at those newly liberated states that cannot, in fact, organize themselves to manage industrial enterprises humanely or to promote exports effectively so as to pay for desired imports. They cannot meet the legitimate expectations of their citizens when anarchic conditions increase and warlordism or ethnonational strife escalates. Thus the miseries experienced by the world's poorest people are increased by industrialization. The paramodern effects of industrialization also hit the richest countries, but we need not say more: industrialization is clearly a mixed blessing that carries tremendous costs as well as benefits for the whole world.

Democracy

The transfer of sovereignty from kings to citizens was eagerly supported in the West by capitalist (bourgeois) forces eager to stabilize the socioeconomic transformations that protected their industrial projects. It also appealed, however, to many other social strata who saw that governments responsive to their interests would help them more than monarchic authoritarianism, especially after secularism had undermined the sacred foundations of kingship. Among the additional benefits they could expect was the increased availability of the goods and services produced by industrialization plus the prized pre-industrial manufactures of non-Western countries that could now be purchased in exchange for cheap exports. Democratization, therefore, was both a cause and a result of industrialization.

The core institution in all modern democracies has been a representative system centering in an assembly whose members were elected by open procedures that enabled citizens to choose persons who would formulate and legitimize public policies and also control the administrative apparatus of governance, its bureaucracy. I have discussed the processes and options involved in this process elsewhere (Riggs 1969, 1997a) and I shall not repeat myself here. However, let me draw attention to the paramodern aspects of democratization. To highlight this point, consider the fundamental distinction between citizens and subjects.

8

Under monarchic rule, there were no citizens. Everyone under the authority of a king or emperor was a subject. When representative government replaced royal authority, the general expectation was that all subjects would become citizens. In practice, however, only some subjects were actually represented. The rest remained subjects because they could not or would not vote or because the assembly could not exercise decisive power over the governing authorities, that is, the bureaucracy and the chief executive. As a result, virtually all so-called democracies have, in fact, been oligarchic democracies, oligocracies as I prefer to call them. In practice, the ratio of citizens to subjects in an oligocracy is variable, but the use of this term compels us to ask about the subjects in any modern state—how many are there, why are they not citizens, and what are the consequences for them?

In principle, the subjects of an oligocracy are worse off than the subjects of a monarchy. At least, under kingly rule, all subjects are equally benefited or oppressed by their rulers—and by the supernatural forces they believed the rites and royal ceremonies could generate. The secularization of legitimacy that accompanied democratization deprived everyone of the comfort that belief in supernatural forces once afforded all the subjects of a king. Unfortunately, while citizens gained by this exchange, subjects lost. In principle, at least, citizens are able, through their representatives in an elected assembly, to improve their prospects in life. However, subjects in a democracy lose the comfort their traditional trust in divine protection gave them but fail to secure the benefits popular representation could promise to voting citizens.

No doubt there are always variations in any oligocracy among its subjects, some of whom are better treated while others are oppressed more brutally. In the American case, the Constitution of 1789 viewed slaves not only as subjects but even depersonalized them as items of property rather than as human beings. Although women were also subjects under this constitution, family solidarity meant that the wives and daughters of leading citizens were often well treated, especially when norms of "chivalry" persisted, but most women suffered oppression based on their gender.

Because of property (and literacy) qualifications, poor people were not enfranchised and also remained subjects. No doubt the emancipation of slaves (as recently implemented by civil-rights legislation) has given de jure (if not always de facto) citizens' rights to African-Americans, and feminist movements have transformed women subjects into citizens. Even so, the American republic

9

remains an oligocracy in which large numbers of citizens fail to vote. They may be viewed as de jure citizens but de facto subjects. Their concerns can easily be ignored by the representatives of voting citizens in American legislative bodies.

Most countries that call themselves democracies have, I believe, failed to transform many subjects into citizens, and, therefore, they are really oligocracies, not democracies. In the present-day world as a whole, therefore, the great majority of people remain subjects in oligocracies and, of course, in quite a few new states—the successor states of the modern empires—authoritarian rule means that virtually all residents are subjects, not citizens. For them, the bitter fruit of paramodernity is greater misery.

Imperialism

Although we normally attribute modern imperialism to industrialism, it also has a close link to democracy. An important rationalization for modern imperialism (but not of traditional imperialism) was the democratic myth that worked at two levels: it rationalized conquests in the name of democracy by claims that conquered peoples would, after a period of tutelage, be given democratic rights; and more importantly, it created expectations in the minds of conquered peoples that were, of course, falsified by imperial practice. Ultimately, however, these expectations helped drive the liberation movements whose ambitious leaders were able to use democratic hopes to help mobilize the popular support they needed.

In all modern empires, the conquered peoples became the subjects of an oligocracy. Rarely, under special circumstances, a few were enfranchised as citizens, most notably in overseas France. Ironically, therefore, while the number of subjects transformed into citizens increased in the homelands of the modern empires, the number who became subjects under imperial domination escalated. Books on the political institutions of modern empires typically focus on how their citizens participate in representative institutions but ignore the way their subjects are excluded. Thus the orthomodern dimensions of democratization are stressed while its paramodern aspects are ignored.

Not surprisingly, the subjects of any oligocracy are not deceived— the more they learn about the benefits of citizenship, the more their anger and sense of injustice grows. Any text that extols the virtues of a modern democracy may enlist the patriotic support of its citizens, but, simultaneously, it enrages its subjects and provokes them to mobilize in support of political movements designed to change their status.

The subjects of any oligocracy can choose between two contrasting positions: the first calls for liberalization of the constitutional barriers to citizenship so that subjects can become partners in the representative institutions of the state; the second calls for liberation so that subjects can establish their own sovereignty and representative institutions. Liberalization has, in fact, transformed many subjects into citizens in quite a few industrialized democracies (oligocracies).

By contrast, although liberation movements in the former possessions of the modern empires have, by the end of the 20th century, created successor states and destroyed the empires, in most of these new states real citizenship has not materialized for most subjects. In many, the regimes are openly autocratic or only formalistically democratic because, despite representative institutions (elections, parties, assemblies), a ruling oligarchy effectively controls the state. The administrative weakness of many of these states also means that the benefits their citizens expected to receive are, in fact, not available. As a result, new political protest (liberation) movements determined to undermine the existing states and effect radical transformations are sure to emerge in many of these countries.

Nationalism

Although the literature on modernization often talks about industrial growth and democratization, it rarely pays much attention to nationalism, although this third pillar of modernity is equally important, in my opinion. There is, of course, a substantial and growing literature on nationalism, and some writers view it as a product of modernity, but, I think, they usually fail to treat its fundamental links as both a cause and consequence of modernity. Rather, they treat it as a separate and regrettable phenomenon, and one that lacks an organic link to contemporary ethnic nationalism.

I cannot review or summarize any of this literature here. I have, however, discussed the subject elsewhere (Riggs 1997b), paying some attention to the absurd argument (in my opinion) that "primordial" identities fuel the contemporary conflicts. No doubt historic myths do provide important symbols to help mobilize people to support liberation movements, and the availability of such myths may, indeed, be a necessary key to success. But that is not to say that the primordial experiences cause today's revolts. If anyone living today could claim descent from the Philistines, they would have plenty to fight about. Primordial wars mean nothing today except in the minds of those who can use the myths to buttress their contemporary struggles.

Far more importantly, we need to focus on the paramodern consequences of nationalism as manifested in the contemporary rise of ethnonationalism, that is, political movements by ethnic communities seeking to become a state and to gain formal recognition of their sovereignty. In order to understand why this has happened, however, we need to distinguish between state nationalism and ethnic nationalism.

State nationalism is a forerunner of ethnic nationalism. It involves the creation of a sense of cultural homogeneity and national identity among the citizens of a state. Proponents of democratization found that the principle of majority rule is more acceptable to citizens who share a common language and other cultural symbols than it is to a culturally heterogeneous population. People are more likely to accept the legitimacy of secularized representative government when they feel that they are part of a single nation rather than a marginalized minority within a dominant nation. Nation-building efforts often gain the support of subjects who learn that, to become citizens, they need to assimilate to the dominant nation. Thus movements toward liberalization by ethnic minorities reinforce the efforts of modern states to promote nation-building.

State nationalism takes a grotesque paramodern form when, instead of assimilating minorities, it seeks to purge them, as Hitler's "National Socialists" did in Germany. Horrors in the name of nationalism are still being perpetrated in some countries under the banner of "ethnic cleansing."

The most devastating consequence of nationalism linked with industrialism, however, took the form of imperialism. Industrialists used democratic processes to win support for nation-building projects because they facilitated their efforts to recruit and manage large number of workers, engineers, and salesmen. However, the drive for industrial expansion has no natural limits, and representative governments often went beyond the reasonable boundaries of nation-building to create multinational empires.

Driven by their economic interests, aggressive industrial democracies hunted for new sources of raw materials and expanded markets throughout the world. They were encouraged not only by capitalists but also by citizens of other social classes who understood that industrialization enabled them to buy valued imports that they could not have afforded without industrialization. Elected assemblies, therefore, represented the interests of a broad constituency when they supported imperial conquests. Democracy, nationalism and industrialism, therefore, reinforced each other in the spread of modern imperialism, perhaps the most damaging aspect of paramodernity.

When we think about imperialism, however, we usually focus on the evils it wrought on conquered peoples, failing to remind ourselves that the citizens of industrial democracies were also victimized. Indeed, the most violent paramodern consequence of imperialism was the interstate warfare between the empires that it caused. It began inconspicuously in remote areas of conquest, but it ended in the metropolitan domain where World Wars I and II were fought. The Cold War, as a final stage of the interimperial struggle, was not overtly nationalistic because neither American nor Russian nationalism could sustain its globalization as a neoimperial contest. Consequently, I believe, these two superpowers put an ideological facade on their gargantuan struggle to mask its true identity as a continuation and final phase of the great interimperial wars of the 20th century.

The paramodern consequences of nationalism acquired a new face when its driving force shifted from the states striving to build nations to the leaders of ethnic communities seeking recognition for themselves and their followers as new states. No doubt these processes overlap, but there is a historical dimension: during the formative centuries of modernity, states created nations, but during the contemporary postimperial phase, since the middle of the 20th century, ethnic nations have been trying to create their own states.

The political effects of the former (earlier) process involved the consolidation of power in modern (oligarchic) democracies. The imperial expansion of some of these states produced a powerful feedback effect in the form of liberation movements and ethnic nationalism among the conquered peoples. Their successes in the anti-imperial struggle have now generated, following the formation of new states, the ironic dilemmas generated by rising ethnic nationalism with movements for sovereignty and further boundary changes.

Ethnic Nationalism

The political strategy of these movements does not involve nonviolent calls for political reform, nor does it usually involve self-enrichment within the status quo (as organized by criminal gangs)

13

nor the replacement of newly established regimes (as in revolutionary movements). Rather, it involves goals of secession or national unification.

Ethnonations whose members form a majority in some part of an existing state mobilize to demand partition in order to create their own new state. When their members live on different sides of existing state borders, they may, instead, call for unification. In either case, they want border changes. Such changes threaten all established states and their rulers because each of them seems to have some precarious borders that could be threatened if the principle that boundaries can be redrawn by self-determination movements were to be widely accepted. Many states, therefore, are willing to join international projects to suppress or contain ethnonational movements that are border-threatening.

Just as democratization generated resentment among the subjects of any oligocracy, provoking them to demand citizenship rights for themselves, so nationalism now produces reactive movements among a growing number of subjects who feel they can never achieve citizenship by reforms. To the degree that their leaders could mobilize followers by appeals to shared grievances and a sense of historical identity, new ethnonational movements were provoked by imperialism and, since liberation, by arbitrary rule in the successor states.

Broadly speaking, three phases flowed into or overlapped each other like tidal waves (tsunamis; see Riggs 1994). During the first phase, modern nationalism in expanding states generated imperialism and spread the utopian dream of a national state.

During the second phase, nationalism evolved in the resistance movements formed to end imperial rule. This phase itself evolved through two subphases. At first, the anti-imperial focus of liberation movements generated an evanescent type of pan-nationalism in which all subjects of an empire, or all residents of a continent, were seen as fellow-nationals. Much of the leadership for these movements emerged in diasporas, that is, among the multi-ethnic subjects who mingled and plotted while living in a metropolitan domain—that is, in Paris, London, New York, and Berlin rather than at home. In the coffee houses and pubs where they met each other and shared their resentments, they created liberation movements against their imperial rulers.

After the modern empires so weakened themselves by world wars that they were compelled to surrender their possessions, the leadership for national movements passed to colonial elites who were living in the possessions, though often after returning from abroad. These co-nationalist movements often linked leaders from diverse minorities within a single possession, but they were quite unrepresentative of all the conquered peoples in a given imperial domain.

It often happened that the leadership of liberation movements came from bureaucrats, persons who had been co-opted by the imperial power to help them govern a possession. For understandable reasons, imperial elites relied on minorities within their domains, people who had often enough collaborated in their conquests because of their own long-standing marginalization by preconquest rulers. Often, too, they were the first to have an opportunity to visit the imperial homeland, where they were trained to assume responsibilities in colonial administration, though often in demeaning secondary roles that provoked their anger and resistance after they returned home.

Without further elaboration, let me pass to the third phase (tsunami), in which, increasingly, the leaders of co-nationalist movements have became the rulers of newly independent states. As controversies and difficulties arise, they increasingly alienate large segments of the population who feel that they are still oppressed by insensitive indigenous rulers who have simply replaced foreign imperialists. In such situations, new sets of leaders emerge and create ethnonationalist movements designed to win sovereignty and independence (or autonomy) for their followers within the context of the postcolonial states.

Often enough, members of a single ethnic nation find themselves living on different sides of two or more interstate boundaries. Infrequently, they were able to persuade their imperial masters to accept a plan that would recombine a divided nation (Togoland, Somalia, and Cameroon provide examples). Far more often, however, ethnic nationalism is rising to demand new boundaries, sovereignty, and independence at the expense of (newly) established states. Violent conflicts, terrorism, and civil wars can be expected as the normal sequel to the rise of ethnonationalist movements. Although nationalism can be blamed as the salient rationale or incentive for this paramodern phenomenon, it is also based on the concurrent development of industrialism and democratization.

Transformations

The new states generated by the collapse of all the modern empires are vulnerable to many unsettling and often tragic consequences.

Among them, revolts and civil strife motivated by ethnic nationalism may be the most conspicuous but it is not the only one. In passing, we need to recognize the other important forms, all of which are equally modern in character. Some are beneficial orthomodern movements, but many, I fear, are stridently paramodern.

Reforms

One response to the paramodern consequences of dem- ocratization that is largely orthomodern in its consequences involves positive and gradualistic efforts to work within a constitutional system to achieve reforms. Such reforms may include policies designed to transform subjects into citizens, by incremental means—civil rights, feminist, and affirmative action programs in many countries, often in concert with international (regional and global) organizations, both governmental and nongovernmental, are examples.

Such reform movements, by extending the range of rep- resentativeness of regimes, bringing many minorities, including women and ethnic communities, into the power structure, empower benign circles which lead, in turn, to improvements in the conditions under which all citizens of a country live. They need to consider constitutional as well as policy reforms. Better rules for making decisions are also needed so that the representative and administrative organs of governance can respond more effectively to the needs of citizens. (More reflections on this theme can be found in Riggs 1997a.)

Corruption

Unfortunately, under anarchic conditions, and taking advantage of the paramodern resources created by industrialization (as mentioned above), criminal gangs or syndicates emerge. Their members seek to enrich themselves by stealing and by killing people, by bribing officials to avoid punishment and even to procure state support for their illegal activities. We may refer to all such projects to undermine society and the state to gain support for alienated groups under the heading of corruption. Of course, vicious circles result. A state's ability to represent and serve its citizens is undermined by corruption, thereby intensifying the spread of anger and the proliferation of illegal activities, including crimes by isolated individuals as well as those managed by well-organized "syndicates."

Gangsters reflect the economic and materialistic goals fostered by industrialization. They seek to enrich themselves by illegal means and criminal violence. Rather than rely on legal and constitutional means, they rely on corruption and terrorism to secure the complaisance of government officials and intimidate those in power. They seek wealth by the most direct means within the political structures of the status quo.

Revolutions

A third response involves the rise of revolutionary movements. Although such movements may reflect the ideological influence of Marxist intellectuals, they are driven by domestic discontents, which may take the classic form of a "proletarian" uprising, generated by the angers of industrial workers, many of whom were urbanized farmers. As Mao Zedong proved in the Chinese case, however, angry peasants can also fuel a revolutionary movement, especially after industrialization has led to widespread marketization and rising pressure from landowners to compel their tenants to produce cash crops for the world market, replacing the traditional subsistence farming that prevailed in pre-industrial societies.

Fascist movements can also manifest the anger of distressed communities outraged by paramodern phenomena including the erosion of their own economic, social and cultural privileges as a result of industrialization and democratization, especially when previously marginalized subject populations are granted citizenship status and rights. Revolutionary movements seek to destroy and replace existing regimes, often on the basis of demands that subject populations replace the citizens of a state.

Organizationally, revolutionary movements tend to be dominated by well-organized groups who have learned how to take full advantage of all the paramodern fruits of industrialism listed above. When such movements succeed, the usual result is the creation of a single-party dictatorship in which, despite lip service to democratic values based on a claim that all the people are represented, in fact, most citizens become subjects under the domination of a small ruling circle able to use the mechanisms of power that were elaborated in the Soviet Union after 1917 and subsequently in Italy and Germany under fascist dictatorships. Revolutionary movements are clearly paramodern consequences of industrialism, democratization, and nationalism (despite lip service in some cases to cosmopolitanism).

Neotraditionalism

Although, on the surface, contemporary neotraditionalist ("fundamentalist") movements seek to restore premodern conditions, I believe that, in fact, they are a fourth type of paramodern movement. We should distinguish, I think, between truly traditional communities—the Amish are an example—and neotraditionalism in which all the available modern technologies (especially for mass communication and organization) are fully employed. Sometimes modern weapons are also used to terrorize opponents. Thus industrialism has provided the tools for neotraditionalism, while, at the same time, it has created a symbolic enemy to be attacked as viciously satanic.

Although supernatural authority is emphasized by neo-traditionalists, they do not try to revive the monarchic institution. Instead, neotraditionalists accept democratic equalitarianism by promising salvation to all those who accept the claims of divine authority made by mediators who promise salvation, peace, and prosperity to all "true" believers, offering equal rights as citizens of a new heaven on earth. Nonbelievers, however, will become subjects vulnerable to severe repression. Thus the distinction between citizens and subjects found in most democracies is also replicated.

Neotraditionalists who control a regime also act like state nationalists in their drive to convert all of their subjects into citizen believers. When they are not in power, however, they are likely to behave like revolutionaries, seeking to overthrow and replace authoritarian regimes. However, in democracies, they may rely mainly on nonviolent means to organize and capture power, but they clearly intend, if they succeed, to suppress all opposition.

Neotraditionalist and secular revolutionary movements resemble each other in their state-transforming rhetoric. In the name of moral absolutism and robust ideologies, they seek to replace existing state elites and transform society, making use of all the modern means of control and social identity that industrialism, nationalism, and democracy have created.

Sovereignty Movements

A fifth type of paramodernity takes the form of ethnic nationalism, as explained above. Increasingly, in the modern world, the aftermath of imperial conquests, including the migration of peoples, especially refugees, have driven sovereignty or self-determination movements designed to secure independence or autonomy for ethnic nations. These movements differ significantly from the four patterns of paramodernity described above. Instead of seeking reform according to constitutionally prescribed rules, revolutionary movements against a regime, or the corruption of those who hold power, ethnic nationalism calls for the partition of states, the rearrangement of boundaries, or the autonomy of ethnic communities.

Because ethnopolitical movements play such a conspicuous and dangerous role in the context of paramodernity, I shall devote the rest of this paper to some further comments about them. First, because these movements often involve boundary changes and cross-boundary migrations, they affect existing states and have international repercussions. I shall, therefore, take a look at the interstate context within which the intrastate symptoms of paramodernity (especially ethnic nationalism) occur. Second, the beneficial (orthomodern) consequences of modernity also need to be considered, especially in order to ask whether or not they can provide solutions for some of the terrible problems of paramodernity. In the context of circular causation, if positive aspects of modernity have negative consequences, may it not also be true that the adverse consequences can generate responses that enhance the beneficial potentials within modernity.

The Global Context

So long as local conflicts do not jeopardize existing borders, the outside world tends to ignore them, claiming that rules against intervention in the internal affairs of sovereign states bars external interference. If ethnic nationalism only involved peoples who live within their own territorial domains, it might be possible to ignore domestic conflicts. In an increasingly interdependent world, however, what happens in any place can have consequences in many other places. Moreover, concerned citizens in all countries feel bonds of human solidarity that lead them to support humanitarian projects and to protest against injustices and oppression wherever it may arise. However, there are several specific reasons why ethnonational conflicts often provoke global concern and action. They are likely to involve migrations and boundary changes.

Refugees

Increasingly genocide ("ethnic cleansing") and revolts produce refugees fleeing across interstate borders. The citizens of Rwanda and Burundi who fled to Zaire, Uganda, and other African countries provide a vivid contemporary example. Others fled zones of conflict in Bosnia, Sudan, Uganda, Burma, Vietnam, Nigeria, Palestine, and many other countries. The flow of refugees creates many problems in the host countries to which they flee: whether they are housed in temporary encampments or given asylum as immigrants, the problems generated by refugees are global in their impact. Violence, economic and humanitarian concerns, and political disputes often follow.

An overlapping problem generated by migrations may be viewed under the rubric of diasporas. Members of any ethnic nation who live outside their homeland may be referred to as a "diaspora," borrowing a word used originally to speak of the Jewish dispersal. Chechens living in Moscow as well as Palestinians, Armenians, Chinese, Tibetans, or Sikhs living in many countries, are examples of different diasporas. Although members of a diaspora often migrate for personal and economic reasons, they often move to escape persecution and the violence of interethnic conflicts. Most members of a diaspora are grateful for the refuge and safe haven provided by host countries, and they often choose to become naturalized citizens.

However, many diaspora people also retain ties to their homeland and participate in its political life and struggles. Indeed, there are many cases where their activism may be more significant than that of ethnonationals living at home. I refer to the whole system of ethnonationals plus fellow ethnics living in diaspora as an ethnic nation. Although ethnonationalism typically provides the most visible and violent evidence of ethnic conflicts in the world today, diaspora mobilization augments them by supporting the flow of information, arms, and leadership for ethnonational movements. Moreover, citizens in diaspora often influence the foreign policy of the states that intervene in these disputes. At many levels, therefore, migrations, especially by refugees, have global effects that lead to external interventions in the domestic politics of states.

Boundary Changes

The likelihood that ethnic nationalism will generate demands for boundary changes has already been mentioned, and I have mentioned the likelihood that they will lead to international reactions. Contemporary situations in Bosnia, Somalia, and Rwanda provide good examples. To the degree that civil wars based on ethnonational revolts do not threaten existing interstate boundaries, the outside world is likely to refrain from intervention. Burma and the Sudan provide good examples.

Even movements to unify divided nations are largely ignored so long as their potential supporters remain internally divided and cannot mobilize much support across existing boundaries: the pan Kurdish, Pushtun, Basque, and Azerbaijan movements probably fall into this category. Although nongovernmental organizations have vigorously protested Jakarta's policy toward the people of Timor, and the UN General Assembly has condemned Indonesia, the outside world has not intervened in any forceful way. Moreover, so long as ethnonational movements are conducted nonviolently, especially within the more democratic countries, there is no reason to expect international intervention to occur.

Clearly in the postimperial age, there is no reason to expect a revival of external interventions inspired by goals of conquest. As Robert Jackson has pointed out, the modern international system maintains a solid front to maintain the de jure status of what he calls quasi states even when, de facto, they lack the effective institutions and infrastructure of a viable modern states (Jackson 1990). It seems predictable, therefore, that although violence, terrorism, and civil wars will escalate in response to the growing pressures of ethnonational movements to achieve sovereignty or reunification, many such movements will be nonviolent, and even violent domestic conflicts may not provoke international intervention except, perhaps, to provide humanitarian relief.

Indigenous Peoples

Although the most visible and violent confrontations arising from the paramodern phenomenon of imperialism can be found in the former overseas possessions of the modern empires, increasingly we can now also see parallel movements by indigenous peoples in many of the countries that were colonized by Europeans as a forerunner of the industrial revolution and the rise of modern empires. Their movements designed to promote autonomy or independence under the mantle of self- determination and compensation for past injustices need to be seen as part of the general phenomenon of paramodernity discussed above.

The rise of liberation movements in the overseas possessions of modern empires came first for a variety of reasons, but the mobilization of a new generation of political activists within the communities that were conquered and settled by Europeans is an inescapable part of the same process. Among the reasons for the long delay is the fact that the conquered peoples overseas were a vast majority of the population, whereas the indigenous peoples are typically a minority among the settlers who have occupied their former lands. In order to understand these movements, however, we need to recognize that they belong to the same long-term paramodern phenomena that have already led to the liberation of new states that were outside the imperial metropoles.

Moreover, it is important to emphasize that the mobilization of indigenous peoples normally leads to nonviolent protests and political action. Because the countries where the indigenous peoples live are, for the most part, industrialized democracies, solutions to their problems can usually be found by means of some kind of autonomy, the creation of a state within a state or a nation within a nation. Moreover, even when they do have a territorial domain that can be recognized and bounded as a "reservation" or a "homeland," a large proportion of the members of these nations have dispersed and are living as citizens outside their own territories.

The discussion that follows will focus on this problem and provides a background for looking at the current concerns expressed by Hawaiians as an "indigenous people" seeking justice by various means and through diverse channels. By viewing the Hawaiian case as a prototype for many similar communities elsewhere in the world, and thinking about the mechanisms of world order that might well be activated to facilitate the solution of these problems, we can move toward a way of thinking about the linkages between local ethnonational concerns and the global system within which such concerns need to be resolved.

Toward Human Security

The basic problem now facing the world, as I see it, is how to make use of the great achievements of orthomodernity in order to overcome their paramodern consequences. This question can be reduced to a problem of human security. Industrialism has produced overpopulation, environmental devastation, and poverty in the midst of plenty. Democratization has replaced monarchic authoritarianism with representative government but also marginalized millions of people as secularized subjects of regimes that are both weak and authoritarian. Nationalism has empowered state nations, enabling them to become both industrialized and democratic, but it has also mobilized a host of stateless ethnic nations that are prone to violence in quasi states where weak authoritarian regimes prevail.

These problems are global and deeply rooted in modernity. To find solutions, we must be able to consider options at all levels, from the global to the local, including the role played by states at intervening regional levels. No doubt states are withering, they are losing functions and authority both upward and downward—to global organizations, both governmental and nongovernmental, and to local communities, groups, and subgovernmental authorities. We need to pay attention at all of these levels—local, regional, and global. The most strategic starting point, I believe, is the intermediate level of states. This is also the most tangible and familiar level.

I believe that democratic states are more capable of dealing with paramodern problems than authoritarian states (whether they be traditional monarchies, single-party dictatorships, or weak quasi states with large areas of anarchy). Among the democratic states, those that are oligarchic in character will be less capable than more fully democratic states. At the structural level, parliamentary regimes are much more likely, in my opinion, than presidentialist regimes to be able to cope with these problems. In part this is because a presidentialist regime can survive only if it is rather oligarchic in character, as is the United States. My reasons for reaching this conclusion are spelled out in Riggs (1997a and 1997c).

Vertical Devolution

A significant contemporary trend that may well ameliorate many paramodern problems can be linked with radical transformation in the functions of states. The phrase "withering of the state" has negative connotations, but it correctly points to an increasingly dynamic movement to surrender state authority both upward and downward to global and local entities. I think of both together as vertical devolution. Surely, states will not disappear: They will continue to perform important functions and remain a stabilizing intermediate force in our increasingly interdependent world system. However, their capacity to abuse power or fail to accomplish necessary tasks can be corrected by appropriate work performed at both higher and lower levels of governance.

The European Union is a good example of upward devolution, but many parallels can be found, especially where specialized authorities have taken over important state functions, including efforts to ameliorate the disasters involved in refugee migrations, the protection of minorities, the regulation of commerce, communications, and transportation, and so forth. Multinational corporations can usefully perform many functions once performed by states, but their capacity to abuse power is also tremendous, and global institutions designed to regulate and control these corporations are also absolutely necessary. In parallel with the corporations spawned for the rise of industrialism, all kinds of nongovernmental international associations are also needed to perform watchdog, humanitarian, scholarly, and aesthetic tasks. They can well replace government in these respects, especially if appropriate means can be found to finance their activities. They need support structures that do not depend on the profit motive or contributions by states.

Downward devolution is well illustrated by the federal structures of authority pioneered by the United States when it created a constitution that recognized the sovereignty of its 13 founding members. Recent events in Washington have reinforced a federalizing movement to devolve more and more authority from the central authorities to the 50 states that now constitute this union. However, a serious limitation constrains the federal principle: all of the constituent states in the United States are, in principle, culturally homogeneous, accepting the same basic national identity.

Some important exceptions do exist, however, as exemplified by the commonwealth status of Puerto Rico and the Northern Marianas, where administrative autonomy and self-government prevail, and the effective autonomy of many native American nations as manifested in self-governing reservations. In Guam, self-government actually exists and formal commonwealth status is under consideration, but in American Samoa, although self-government prevails, the move toward commonwealth status has been blocked by opponents who fear that it would undermine traditional land tenure and chiefly rights. Constitutionally, full recognition of political and cultural autonomy requires something more than federal devolution of power.

I think of such a status as that of an addominium in which autonomous jurisdictions are not subject to the authority of elected assemblies in which they are constitutionally represented. The status of the Isle of Man and the Channel Islands in relation to the United Kingdom may be viewed as an example of what I have in mind. For reasons elaborated elsewhere, I think addominiums are more like to arise in parliamentary than presidentialist regimes (Riggs 1997a). An important initiative taken by Liechtenstein in the United Nations calls for more formal support and recognition of administrative autonomy as a status, short of full independence, that would permit states like Chechnya to accept self-rule while remaining part of the Russian Federation. Of course, de facto, all kinds of self-governing entities within a modern state can be established outside the formal structures of governance. The literature on civil society celebrates such possibilities by calling attention to the many ways in which nongovernmental organizations (including corporations, associations, churches, clubs, and sodalities of many kinds) can arise between the nuclear family and the state to take over a wide variety of social functions.

Actually, I think, a quasi-official kind of personal sovereignty is also possible. And it may well be illustrated by the "corporations" organized by indigenous nations in Alaska. The model they follow is not that of a territorial state but rather that of a private corporation. All members of an ethnic nation have the right to elect its governing boards and control the properties and activities it sponsors even though there is no territorial boundary to separate its members from nonmembers. Communities now seeking sovereignty in the United States—like Hawaiians in Hawaii—might do well to look at these Alaskan Indian corporations to develop some useful ideas about how their own needs can be met within the framework of the American state.

Increasingly, the ability of states to oppress their subjects and represent their citizens effectively can, I think, be enhanced by both the upward and downward devolution of state powers. By this means many of the effective negative effects of paramodernity can, I hope, be ameliorated by the gradual emergence of a new phase of late modernity in which its most dangerous and destructive side effects can be counteracted.

Social Science Research

A great deal of research is urgently needed to test the hypotheses offered above and to find appropriate solutions. If we consider the social sciences as a modern tool available to help us understand problems and find solutions for them, then we should be able to view the social sciences as part of our orthomodern resources. Unfortunately, however, the tendency toward specialization, which underlies much of modernity, especially in the processes of industrialization, has seriously handicapped us in our quest for solutions to concrete problems in the real world. Modernity itself has social, economic, political, psychological, cultural, historical, and geographic aspects that, as I have tried to show above, are part of a seamless web. Insofar as we try to analyze and solve these problems separately—for example, economics for industrialization, politics for democratization, and social/cultural perspectives for nationalism—we are sure to fail. Only by pulling together the insights and methods of all the social sciences can we ultimately succeed in finding better solutions—at least, that is my belief.

We are only, I think, at the beginning of a long-term process. The depth and connectedness of all the paramodern problems are just beginning to attract the attention of scholars, politicians, and community leaders. If we can link the efforts of the best minds modern scholarship has produced, with the common sense and good will of millions of ordinary people, perhaps we shall be able to forestall some of the most dangerous consequences of modernity and find a way to overcome them in the interest of growing security, peace, and health for our global community.

Note

1. When I first wrote *malody* in the title of this article, it was a spelling error or was it a blip of the unconscious? I soon saw that it is a useful blend of *malady* and *melody*, a word that could well symbolize both the pleasant and the unpleasant aspects of something like modernity. Many aspects of modernity—including industrialism, nationalism, and democracy—please us and cause rejoicing when they are combined in the ideal form of a national state. Unfortunately, these same dimensions of modernity also wreak havoc in the world today as manifested in imperialism, class struggle, and single-party dictatorships, a global population explosion, environmental degradation, growing poverty in the midst of plenty, crime, anomie, and the escalating violence caused by ethnonational revolts and genocide in the name of ethnic cleansing. Perhaps the melodies of social science research can help us discover ways to cure the maladies of modernity.

CHAPTER 2

World Politics and Regional Formations

T. V. Sathyamurthy

As we enter the new millennium, the future of the world has once again become the subject of close scrutiny. This is particularly the case in light of the unfolding changes of immense political significance at a number of different levels—international, regional, national, and local. I focus here on some of the crucial aspects of the transformations at each of these levels and the interrelationships between the different levels.

An equilibrium, stable despite being subjected to the major global tensions and contradictions that rapidly developed in the aftermath of the world war, may have been replaced by another—at best metastable, perhaps even unstable, and certainly of an unpredictable character, since the end of the Cold War a little over a decade ago. With the precipitate removal of one of the major contradictions of the postwar world, the process of adjustment in a radically modified international setting has been fraught with unanticipated difficulties— not only by domestic political opposition forces in the former Soviet Union and Eastern Europe but also Western (and in particular, American) antagonism toward communism. These difficulties are amply and dramatically reflected in the political sea of change signaled in the former Soviet Union and Eastern Europe by the unleashing of forces that had been widely assumed to have disappeared under communist rule extending over a period of four to seven decades.

The radical thrust of political change involving the global reconfiguration of power now under way is provided by Asia (in particular, Far Eastern Asia). Here, I address three general questions:

1. How best can the essential changes in the configuration of forces during the contemporary phase of international relations be characterized?

2. How can the rapidly changing face of Asia be best understood?
3. What is the most satisfactory way to make sense of the terms of discourse of interregional political and economic comparisons within Asia?

A Retrospective

We are familiar with the conventional literature on the Cold War, which is firmly rooted in analyses of its essentially *Realpolitik* character as a clash of interests involving military security on a global scale, economic competition, cultural legacy, and political domination. The emergence of ideological antagonism subsuming, if not replacing, territorial ambition as the potent motivating principle of international competition coincided with the rise of the Soviet Union to the position of a world power following its share of the victory over fascism in World War II. For the first time since the Bolshevik revolution, the Soviet Union came to be regarded by the United States and the West as a foe worthy of their steel.

In the postwar era, the territorial ambitions of the great powers widened and deepened. They pursued the political aim of converting the minds of men and women in different parts of the world (especially the "uncommitted" areas) to the virtues of "socialism" or "democracy"—each of these two portmanteau terms being defined in a narrow, hegemonic sense rather than in a wide, far-ranging, open-ended, and undogmatic perspective. Keeping larger extents of territory within the sphere of influence of one or other of the supreme protagonists came to assume subsidiary importance. Territory increasingly took on significance as a means to the much more important end of bringing larger and larger numbers of people under the influence of one or other of the two major ideological orientations associated with the superpowers.

The North American and Western literature on postwar international relations has, however, rigidly adhered to *Realpolitik* formulations that have largely failed to capture the nuances and variations introduced by an interlinking between traditional (i.e., geopolitical) objectives and objectives of an essentially ideological and psychological character. By the same token, the "revisionist" literature on the Cold War, often critical of the United States and the West or partially exonerating the Soviet Union of primary culpability, has also been restricted in scope.

In contrast to both these stands, the governments on either side of the ideological divide tended to be more explicit on the question of ideological competition, coexistence, and hegemony. Military security—globalized in order to advance the crucial aims of national or Western security, economic security through making the world safe for and dependent on capitalist penetration and global market domination, and propagating cultural homogeneity on a worldwide scale, have become inextricably intertwined. For its part, the Soviet Union found, to its cost, that its resources could not be stretched beyond the narrow and essentially counterproductive confines of military security and the limitations imposed by global geostrategic imperatives to pay for its psychological, ideological, cultural, and economic objectives on the plane of international (or, for that matter, domestic) politics.

For my part, I have found a dialectical framework much more useful and resonant as a guide to understanding the configuration of forces in international relations during the Cold War epoch. Three major contradictions gathered momentum in the immediate aftermath of the war. Their interactions and inflections shaped the world for five decades. They encompassed the strategies and counterstrategies of the ideologically differentiated East and West in the economically differentiated South and North.

Moreover, they contributed to the emergence of new configurations of power out of the impact of East-West relations on North-South relations within a world shrinking fast under the influence of a complex network of communications and information technology. Above all, they impinged in profound ways on the modalities specific to the three major divisions of the world—that is, the First (consisting of industrialized, capitalist countries), Second (consisting of socialist/communist countries), and Third (consisting of former colonial and poor countries) Worlds. These contradictions also define the limits of conflict—between, on the one hand, deterrence in the realm of nuclear inter-superpower conflict as expressed in the competition engendered in one of the three major contradictions; and, on the other, overt war of damaging proportions, enjoined on warring parties by the essential properties of another major contradiction.

Thus while *Realpolitik* can by no means be ignored in explanations of the day-to-day behavior of superpower blocs and big powers in general, it does not constitute a sufficient basis for an understanding of the complexities of international politics. International relations during the four decades of the Cold War were embedded in three mutually interacting and closely interconnected major contradictions. The shaping of these contradictions and their outcome constitute the stuff of international relations during the second half of this century. The conflicts were reflected in the arms race, at negotiating tables, on the battlefield, in the appropriation of new strategic areas, and in the scientific, technological, and economic competition between the two blocs and within each bloc. The major contradictions of the world during the Cold War period can be characterized as follows:

1. The contradiction between the two superpowers and their allies, publicly expressed in the idiom of ideological hegemony, with a subtext imbricated with a calculus of military power and economic influence and their extension as major ingredients of security and interest (national, supranational, and global). In other words, while the long-term aims of hegemony were ideological in character, the day-to-day practice of competition, confrontation, and negotiation was rooted in an emphasis on considerations of a *Realpolitik* nature.

2. The contradiction within the socialist bloc that developed even during the late 1940s (spearheaded by Tito of Yugoslavia) and had its origins in the differences within the Communist Party of the Soviet Union (CPSU), the Comintern, and the Chinese Communist Party (CCP), as well as between them, over the question of strategy and tactics to be followed in the conduct of the Chinese revolution. Its public airing for the first time in 1957 represented the beginning of a new and more serious phase of an already well-developed ideological conflict within the communist world.

3. The contradiction between the forces of national liberation on the one hand and the forces of imperialism (in particular, U.S. imperialism) on the other. From 1968 until the end of the Cold War, formulations of this contradiction varied between those who regarded U.S. imperialism as the main enemy of the Third World and those who regarded U.S. imperialism *and* Soviet "social imperialism" as the two equally dangerous foes with which it had to contend. The conflict between the forces of imperialism and the forces of national liberation carried far greater ideological (as differentiated from power political) weight in both the long and short-term perspectives. The origins of the contradiction go back to the middle phase of the Chinese revolution (from the mid-1930s onward) when, under Mao's leadership, the revolutionary struggle of the Chinese Communist Party encompassed the national liberation struggle—fighting the enemy on three fronts: on the international front with special

reference to imperialism going back in history to the 19th century; on the military front with reference to Japan's armed conquest of China; and on the domestic political front against the Kuomintang (KMT).

To these must be added the tensions and contradictions within the Western world that were bound to surface with the assertion of France as a national power in the West (after putting behind its lackluster performance during the Second World War and its defeat at the hands of the forces of national liberation, first in Indochina, and subsequently in Algeria), the gradual emergence of the European Economic Community (EEC) and its transformation into the European Community (EC) and the European Union (EU), and the rise of Japan as an economic power of great global magnitude.

The degree to which each of these contradictions was antagonistic at any given moment, and the trajectory of each contradiction over time, is a fascinating subject to which hindsight can be profitably applied for the lessons that it might contain for the future.

For analytic purposes, it would be appropriate to take each of the three major contradictions in turn, while remembering that their overall impact on the world was joint, integrally cumulative, and combined, rather than separate, arithmetically additive, and isolated. After the first decade of the postwar era, a change of gear of foreign policy in the Soviet Union brought about by Stalin's successors was clearly discernible. An apparently antagonistic contradiction settled down to a new register, encompassing the relations between unequal superpowers. This was marked by a lessening of inequality between them, at least in certain specific spheres of development, and by peaceful competition and coexistence between the two sides that signified an increasingly nonantagonistic phase in which the conflicts were confined to more or less precisely defined limits. This pattern of relationship was not negated even by such serious perturbations as the Cuban missile crisis or Soviet military intervention in Afghanistan (1979–1987) portended.

With the end of the wars of national liberation in Indochina, a new phase of the bilateral relations between the Soviet Union and the United States began. This was paralleled by a similar change in Europe in the multilateral relations embracing the North Atlantic Treaty Organization (NATO) powers, on the one hand, and the Eastern bloc on the other. With the ideological dimension of the Cold War antagonism was now confined to the field of conflict between the United States (without much moral or material support from its allies) and the forces of national liberation, which were in an advanced state of development in certain parts of the world. The quotidian relations between the protagonists of the First and Second Worlds (and, increasingly since 1972, including China) in general, and the Soviet Union and the United States in particular, took on an almost conventional appearance familiar to students of international relations before the war. In other words, beneath a thin layer of ideological icing, the terms of reference of diplomacy, foreign policy, and international relations were largely dictated by considerations of *Realpolitik* rather than a burning desire to conquer the minds of men and women.

In sharp contrast to the first major contradiction, the third major contradiction, with its roots stretching back to the early postwar years, provided the arena for a fateful clash between ideology and *Realpolitik*. The national liberation struggle can be characterized as a means (1) of eradicating imperialism root and branch, (2) of establishing new structures of power, and (3) of interweaving a nonnegotiable form of nationalism[1] with socialist construction.[2] As such, it was as novel a feature of the international relations of large parts of the Third World as nuclear war was in the international politics of the First and Second worlds.

As far as the United States was concerned, initial tolerance of militant nationalism gave way to implacable hostility toward full-fledged national liberation movements, as in Indochina. Tolerance had included certain elements of incipient national liberation struggle—as in the case of Indonesia up to 1948—in preference to a continuation of colonial rule. The logic of the domino theory, invented in order to justify American military intervention in such areas, was predicated on fears of an economic nature to which strategic considerations were of course closely linked.

The confrontation with Indochina was seen by the United States as global in character and scope. For the former, however, it was specific, local, and national; its aim was to free Indochina from the stranglehold of imperialism and to liberate it as much from the economic as from the strategic domination of the United States.

The third major contradiction of the postwar world was thus played out on two levels. For the United States, it was an ideological struggle in which *Realpolitik and* strategic considerations mattered greatly. For the national liberation movements themselves, the struggle was of paramount importance on an ideological level and essentially of a defensive nature on a military level. As it was undertaken as a fight to the finish, the elements of negotiation and compromise were suppressed until the final stages of the conflict when the outcome of the protracted struggle between the two sides was no longer in doubt.

The second major contradiction of the world was confined to its socialist half and hinged directly on the two visions of the world proletarian revolution that came into conflict as the construction of socialism got under way in China. Even from the mid-1920s onward, a number of ideological differences over the correct path to revolution that the CCP should pursue, generally expressed through the medium of the Comintern and the Soviet emissaries to China, had begun to fester in interparty relations. The decisive defeat of the Soviet (i.e., Stalin's) line on the Chinese revolution and the assumption of control over the strategy and tactics of the national liberation struggle in China under Mao's leadership (1936–1937) led to the emergence of an alternative to the template of world proletarian revolution imposed on the international communist experience by the Bolshevik Party.

Even from the late 1930s onward, the Chinese revolutionary strategy was adopted to varying degrees by the national liberation forces in different parts of Southeast Asia, while from the 1950s onward, its appeal spread to other parts of the colonial world as well as Latin America. In South Asian countries, national independence movements,[3] opposed to the strategy of national liberation, constituted the political norm. But even in this region, pockets of peasant as well as popular insurrectionary resistance did emerge here and there, which testified to the undoubted appeal of the anti-imperialist national liberation strategy among certain segments of the population.

During the 1960s, the ideological rupture between China and the Soviet Union[4] led to a vertical shift in the various communist movements that spread throughout the world, including countries with strong communist parties such as Italy. Thus, during the 1960s, there were two major centers of communism propagating rival versions of revolutionary ideology and world politics. Within the socialist half of the world, at least five different types of communist practice were discernible where the Communist Party controlled state power—as exemplified in the Soviet Union and Eastern Europe, Yugoslavia, Albania, China, and Cuba.

This great ideological schism went largely unnoticed in the mainstream Western literature on international relations until 1968, while policy circles in the United States (and Western Europe, to a lesser degree) attached little weight to its salience in the global reckoning. The

Soviet invasion of Czechoslovakia in 1968, followed in 1969 by a menacing military confrontation between the USSR and China, betokened a level of antagonism between the two major socialist powers before which the habitual hostility between the USSR and the United States paled into insignificance. For their part, the Western powers were persuaded that for China to characterize the Soviet Union as "social imperialist" constituted an unmistakable indication of the seriousness of the rupture between the two major communist powers.

The taming of the first major contradiction followed an uneven path. During the 1950s and 1960s, acute tension in Europe was followed by an uneasy modus vivendi between the two sides that enabled a partial restoration of the status quo. Détente in Europe gave the United States and the USSR (especially Brezhnev and Nixon) the opportunity to introduce new modulations into the Cold War system that appeared to temper its original harshness and severity. In other parts of the world, the two superpowers realized that their interests in third areas were variant, conflicting, and competitive in certain aspects, but congruent, mutual, and complementary in others. Thus, for example, as the national liberation struggles in Indochina reached their different climactic moments during the early 1970s, the U.S. desire to cut its losses and leave the battlefield, and the Soviet Union's lack of appetite for any development that challenged the status quo as defined by the postcolonial national boundaries bequeathed by the colonial powers were the obverse and reverse of the same coin.

During the decade between the end of the wars of national liberation in Indochina and the emergence of Gorbachev as the First Secretary of the CPSU and chief executive of the Soviet state, fundamental changes were under way in the international arena that radically transformed the character of the major contradictions of the postwar world:

1. In the aftermath of comprehensive defeat in the Indochina wars of national liberation, the United States forged a new strategy to avenge its humiliation. Under Reagan, the United States returned to the profoundly anticommunist theme underlying Truman's policy. Four decades from the beginning of the Cold War, American policy had thus come full circle. No longer satisfied with *Realpolitik* games and demarcating rival spheres of influence, the United States during the 1980s pursued the aim of destroying the "evil empire" of the Soviet Union by bringing its combined military, economic, political, and international power to bear on the Eastern bloc as a whole.

The success of the American project exceeded the most optimistic expectations of the Western world. Even before Reagan left office, he could see the communist bloc in Europe crumble and effloresce. With its command over the technology of communications, the United States simplified and exaggerated the threat faced by the West from the alien world of communism. Economic strangulation and growing domestic disenchantment in Eastern Europe with democratic centralism prepared the way for the demolition of the political edifice built on communist ideology. By 1990, an entire empire comprising one side of the equation, balancing the two superpowers on an ideological fulcrum of contradiction, collapsed. The first major contradiction of the world thus vanished in thin air.

2. Even though it was counted as socialist in certain respects, its dramatic change of direction after the deaths of Prime Minister Zhou Enlai and Chairman Mao Zedong, marked China out as a dynamic, potentially powerful and economically compatible competitor rather than as a political enemy subscribing to a dangerous doctrine. The new policies in China led to the so-called four modernizations, the policy of opening its doors to the outside world, as well as liberalization, globalization, modernization, and marketization of its economy

3. The rise of Islam as a powerful international political force acquired ideological significance from the 1970s onward. Not only did Islam capture state power after winning an outright struggle against the Shah of Iran, who was one of America's closest allies and protégés, but it also spread its influence far and wide among Muslim populations governed by leaders enjoying the support of the United States.

4. Throughout the 1980s, under Deng Xiaoping's leadership, China set in motion policies of "damage limitation" toward the Soviet Union.[5] In any case, with one of the epicenters of communism wiped out by the dramatic evaporation of the ideology from the whole of eastern Europe, the second major contradiction of the postwar world, like the first, went into desuetude even before the Soviet Union ceased to exist.

5. The status of "national liberation" as a political force, however, developed along complex lines after the end of the wars of national liberation in Indochina. I shall only hint at some of the crucial aspects of its ambiguous transformation(s). National liberation, in the classic and pristine anti-imperialist sense, had grown wings in different parts of the world during the 1970s and

1980s. In Central America, the movements in Nicaragua, El Salvador, and Guatemala assumed an uncompromising force, even though, in recent years, their revolutionary character has been affected by the vicissitudes of American interventionism.[6]

In the former Portuguese colonies of Africa, in Zimbabwe, in South Africa, in Yemen, in Ethiopia, in Eritrea, and elsewhere, political movements and parties engaged in national liberation struggles. These struggles often entered into negotiations with imperialism or the colonial power or with domestic political forces opposed to the guerrillas. They invariably led to the formation of new independent states.

In a world radically challenged by the collapse of communism, the political future of national liberation as we know it from postwar experience is problematic to say the least. At least a temporary end to polarization of power between two rival centers, dominance of the world political economy by the forces of capitalism, and the gradual appearance of alternative and new centers of capitalist development along the so-called Pacific Rim are factors to consider in this equation.

Even so, the fact that states established as a result of national liberation struggles have been unable to realize their dream of autonomy and political liberation from imperialist domination, ought not to obscure certain new and portentous developments in the rapidly changing relationship between the rich and the poor of the world.

The Third World economies dominated by the World Bank and the International Monetary Fund (IMF) have developed layers of vast thickness spreading through the bottom of the society. These constitute the poor, the weaker segments of society, and accumulations of ever larger numbers of people differentiating downward along a spiral of deprivation. Despite their present relatively anomic condition, they nevertheless represent a potential challenge to the inequalities that have been bred in all societies, and particularly in Third World and former European communist countries.

Prospective

Against a cursory background along these lines, we can attempt to formulate tentative answers to the three questions posed above. First, in contemporary international politics, two of the three major contradictions of the postwar world (viz., the first and the second) are no longer operative. The disappearance of these contradictions has, to a large extent, driven the third major contradiction, still extant and potentially significant, underground.

Second, even though these developments have been followed by premature jubilation among some intellectuals heralding the end of history, closer scrutiny of the political conditions should alert us to the appearance of new vectors in international relations. Changing economic balances between different parts of the world can be reasonably viewed as harbingers of fresh conflicts and contradictions.

Third, the fact that communism has been removed from the first major contradiction and that national liberation in the third major contradiction has become muted in recent years does not mean that the forces of imperialism have assumed a state of passivity. On the contrary, they are still very active, and their role in world politics and impact upon various regions and different layers of societies (more appropriately, different classes of people) are bound to give rise to fresh challenges that are likely to assume the form of new contradictions.

Let us now return to a brief discussion of the changing dynamic of the realignment of forces that has been under way since the disappearance of the first and second major contradictions of the Cold War era. As we approach the next millennium, we are witnessing a veritable explosion of economic energy accompanying the development of capitalism on a worldwide scale with no other economic system to challenge its hegemony. To a far greater extent than ever before, capitalism may be said to have broken national and regional barriers in its search for global identity and pervasiveness. Marketization and consumption, like investment and production, know no national or regional bounds.

However, even though nation-states and new structures of regional power (the preeminent example of these being the EEC/EC/EU) continue to modulate the process of globalization, marketization, privatization, and liberalization, they also continue to serve as a bridge between the particular and specific interests and needs of national societies. They also respond to the requirements of rapidly globalizing capital, which thrives on competition between different political units. Of considerable importance to our discussion is the reorientation of the long-established capitalist regions of the world on the one hand and the new entrants to the world capitalist club on the other. Together they constitute the emerging configuration of forces that provide the basis for new contradictions in the coming millennium.

The emerging configuration of forces in the world significantly differs from the hegemonic order that developed in the aftermath of the war in the following aspects:

1. The conflict between alternative ways of organizing political, economic, and social life in the national and international spheres represented by capitalism (and its questionable and debatable identification with democracy) and communism (and its problematic egalitarian credentials) has ended, with the former victorious and the latter vanquished.

2. The assumption that the status quo embodied in the Cold War would continue indefinitely gave rise to theoretical contributions and intellectual justifications that propounded an evolving convergence over time between the two mutually antagonistic if not actively hostile socioeconomic systems. It also suggested the end of "ideology," and the development of a global "postindustrial" consensus. However, the sudden collapse of communism appears to have inspired a new rash of theories variously heralding the end of history following the liberal triumph of the 1980s, or more ominously, conveying a foreboding of Armageddon involving a clash of civilizations.

It is interesting to note that such theories have emanated mostly from the United States and would appear to reflect a preoccupation with maintaining its dominance of the post-Soviet transformations of the world system. There is also more than a hint of hubris in operation in the minds of those who take it upon themselves to theorize with frameworks that have terms of reference sufficiently skewed to introduce significant distortions of reality.

Moreover, there is an asymmetry between the two sides—in this case, America and Asia—which stems from an absence of preoccupation with speculative stances or theories among Asian (and germane to this discussion, Chinese) intellectuals embodying hegemonic aspirations. Such asymmetry is rooted in the radically different fields of vision within which the two sides articulate their positions. This difference can be characterized as follows:

It originates in the Western (and American in particular) view of Asia as an *integral* part of the West's hegemonic security and economic interests.

Different parts of Asia, however, are animated by entirely different concerns. They do not regard the West or the United States as in any way a part of *their* security concern. Thus, while U.S. interest in Asia is geostrategically inclusive and intrusive, Asia's interest in America is almost entirely uninclusive and unintrusive in character.[7] Attention is focused on the opportunity provided by global competition under the banner of development of market forces under capitalism to release Asia from the stranglehold of Western hegemony in general and American economic and political dominance in particular.

This process will, in all probability, be accompanied by reorientations throughout Asia that are likely to result in new alignments. The alignments could turn out to be between China, Korea, and Japan; between each of these and Russia (Asian Russia); between Japan and Southeast Asia (and Australasia); between China and Southeast Asia; between China and South Asia; between South Asia and West (and Central) Asia (i.e., the Middle East); and between South Asia and Southeast Asia. Such alignments would radically alter the configuration of forces in the world as a whole and in Asia in particular.

Against such powerful winds of change aiding transformations of millennial scope, influential intellectuals seem inclined to attach disproportionate importance to factors such as the rise of Islam or the civilizational imperatives driving non-Western societies (e.g., China) to an inevitable clash with the West. This is in accordance with the classic journalistic device—"simplify and exaggerate." But in this instance, the device has been elevated to a level of systematic editorial practice by a number of opinion-building organs of the media. The complexity and magnitude of the real problems are being turned around before our very eyes.

3. How best can the emerging configuration of forces in the world be characterized and what portent might they contain? Let us start with the West, move East (Asia as differentiated from the East of the Cold War era) and South. The United States is undoubtedly the greatest beneficiary of the end of communism. In place of the Soviet Union is a Commonwealth of (10) Independent States (CIS), of which Russia is historically and militarily the power of greatest significance, albeit much reduced in stature. And East Europe, which the Soviet Union turned into a buffer zone between the East and the West, has reverted to the Western sphere of influence.

However, the former Soviet Union and Eastern Europe have suffered a great psychological, military, economic, and political deflation and seem to be suspended in limbo. Their lurch toward democracy and leap into capitalist economic organization have stirred up latent tensions, of which those familiar to the precommunist ancestors in the spheres of national and ethnic separatism and antagonism have undergone a fierce revival and re-intensification. The supersession of narrow national/ethnic consciousness by a wider ideological identity accompanied by an elimination of atavistic memories of the past was thus only superficial and temporary in character. By the same token, the failure of the communist parties to debureaucratize and democratize their regimes created huge problems for the legatees of a sclerotic political system. In the space for reform created by the dramatic political change of the late 1980s and early 1990s, anomic social violence and anarchic tendencies entered, rendering democratic changes difficult to accomplish.

In the reconfiguration of political forces following the Cold War, we must not lose sight of realignments internal to the West, and here we include in the West not only Europe but also Japan. Nor ought we to forget that Japan is both a modern economic power *and* an Asian country with a powerful stake in the on-going economic, political, and strategic transformations of that continent. These realignments are potential sources of contradiction within the giant tridentine economic superpower of the world.[8] Moreover, these radical changes are fueled by new ramifications of capital in a world of shrinking national boundaries and increasing fiscal porosity and are accompanied by an almost evangelical zeal with which latter-day converts to capitalism and newly opened areas of capitalist penetration foster the expansion of markets.

During the next twenty years, China (with the integration of Hong Kong followed by Macao and, eventually, Taiwan) will almost certainly experience an exponential surge in its economic performance. Assuming that the Chinese economy continues to maintain the pace to which it has grown accustomed during the last 15 years of globalization and liberalization, its emergence as an economic superpower can be all but taken for granted. Such a development will not only affect the dynamic of Japan's role in a revitalized East Asia, with the Pacific Rim becoming a magnet attracting capital and surplus accumulation to unprecedented levels, but also may well introduce new stresses and strains in Sino-American economic and political relations. China's self-image as an Asian power seeking to carve out for itself a rising economic destiny and a sphere of influence of continental dimensions will almost certainly spill over into new forms of contention and antagonism in its relations with the United States.

It is highly unlikely that the United States will allow a radical displacement of the center of gravity of world capitalism. Present arrangements provide for intracapitalist economic and political cooperation while initiatives are controlled by a consortium of powers consisting of the United States, Japan, and the European Community (with the help of international banks). As China pursues an aggressive policy of capturing markets in the rest of Asia (as well as of appropriating a lion's share of the domestic market), conflicts between China and the United States will become unavoidable. These conflicts may well develop into a major world contradiction with unpredictable consequences for the internal cohesion of the triangle constituted by the United States, the EC, and Japan in the world as we know it today.

In other words, an enlargement of conflict between the United States and China could well provoke division and contradictions *within* the Western alliance (including Japan). It is probable that when China reaches the stage of economic development at which it would fulfil the qualifications needed to join the G-7, the United States will invent political obstacles in order to prevent its admission into the club.[9] It is well within the realm of the possible that we shall then witness an inversion, on a global level, of the "One country, Two systems" phenomenon of our own day into a "One world, Two systems" formula with the rider that both systems would be capitalist, modern, global, privatized, market-driven, and liberal!

The potential major contradiction of the world in the 21st century may well crystallize around the project of modernization and globalization of the Chinese economy. As in the case of Japan during the second half of the 20th century, so too in the China of the first half of the next century, its continued low-profile projection of itself in the military sphere[10] is likely to be more than offset by spectacular economic performance.

The great American preoccupation throughout the Cold War was with loss of markets and cheap sources of raw material in different parts of the world. The United States feared that national liberation struggles would undermine its dominance in these vital areas of global development of capitalism. Now that the world has changed and anti-imperialist national liberation struggles have been thrown out of gear, the path of capitalist development has been cleared of obstacles to the processes of globalization and liberalization. Or, so it would seem.[11]

Ironically, however, the determination of China to become a full fledged member of the capitalist club, and the likely emergence of India as an unevenly but substantially developed though dependent capitalist economy, can have consequences for the United States that are far from palatable.

First, access to raw materials can no longer be controlled from afar; they will have to be shared among a large number of gigantic competing capitalist economies. Second, if China and India develop at their present rates, they will swell the ranks of the world's middle classes (on an upward consumption curve) by at least another billion in 20 years, thus outnumbering by a large margin the bourgeoisie of the whole of the rest of the world.

The crisis of "sustainability," not to mention global pollution levels, will reach proportions hitherto undreamed of. The West in general and the United States in particular will have to devise new strategies, including a possible, arguably voluntary, lowering of the living standards of their own middle classes or facing the alternative of conflict with the new Asian members of the world capitalist club. Paradoxically, the dialectic of the post–Cold War era of "doors opening" in third areas of the world may well give rise to consequences not dissimilar to those feared during the era of national liberation struggles.[12] The rise of new poles of growth within a globalized capitalist system will in all likelihood lead to a clash between its established dominant and newly emergent segments. Not a clash of civilizations, but a clash of economic wills— the will to maintain predominance and advantage on the one side and, on the other, the will to develop to the hilt.

Let us now move south in the Asian context. The emerging picture can be completed with a brief reference to the formation of regional identities in Southeast Asia and South Asia. We have already noted that in North and East Asia, two major economic forces are on the threshold of radical change. Japan is undergoing a process of readjustment of its postwar role as a Western economic power of global significance. Japan is also becoming an increasingly vigorous member of an emergent cohort of Asian economic giants establishing powerful links with China, Southeast Asia and (to a lesser extent) South Asia.

Despite its relatively uneven development, China enjoys the advantages that go with its continental size. Japan's great opportunity lay in its Phoenix-like rise from the ashes of Armageddon to become one of the economic superpowers of the century. Unlike either China or Japan, until the 1960s, the Association of Southeast Asian Nations (ASEAN) members were embroiled in internal and regional struggles that stood in the way of rapid economic development. The region as a whole became a theater of tension between nationalist, pro-American, and pro-Communist political forces. However, the entire region was somewhat less susceptible to uneven development than South Asia or even China, though it started from a low threshold of industrialization and modernization.

During the last three decades, the different parts of the region—from the vast archipelago of Indonesia to relatively small nations—have come together to forge close institutional links and programs of mutual cooperation and division of labor in the spheres of investment, production, and export. In the process, they have learned the art of promoting their collective or regional identity without allowing themselves to be held back by rigid received ideas of national sovereignty. So much so that ASEAN is second only to the EU in contemporary world politics in the quality and level of economic performance that it has achieved through a combination of techniques and practices based on the principles of integration, complexity, and subsidiarity.

As a region, Southeast Asia is not in the same league as Japan or China (given the latter's potential). Nevertheless, it represents a *tranche* of Asian economic development of considerable magnitude and importance, still continuing to rise on an upward curve. Southeast Asia has thus carved out for itself a dynamic role to play, even allowing for the radical political changes that await some countries of the region (e.g., Indonesia) in the near future.

In striking contrast to Southeast Asia, South Asian countries[13] (mostly postcolonial nations with a background of British colonial rule) have been stuck in a groove for far too long a time. As a region, South Asia has not changed radically. Even recent injections of strong doses of modernization and liberalization, globalization and marketization have not quite awakened South Asian nation-states from their prolonged state of postcolonial torpor. Among the main characteristics marking the South Asian cohorts from their Southeast Asian counterparts are:

1. South Asian countries have been unable to shed the legacy of interregional, intercommunal, interethnic, and interreligious tensions bequeathed by colonial rule. Far from diluting them and blazing new trails of mutual cooperation, the dominant classes in control of state structures in these countries have invariably sought to exploit the various tensions present in the society for political purposes and as breeding ground for new conflicts. The subordination of social ends to sectional gain has been an enduring feature of intra–ruling-class conflicts in different countries of the region.

2. In the economic sphere, entrenched agrarian structures have proved difficult to reform. Even though the capitalist mode of production has penetrated agriculture, precapitalist relations of production as well as traditional social hierarchies have continued to flourish. The political consequences of cohabitation, within the economic base, of two fundamentally opposed forces of production, have remained counterproductive to rapid economic growth.

At the same time, technological self-reliance has developed only partially even in India, which has claimed credit for a long-term policy of self-sufficiency and autonomous development. The success of the forces of globalization and modernization throughout South Asia has been much less efficacious than in Southeast Asia as a whole or, for that matter, any other region of Asia. Uneven development in an era of central planning (1950s–1980s, especially in India and Sri Lanka) has reproduced itself under different conditions during the present epoch of modernization (starting in the 1990s). As a consequence, the rate of economic growth of South Asia can be expected to continue to fall drastically behind the rate of economic growth of Southeast Asia.

3. Throughout the first five decades of the postcolonial history of the region, relations between South Asian countries have been fraught with conflict. Conflicts have ensued over borders, over territorial and irredentist disputes, over ideological questions (e.g., secular democracy versus theocratic autocracy), over ethnic separatism and national fission (e.g., Sri Lanka), over questions relating to "internal colonialism" (leading, for example, to the breakup of Pakistan and the establishment of Bangladesh and subsequently to tensions between the Center and Punjab on the one hand and sister provinces of Pakistan on the other). Such conflicts also are reflected in the aftermath of Soviet military intervention in Afghanistan and the civil strife that followed as well as in the predicament of the small landlocked kingdoms of Nepal and Bhutan with a big regional power breathing down their necks.

The arrogant behavior of India toward the other South Asian countries, its doomed China policy of the 1960s and 1970s, the intransigence of India and Pakistan over Kashmir, and India's uneven record on the Tamil question relating to Sri Lanka have been among the serious obstacles blocking social and economic progress in the region as a whole.

A lion's share of responsibility for South Asia's miserable record in the maintenance of intraregional peace belongs thus to India, which, under the dominance of the Congress Party, tended to treat the region more as its fiefdom than as a community of equal, separate, independent sovereign states. Non-Congress coalitions (as well as the Congress government that was briefly presided over by Lal Bahadur Shastri), however, have pursued policies clearly accented toward tempering the inequalities of intercourse. But the Congress Party has not yet remained continuously out of power for a sufficient length of time to create conditions that would favor a breaking of the mold in which the international relations of South Asia have been set.

4. Unlike the postcolonial developmental experience of Southeast Asian societies (which has been marked by *relatively* less severe forms of poverty at the lower levels), that of South Asian countries has been not only extremely uneven but also accompanied by an intensification of poverty. This is reflected in an acute downward differentiation along a vertical axis among *all* social strands; a systematic disempowerment of large segments of society; a drastic shrinkage of social opportunities; and, massive deprivation caused by a lack of entitlement to elementary civic democratic and social rights to education, health, and employment of a vast majority of the population.

Thus, in India, to cite a ready example, a majority of the population has sunk to such depths of deprivation that they lie submerged beneath even the officially defined poverty line. By the same token, the Sri Lankan economy, which, during the early years of independence, held promise of an adequate welfare policy, is plagued by poverty at levels comparable to those prevailing elsewhere in the region. Poverty in Bangladesh is experienced in rural areas through agricultural involution and in the towns through a grossly dependent, partially criminalized and stagnant urban economy. Long periods of military rule and endemic corruption of civilian political parties have also contributed to an intensification of poverty in countries such as Bangladesh and Pakistan.

The state is by far the most puissant political actor in South Asian as in East Asian and Southeast Asian countries. However, its social foundations radically differ between these regions. Starting from an advanced economic base, Japan rebuilt itself under postwar American occupation and a regime of "liberal democratization" of the civilian polity. China, under the CCP rigorously pursued a dynamic policy during the 1949–1979 period. Preceded by a highly enlightened radical economic policy that belonged to the Yenan era, China eradicated poverty and enabled the lowest rungs of society to secure the basic entitlements of health, housing, literacy and education, employment, minimum welfare, and democratic political participation at the local level (the term "democratic" being radically differently understood in this context from the standard Western view).

In South Korea and Taiwan, economic development was pursued with the help of huge amounts of money made available by the United States (an almost suzerain presence in both countries) as well as drastic land reform radically altering the productive agricultural base. In Southeast Asian countries, despite a lack of clear commitment to eradication of poverty, the new states would appear to have built their economic edifices in social milieux that have been significantly less harsh than in South Asia. This is the case regardless of whether the regimes were under the control of populist governments such as Indonesia under Sukarno's leadership, or Malaysia under UMNO, or a civil-military hybrid such as Thailand or Indonesia since the overthrow of Sukarno in 1965. In contrast to all the other regions of Asia, throughout South Asia the state has, on balance, played a negative role in relation to the economic position of the mass of the population which has steadily worsened over the years. At the same time, state power has been generously deployed toward the creation of a substantial minority belonging to the middle class (numbering about 300 million in India, 50 million in Pakistan, 5 million in Sri Lanka, 15 million in Bangladesh, with far fewer in Afghanistan, Nepal, and Bhutan).

A comparative analysis of the structure of poverty in the different regions of Asia and in different countries within each region can throw light on the political pressure points that are developing in different societies in the domestic, regional, and international contexts. Of particular relevance here is the question of intensification of poverty and uneven development in China, recently opened to the outside world, against a background of three decades of successful struggle to remove mass deprivation within a "closed system."

However, the price of dependent and centralized development has been exacted in the form of an accelerating "democratic deficit" (in electoral polities) or outright "authoritarianism" (in states that oscillate between absolutism of one kind or another— e.g., "military rule" to "feudal" or "fundamentalist" structures of authority). Horizontal social contradictions invariably lend themselves to intra–ruling-class accommodation. By contrast, vertical social contradictions (e.g., between the state and the mass of the people, between industrial capital and labor, between the rich and middle peasantry and the poor peasantry and landless labor, between men and women in the family and at the workplace) tend to intensify with development. A general factor underlying this phenomenon is the differentiation between the upwardly mobile better off and the downwardly mobile worse off, resulting in an exacerbation of poverty and deprivation.

5. Seen from the grassroots, the structure of the state in South Asia (as indeed in other parts of Asia, to differing degrees) constitutes an alienating if not a positively repellent sight. In countries such as India in which some form of token decentralization *(panchayati raj)* of power has been reluctantly brought into place, local structures to which power has been devolved (with few exceptions) take no steps to spread out the benefits of decentralized power to the population as a whole. A yawning gap separates the local "haves" who monopolize the resources and the mass of the local poor. Environmental and ecological damage and abuse inflicted by development projects affect the latter while the benefits flow to the former.

In all countries of South Asia, democratic consciousness and an awareness of civil rights have grown among the poorer sections. A minimal impact of this expanding sense of political identity can be seen in the alacrity and thoroughness with which the mass of the electorate periodically wipes the slate clean of legislators and parties with a manifestly corrupt record. However, the electoral precocity of the mass of the people is by no means sufficient to change the agenda of the state or the commitment of the dominant classes to further their own class interests. This is done with the assistance, needless to add, of their international mentors and supporters rather than to the common interests of *all* classes of society.

An enormous rift has developed during the last three decades between political parties whose horizon does not reach beyond the narrow confines of the classes that they represent. These class interests are refracted through a variety of prisms—viz., of regional, communal, social, ethnic, religious, gender-based, and cultural differentiation and discrimination) on the one hand and, on the other, the vast and expanding mass of (undifferentiated) poor. This has led to a growing realization that democratic ends cannot be vouchsafed by the existing modalities of state power and socioeconomic development.

Thus we have been witnessing a growth of political and social movements addressing problems of an immediate nature, including how to survive under conditions of increasingly harsh and ruthless exploitation at the hands of the structures of the state and of the local power-holders, and how to safeguard the environment and customarily available local resources for subsistence from the depredations of "developers."

In India, Sri Lanka, Bangladesh, and Nepal, a vast number of local movements of resistance has registered remarkable though still limited successes, despite their continuing to remain parochially based and confined to single (or a small clutch of) issues. However, the important insight arising out of this observation is that *democratic participation* cannot be guaranteed simply by writing a constitution or by constructing instrumentalities of state.

The signal failure of the existing system of power in this area, during the last five decades, to acknowledge the need for giving political participation due importance has resulted in the democratic initiative passing into the hands of the mass of the people (in the first instance, at the local level).

The state in South Asia is thus at a crossroads. To cooperate with their democratically aroused peoples or to resist them, that is the question. Resistance to an unheeding state has been the language of the poor in the face of opposition. How will the class forces that control the levers of state power respond to the new political consciousness that is spreading throughout the lower rungs of society? The task of finding the answers to these questions is of crucial relevance to our concern.

I began this paper with a reference to contemporary developments in global interrelationships. Let me conclude by briefly returning to the same theme. The highly uneven all-Asia picture contains clear indications of the extreme weakness of the South Asian regions, the qualitative gap between South Asia and Southeast Asia, and the momentum (in systemic terms) gained during the last two decades by North and Northeast Asia in general and China in particular. South Asian countries have only recently begun to emerge gradually from a long night of darkness symbolized by the India-Pakistan pyrrhic conflict and India's repeated attempts to dominate the region into a new era marked by lesser mutual suspicion if not greater trust.

This slow change has been signaled by the evolution of the South Asian Association for Regional Cooperation (SAARC), since its inception in 1983, into a forum for discussions of common problems faced by the region and a scaling down of India's ambitions through the adumbration of a new line of approach to regional issues embodied in what in regional patois has come to be known as the "Gujral doctrine."[14]

Even so, the SAARC is a far weaker intergovernmental body than the ASEAN and lags much behind the latter in the economic promise that it holds for the future, while it is true that both share the same kind of allergy to democratic politics. The weakness of the SAARC in general and India (as its largest member) in particular is highlighted by the fact that whereas ASEAN invites China and Japan to attend its meetings on trade, India has to date been unable to secure similar recognition of its international status as an Asian power. Thus, in such shifts of power as may now be under way between Asia and the West, South Asia will continue to occupy the lowest position in the emerging pecking order to which globalization will eventually lead.

Conclusion

Social science can contribute to new initiatives in the related spheres of reduction of poverty and empowerment of the weaker segments of society only by a radical alteration of the structure and contents of its discourse. It ought to start with an explicit recognition of the roots of mass poverty in the rapacious exploitation arising out of the penetration of a combination of forces—of global capitalism, of imperial power, and of state power dominated by different segments of indigenous capital.

Social science discourse should provide more and more space for the exploration of participatory democracy instead of concentrating on the virtues of "good governance," invoking the salience of "security" (i.e., the preservation of the status quo), and placing the "state" as the centerpiece of discussions of development and change. Research ought to focus greater attention on the contrast between the anatomy of competition (which lies at the heart of capitalist economic development) and the new enterprise of complementation and cooperation. Without such cooperation, poverty cannot be eradicated and "security" in its deepest meaning cannot be guaranteed between different segments of any given society, between different societies in any given region, and between region and region.

Notes
1. In contrast to the other major brand of nationalism, which invariably led to deals between the parties waging struggles for independence and the metropolitan colonial power, as, for example, in India.

2. The first revolutionary movement adopting this form of all-out struggle being the Chinese Communist Party after Yenan—that is, between 1937 and 1949.

3. These struggles were invariably waged with the aim of securing a negotiated transfer of power from the metropolitan governments.

4. Ironically, the Sino-Soviet dispute coincided with détente in the relations between the superpowers, leading to a partial normalization of relations embracing the first major contradiction.

5. China has pursued a friendly policy toward all the ten members of the Commonwealth of Independent States (CIS), sprung from the former Soviet Union in general and Russia in particular, since 1991.

6. Largely since the successful conclusion of the Nicaraguan liberation in 1979 by FNLS guerrillas.

7. It is ironic that even 20 years ago China's record of advancing global theories was phenomenal to say the least. Mao Zedong and Zhou Enlai were leading figures in this field. Yet this strand of making sense, intellectually, of the world of the present and the future appears to have gone into prolonged disuse.

8. I have deliberately refrained from referring to the immense potential for the development of a serious contradiction between the United States and Western Europe (notwithstanding the expansion of NATO) as Russo-German relations are strengthened and consolidated. My reluctance in this regard is inherent in any serious *longue durée* view informed by the wisdom embodied in the apothegm "We will never know how our actions will turn out." It is useful to remember that West Germany's *Ostpolitik* was after all the first step in the process that ultimately led to the reunification of Germany. Who can foretell the destiny to which Germany's *Mittel Europa* policy toward Russia might lead in the early decades of the new millennium and what its impact will be on the West as a whole and on America in particular?

9. By the same token, Japan may well lobby for China's admission into the G-7 system!

10. After all, it was one of Mao's oft-repeated remark that there was no substitute for a well-equipped, technologically sophisticated, and modern army. Guerrilla armies were necessary for survival in struggles against militarily superior enemies, but their international significance was limited. Without a modern army functioning at the highest level of technological efficiency, it would be impossible to compete with other countries globally.

11. I have not included in this discussion any reference to the inherently crisis-ridden character of the development of capitalism and the great risks that are entailed in the current phase of globalization. A future

crisis of capitalism could well trigger interimperialist conflicts on a large scale involving old, established capitalist powers on one hand and new Asian entrants into the capitalist club (in particular, China) on the other, with Japan hovering between the two.

12. Especially as prefigured in the indiscriminate use of the metaphor of the domino.

13. Afghanistan, Bangladesh, Bhutan, India, Maldives, Nepal, Pakistan, and Sri Lanka.

14. A. B. Vajpayee, the foreign minister of the Janata government (1977–1980) and I. K. Gujral, the foreign minister of the National Front government (1989–1990) and foreign minister and prime minister of the United Front governments (1996–1997 and 1997–), altered the style and substance of India's foreign policy marginally for the better. I. K. Gujral, in particular, has enunciated a neighbor-friendly foreign policy under the terms of which India should be more generous to and expect less from the other powers of the region.

CHAPTER 3

Regionalism and Globalism in Asia Pacific

Joseph A. Camilleri

Fashionable though it has become, regionalism remains a multidimensional, ambiguous, and highly elusive concept that can obscure as much as clarify the modalities and implications of functional and institutional interaction. One of the more helpful theoretical expositions is that offered by Andrew Hurrell, who subdivides the notion of regionalism into five categories: regionalization, regional awareness and identity, regional interstate cooperation, state-promoted regional integration, and regional cohesion (Hurrell 1995, 37–73). By endowing each category with distinctive meaning and content, he is able to retain the richness and complexity of the concept, while highlighting the diverse and at times contradictory pressures to which it is invariably subjected in practice. Given that the third and fourth categories are closely connected in that they both focus on the role of the state, the intention here is to conflate them into one category, the emphasis being on the negotiation and development of interstate agreements, regimes, and institutions. As for the fifth category, it may be more helpful to postpone consideration of the potential for regional cohesion to a later stage, since it represents the combined impact of the other four categories. To these three categories borrowed from Hurrell's analytical framework a fourth will be added, which specifically draws attention to the emergence of dual-track diplomacy, foreshadowing the subsequent and more detailed discussion of the contribution of nonstate actors and civil society more generally to the processes of regionalization.

Though regionalism clearly lends itself to comparative analysis, care must be taken to avoid the trap of assessing Asia-Pacific regionalism purely in terms of the European experience. Here it may be useful to distinguish between de jure integration, which has made considerable headway in Western Europe, and de facto integration, which is perhaps more attuned to the circumstances of Asia Pacific. It is also well to remember that integrative processes in each of the three subregions are likely to proceed at a different pace, assume different forms, and have differential, even contradictory effects on the region as a whole.

Regionalization

Hurrell uses the term "regionalization" to refer to the complex network of flows across state boundaries, involving the movement of goods and services, capital, technology, information and people. He lays particular stress on the role of markets and private economic actors, including transnational firms and regional business networks, in establishing higher levels of economic specialization and interdependence within a given geographical region. Trade and investment flows, international mergers and takeovers, and regional production alliances are seen as key indicators of regionalization. Trade is perhaps the most striking manifestation of Asia-Pacific economic regionalization. Intra-Asian trade now accounts for about 45 percent of East Asia's total trade. Between 1980 and 1992 Asia's share of exports originating in Asian newly industrializing economies rose from 32.2 percent to 43.5 percent. During the same period, the comparable share for the ASEAN countries fell slightly but rose sharply for China from 52.9 percent to 70.3 percent, and the United States from 21.2 percent to 26.3 percent (Katzenstein 1996, 126). In the case of China, the last few years have seen much higher levels of economic interaction with the rest of Asia. Sino-Japanese trade reached $39 billion in 1993. Japan was now China's largest trading partner, while China was Japan's second largest trading partner. Hong Kong, Taiwan, South Korea, Singapore, and Thailand are now also among China's top ten trading partners. Bilateral trade between China and Taiwan increased from $77 million in 1979 to $14.4 billion in 1993. According to one estimate, South Korea will displace Japan as China's largest trading partner by the end of the century, with bilateral trade expected to rise from $11.7 billion in 1994 to $56 billion in the space of six years (Hu 1996, 45–46).

The regional concentration of trade is but one of several indicators. Of particular significance has been the accelerated relocation of Japanese production in different parts of Asia, thereby establishing Japan as "the undisputed leader in Asia in terms of technology, capital goods, and economic aid" (Katzenstein 1996,

128). Having achieved a secure foothold in Korea and Taiwan, Japan has since rapidly expanded its stake in the ASEAN economies and is now developing a substantial presence in China and Indochina. In each case Japanese firms have taken advantage of lower labor costs and highly favorable fiscal and other regulatory conditions to meet the growing demand for producer and consumer goods in these countries. Another important factor contributing to regional economic integration has been the economic growth of "Greater China," with overseas Chinese currently accounting for nearly four-fifths of direct foreign investment in the People's Republic of China (PRC). To give but one example, the four Special Economic Zones in Guangdong and Fujian have become increasingly enmeshed with the economies of Hong Kong, Macau, Taiwan, and the Chinese business communities of Southeast Asia. China is now the third largest recipient of foreign investment from Hong Kong, Taiwan, South Korea, Singapore, and Thailand. The interpenetration of national economies is also stimulated by the exponential growth of financial flows across national boundaries, coupled with the increasing dominance of intracompany as a proportion of bilateral trade. Intracompany trade currently accounts for nearly four-fifths of Japan's total exports and half of its imports (Encarnation 1994, 2). Complementing and reinforcing these transnational production structures is the emergence of such regional economic zones as the Johor–Singapore–Riau growth triangle, the Indonesia–Malaysia–Thailand growth triangle, the East Asia growth area, the Southern China growth triangle, and the Tumen River Delta Economic Zone (Thant, Tang, and Kakaza 1995; Jordon and Khanna 1995, 433–462). Finally mention must be made of the increasing mobility of labor, with the strongly performing economies of the region attracting large numbers of legal and illegal immigrants.

There are, however, clear limits to the extent, intensity and efficiency of these economic and functional linkages. There are many states (Cambodia, Laos, North Korea, several of the Pacific island states) and many areas within states (e.g., noncoastal areas of China, parts of Burma, and the Russian Far East), where these linkages are nonexistent or at best tenuous. Moreover, many of the linkages that are said to contribute to regional interdependence (e.g., Japan-ASEAN trade and investment flows) are acutely asymmetrical and to that extent likely to promote social and political tensions both within and across national boundaries. The negative implications of regional financial linkages were most dramatically demonstrated in the East Asian crisis of 1997 (Bello 1998). Like a pebble dropped into a pond, the depreciation of the Thai baht on 2 July 1997 spread its ripples with remarkable speed through to the Philippines, Malaysia, and Indonesia and then to South Korea, Singapore, and Hong Kong. The impact on Japan and China, though less direct or immediate, was by no means insubstantial. It was as if a powerful transmission belt comprised of a number of intricate but connected mechanisms had helped to spread the disease from one country to another.

Regional Identity

Notwithstanding these unmistakable asymmetries and the domestic fissiparous tendencies that they mirror and reinforce, regionalization in Asia Pacific is also reflected in the development of a wide range of transnational flows and social networks. This trend is still very much at an embryonic stage, but there is enough evidence to suggest the emergence of new forms of identity, or at least new attitudes and perceptions, which bypass but also influence the conscious policies of existing territorially defined states.

For observers wedded to a Eurocentric perspective, national differences still seem pervasive. A case in point is the sharp tension that still separates Japan from many of its neighbors, notably Korea and China, for whom Japanese aggression and brutality in the Second World War remain a major source of friction. According to Aaron Friedberg, Asian nationalism rooted firstly in ethnic and racial differences is "a reflection of the region's diversity, its geographical dispersal, its troubled past and its lack to date of the soothing interconnections that have existed for some time in Western Europe (Friedberg 1993/94, 17). Numerous conflicts over the delineation of land frontiers or maritime boundaries and disputed control over newly discovered natural resources are portrayed as the geopolitical or geoeconomic expression of deeper national animosities. History is itself a subject of disagreement, with different Asian societies (e.g., China and Japan) intent on reconstructing the past in ways which serve national purposes and accentuate the national divide. The extreme sensitivity surrounding such issues as the content of history textbooks and the commemoration of past wars is seen as evidence of the absence of cultural affinities. A sharp contrast is thus drawn between Europe, where "political similarities are supported by rough cultural unity," and the Pacific, where "the similarities are barely skin deep" (Segal 1993, 179–181).

In recent years an opposing view has emerged highlighting the signs of a growing Asian identity, with frequent references to such notions as "Asian values" (Zakaria 1994; Kausikan 1993), the "Pacific Way" (Mahbubani 1995), and an Asian "strategic culture." Exponents of the Asian identity thesis have tended to reaffirm the principles of sovereignty and noninterference in interstate relations, to challenge universalist claims of human rights, and to emphasize instead duties and obligations, respect for authority, and forms of economic and political organization that privilege social harmony and family and kinship ties. It is doubtful, however, whether this social cosmology, sometimes labeled as Confucian, accurately reflects the diversity of Asia's religious and cultural traditions, let alone the much wider cultural net, which encompasses Australia, New Zealand, Canada, and the United States.

There is reason, then, to question the facile formulations that depict the region as either culturally cohesive or hopelessly fragmented. A more plausible assessment is of a region which, though incorporating a great many ethical and normative influences, is nevertheless, by dint of increasing social and economic interaction, developing a heightened sense of common interests, perhaps common destinies. Contributing to this outcome is the consumerist culture of middle-class capitalism, coupled with the homogenizing impact of economic regionalization and globalization, and as a consequence of this an emerging cultural and political discourse that, though it cannot always reconcile differences, must in practice negotiate agreements across a wide range of issues, including trade, human rights, security, and environment.

Interstate Agreements, Regimes, and Institutions

In the course of the last 50 years, Asia Pacific has witnessed a great deal of regionalist activity involving the negotiation and implementation of interstate norms, agreements, and regimes. Even during the Cold War, cooperative arrangements flourished on many fronts. Political and strategic cooperation was shaped largely by the dictates of ideological bipolarity, hence the proliferation of bilateral and multilateral alliances and security arrangements (e.g., U.S.-Japan alliance, ANZUS treaty, Sino-Soviet alliance, Southeast Asia Treaty Organization) within which the United States and to a lesser extent the Soviet Union exercised a hegemonic role. U.S. hegemony was generally more solidly grounded for it rested on a number of economic arrangements reflecting in different forms and to varying degrees American preeminence within the world economy. By the same token, a number of organizations established between 1945 and 1975 bore the imprimatur of the United States or had as their primary focus the containment of communism (e.g., Far Eastern Commission and Allied Council for Japan, Asian Development Bank, Asian and Pacific Council). A great many other organizations were much less constrained either by the logic of Cold War antagonisms or the primacy of U.S. strategic interests. Some institutional arrangements were directly or indirectly created by the United Nations (e.g., Economic Commission for Asia and the Far East, Asia-Pacific Institute for Broadcasting Development). Others resulted primarily from the initiatives of Japan (e.g., Asian Productivity Organization, Asia Pacific Parliamentary Union, Ministerial Conference for the Economic Development of Southeast Asia), Australia (e.g., Colombo Plan, South Pacific Commission, Central Banks of Southeast Asia, Australia and New Zealand), or one or more Southeast Asian states (e.g., Asia-Pacific Postal Union, Association of Southeast Asia, Association for Science Cooperation in Asia, Cultural and Social Center for the Asia and Pacific Region). To a greater or lesser extent, most of the organizations created during the 1950s and 1960s were subject to a number of limitations: *geographical* (i.e., they were confined to a particular subregion), *temporal* (i.e., they operated over a relatively short time span), *functional* (i.e., their responsibilities extended to the performance of a few technical tasks), *ideological* (i.e., they were designed to promote the interests or worldviews of a particular camp and were therefore *exclusivist* in membership). They nevertheless contributed to the development of regional diplomacy and a culture of technical and economic cooperation. But it was only after the end of the Vietnam war and the decline of Cold War rivalries that the institutionalization of norms would gather pace over the entire Asia-Pacific region and across the spectrum of issues.

The 1970s are best characterized as a period of transition, during which ASEAN gradually assumed a pivotal role in regional institution-building. Though formed in 1967 with the express purpose of promoting active collaboration and mutual assistance in the economic, social, cultural, technical, scientific, and administrative fields, ASEAN would over time develop a comprehensive security framework, which Michael Leifer has aptly described as an institutionalized vehicle "for intra-mural conflict avoidance and management" on the one hand, and "extra-mural management of order" on the other (Leifer 1995, 132–133). When the Bangkok Declaration was signed in August 1967, it could be argued that there was little binding together the five founding members of ASEAN except a common desire to contain threats to internal security, normally associated with the activities of revolutionary or secessionist movements. Anticommunism was perhaps the ideological glue that helped to cement an otherwise disparate group of states, whose elites were often suspicious of each other's intentions and embroiled in a series of territorial and other diplomatic disputes.

Partly in response to but also in anticipation of the decline of Cold War rivalries, ASEAN's conception of regional security cooperation gradually assumed a more encompassing perspective, with greater emphasis on uncertainties rather than external threats, and confidence-building measures rather than zero-sum perceptions. Increasingly, the accent was on inclusiveness, that is, on ensuring maximum participation in the dialogue, regardless of differences in levels of economic development, ideological orientation, or geostrategic location. As a consequence, ASEAN membership was progressively expanded with a view to encompassing the whole of Southeast Asia, and, as we shall see, the number of dialogue partners substantially increased, eventually incorporating the greater part of the Asia-Pacific region.

By the late 1980s several independent but closely interacting influences, not least ASEAN's catalytic role in regional diplomacy, were conducive to a number of region-wide proposals and initiatives. The most important of these initiatives were the ASEAN Post-Ministerial Conference (ASEAN PMC), the ASEAN Regional Forum (ARF), and the Asia Pacific Economic Cooperation (APEC) process. Throughout the 1970s ASEAN had established a series of bilateral dialogues—with the European Community in 1972, Australia in 1974, New Zealand in 1975, UNDP in 1976, and Canada, Japan, and the United States in 1977—as a means of promoting economic cooperation, in such areas as agriculture, fishing, forestry, communications, air transportation, shipping, trade, and stabilization of commodity prices. With the progressive widening of ASEAN's membership and agenda, this dialogue framework eventually paved the way for the ASEAN Prime Ministerial Conference (ASEAN PMC), which, by bringing together all the dialogue partners at the same table, established an embryonic institutional infrastructure, including meetings of senior officials (SOMs) of the ASEAN states and the dialogue partners. The ensuing exchange of views on political and security issues signaled a broadening of the security dialogue in that it now encompassed the wider Asia-Pacific region. Several limitations were nevertheless still apparent. The ASEAN PMC has found it difficult to grapple with the more sensitive subregional issues (e.g., Korea, Russo-Japanese territorial dispute) or to develop the principles that might guide and nurture the security dialogue. The task has proved especially difficult in the face of significant differences between ASEAN and its Western interlocutors, especially in relation to the unconventional aspects of comprehensive security (e.g., environment, human rights, good governance). The decision to establish the ASEAN Regional Forum was taken partly with a view to overcoming some, though by no means all, of these limitations.

As in the field of security so in economic relations, the notion of an emerging "Pacific Community" had been steadily gaining ground throughout the 1960s and 1970s. Japan and Australia often took the lead in encouraging the establishment of new institutions, notably the Pacific Basin Economic Council (PBEC) in 1967 and the Pacific Economic Cooperation Council (PECC) in 1980. These institutional developments, pioneered in many instances by business and academia as much as by government, prepared the ground for a major Australian diplomatic initiative in 1988, which came to fruition in 1989 with the formation of APEC (Hellman 1995). Operating initially as a purely consultative forum, APEC brought together representatives from Japan, the United States, Canada, the Republic of Korea, Australia, New Zealand, and the six member states of ASEAN. It aimed at facilitating the exchange of information between member economies, pressing for a successful conclusion of the Uruguay Round of GATT negotiations, and fostering trade and investment liberalization within the Asia-Pacific region. By 1996 APEC's membership had been expanded to include China, Taiwan, Hong Kong, Papua New Guinea, Mexico, and Chile. Though having only a minimal secretariat and a relatively small budget at its disposal, APEC soon developed an extensive network of ministerial and senior official meetings, committees, and working groups. Under the impetus provided by its annual Leaders Meetings, the first of which was held in Seattle in November 1993, the APEC project entered a new phase, which is specifically aimed at trade liberalization through negotiated agreements for the removal of tariff and nontariff barriers. At their fourth summit in Subic in November 1996, the APEC leaders were ready to launch the implementation phase of their free trade and investment agenda. Agreement was also reached on a number of business facilitation measures and the engagement of the business sector as a full partner in the APEC process. APEC was rapidly emerging as a private-sector-driven multilateral process but with the state performing a key coordinating and legitimizing role.

Second-Track Diplomacy

A distinctive feature of Asia-Pacific regional diplomacy has been the emergence of nongovernmental exchanges and institutional linkages known as second-track diplomacy. These mechanisms, which involve academics, business people, and government officials participating in their personal rather than official capacity, have provided a useful vehicle for "unofficial" or "quasi-official" dialogue (Harris 1996; Woods 1993). Though such mechanisms have also emerged in other regions, in Asia Pacific there appears to have been greater acceptance of direct links between second-track and governmental processes, particularly with respect to policy development and even policy application. Second-track diplomacy first made its mark in the economic area with the creation of the Pacific Trade and Development Conference, PBEC, and PECC. The lack of intergovernmental institutions, particularly in the area of trade and investment, and the limited institutional expertise and bureaucratic infrastructure at the disposal of postcolonial governments, coupled with increasing pressures from regional business and academic elites for greater policy coordination, created a psychological climate highly favorable to the development of informal or semiformal regional dialogues.

Second-track diplomacy has also been an important feature of ASEAN multilateralism, hence the active encouragement given to policy-oriented ASEAN scholars and analysts. ASEAN-ISIS, a nongovernmental association comprising Southeast Asia's most important institutes and think tanks on security-related issues, assumed a pivotal role in the development of second-track diplomacy and in the generation of policy ideas that helped to shape the ASEAN PMC agenda and eventually paved the way for the formation of the ASEAN Regional Forum. Quite apart from the support given to institutes and think tanks, ASEAN has given its blessing to specific second-track initiatives designed to resolve, or at least contain, intractable regional conflicts. The two most important initiatives to date have both been spearheaded by Indonesia. In the case of the Cambodian conflict, the Jakarta Informal Meetings of 1988–1989 enabled Indonesia to assume a limited mediating role, but with ASEAN performing a useful legitimizing and monitoring function. In response to the Spratlys dispute Indonesia has since 1990 hosted a series of unofficial workshops that have at least provided a forum acceptable to all the South China Sea states. Second-track diplomacy has in both instances served as a valuable confidence-building exercise and enabled ASEAN to assume a higher diplomatic profile than would otherwise have been possible.

ASEAN-inspired initiatives have been complemented by numerous other second-track mechanisms. Some have been region-wide in scope or participation (e.g., Asia-Pacific Roundtable, Asia Pacific Peace Research Association), whereas others have had a geographically more restricted or subregional focus (e.g., North Pacific Cooperative Security Dialogue, Northeast Asia Cooperation Dialogue). Some have operated over a limited time span (e.g., ASEAN-United Nations Workshops on Co-operation for Peace and Preventive Diplomacy), while others have a longer-term horizon (e.g., Pacific Symposium, ASEAN-Japan Dialogue, International Security Forum). Some are issue- or conflict-specific (e.g., Asia-Pacific Dialogue on Maritime Security), while others embrace a wide-ranging agenda (e.g., Commission for a New Asia, Asia Pacific Forum, Kathmandu Regional Centre for Peace and Disarmament in Asia-Pacific). Notwithstanding these differences in scope, geographical reach, and membership (Evans 1994, 132–136), nongovernmental processes have added considerable breadth and depth to the regional security dialogue, spanning, as they do, every country in the region, a great many areas of expertise, and a wide spectrum of opinion. The inclusiveness of the second-track multilateral process, coupled with its relative informality, has facilitated the formation, cross-fertilization, and refinement of ideas and proposals, many of which have subsequently percolated through to the more formalized institutions of first-track diplomacy (Evans 1995, 205–206).

Perhaps the most encompassing multilateral mechanism to have emerged from the rapidly developing nongovernmental dialogue on Asia-Pacific security is the Council for Security and Cooperation in Asia Pacific (CSCAP) (Evans and Ball 1994). Established formally in 1993 by ten founding institutes, many of which belonged to or were clearly linked to ASEAN ISIS, CSCAP's principal function is described in its charter as "providing a structured process for regional confidence building and security co-operation" in Asia Pacific. It seeks to promote discussion between scholars and officials, convening regional and international meetings to consider political-security issues, establishing links and exchanging information with institutions in other parts of the world, and producing and disseminating publications arising from its various deliberations. Thus far its contribution to the security dialogue has revolved largely around the work of its Steering Committee, its national Member Committees (more than a dozen of which have already been formed), and four Working Groups (Maritime Cooperation, North Pacific Dialogue, Cooperative and Comprehensive Security, and CSBMs). Though it is far too early to tell how influential CSCAP will be, its claim to inclusiveness reinforced by China's participation, the support it enjoys from a number of governments, and its extensive contacts among the leading research institutions of the region hold considerable promise for the future.

The Globalism-Regionalism Dialectic

Enough has been said to indicate the quantitative and qualitative growth of institutional processes and mechanisms that has characterized the Asia-Pacific region, especially over the last two decades. Regionalism, particularly in its more recent manifestations, can be understood largely as a response to globalization of the political and economic structures within which regions and states are embedded. Turning first to the international strategic environment, it is clear that over the last three decades the international configuration of power and "the dynamic of power-political competition" have been substantially transformed. Whereas in the aftermath of the Second World War regionalist alignment tended to reflect the imperatives of ideological and strategic bipolarity, the more recent period has been characterized by the collapse or far-reaching reorganization of Cold War alliances, the dissipation of ideological tensions across the East/West divide, the breakup of the Soviet Union and with it the steep decline of Russian power, and a marked shift toward multipolarity. Perhaps the role and status of the United States constitutes the single most ambiguous element in these new geopolitical circumstances, for the world's only remaining superpower (i.e., the only state capable of projecting force on a global scale) is finding it increasingly difficult to translate military capability into political influence. While it continues to enjoy a residual primacy in world affairs, which it is unlikely to surrender in the near future, the maintenance of a global military presence represents a severe financial drain on the U.S. economy, hence the increasing emphasis which successive U.S. administrations have placed on burden-sharing.

It is hardly surprising, then, that with the virtual disappearance of the Communist threat, the decline or at least qualitative retreat of "Pax Americana," and the corresponding rise of new centers of power in Asia Pacific, notably China and Japan, small, middle, and great powers alike should be reconsidering their response to the security dilemma. While the uncertainties posed by the disintegration of the Cold War system may have inclined a number of Asian governments to look favorably on a continuing U.S. military presence, there has been an equally strong and widespread inclination to explore possibilities for a more inclusive security framework that would more accurately reflect the political realities of a multipolar world. With the end of the Cold War, regional inclusiveness across the ideological and core-periphery divides has become a more feasible and attractive strategy.

Indicative of the new trend has been the gradual shift in U.S. and Japanese attitudes toward the new regionalism. During the 1980s the United States could see little merit in any new arrangement that might erode its strategic, and especially naval, preeminence in the region or that might weaken or delegitimize any of its existing security arrangements. The view in Washington, at least under Reagan and in the early years of the Bush administration, was that a U.S.-centered unipolar security system offered the best prospects for maintaining regional stability. By the early 1990s, however, a policy shift was under way. Secretary of State Baker now countenanced a new Asia-Pacific architecture that would comprise a framework for economic integration, a commitment to democratization, and a revamped defense structure for the region (Baker 1991/92). For its part, the Clinton administration embraced the concept of multilateral security dialogue as one of the four pillars of the "new Pacific Community," expressed support for several potential arenas of dialogue, including the ASEAN PMC and APEC, and called for the establishment of "new mechanisms to manage or prevent emerging regional problems". Several considerations had no doubt contributed to Washington's reappraisal of its options, but none was more important than its realization that U.S. power could no longer perform the coordinating role characteristic of the Cold War period. As Manning and Stern have argued, "the two traditional pillars of American predominance in Asia—US economic muscle from its markets and overall financial presence and US security muscle from its bilateral alliances and military bases—are both diminishing assets" (Manning and Stern 1994, 85). To put it differently, a continuing U.S. military presence in Asia Pacific is not enough to contain Chinese power and influence, offer a comprehensive guarantee of regional security, provide acceptable opportunities for more substantial Japanese involvement in regional affairs, or more generally cope with the challenges of increasing economic interdependence and the realignment of power.

Though equally skeptical at first, the Japanese government

became increasingly sympathetic to the advocacy of regional multilateralism. While still preferring a bilateral framework for dealing with such issues as the Northern Territories dispute with Russia or the alliance with the United States, Japan could now see advantages in both ad hoc and more permanent institutional mechanisms. These might, for example, help to legitimize a more assertive Japanese role in regional diplomacy, while at the same time allaying Chinese, Southeast Asian, and Australian anxieties. Such mechanisms might also place additional constraints on Chinese or U.S. unilateral action, which might otherwise prove highly damaging to Japanese interests, whether in the economic or strategic arenas. Significantly, at the ASEAN Post-Ministerial Conference of July 1991, the Japanese foreign minister, Taro Nakayama, while endorsing the ASEAN PMC's role as "the most important forum" for regional dialogue, went on to advocate new mechanisms and frameworks, and in particular the establishment of an Asia-Pacific "forum for political dialogue" designed to promote mutual reassurance. To this end, he proposed the formation of a senior officials meeting to consider options and report to a future meeting of the ASEAN PMC (Nakayama 1991). Conscious of the volatility of its post–Cold War environment, Japan was seeking to become a more independent actor, in part by embedding its role in both established and newly emerging global and regional institutions.

In due course even China became more amenable to multilateral dialogue, in part because it saw this as an opportunity to play a more active role in regional affairs and establish its credentials as a new center of power in the region, but in ways that would not fuel fears of an emerging Chinese threat. In other words, by the early 1990s each of the three principal regional powers was willing, in response to the rapidly changing circumstances of global geopolitics, to entertain at least the modest development of regional and subregional arrangements. It was, however, left to small and middle powers, notably Australia and ASEAN, and to a lesser extent Canada, to take advantage of the more favorable political and ideological climate. Though activated by somewhat different objectives, they sought to promote, through a range of proposals and initiatives, new or expanded cooperative arrangements that might simultaneously restrain the exercise of actual or potential hegemonic power and serve as a forum for negotiation, if not reconciliation, of the conflicting interests of actual or aspiring hegemons. Here it is worth stressing the leadership role of ASEAN and the particular diplomatic style most closely associated with ASEAN's practice, with its emphasis on longer time horizons and policy perspectives, informal structures and processes, consensual approaches to decision making, multidimensional notions of security, and the principle of noninterference in the internal affairs of other countries (Ball 1993; Hassan 1995, 12–13). All of these principles have helped to make multilateralism both more enticing and less threatening than might otherwise be the case. This is not to say that everyone in ASEAN marched to the same tune. Witness, for example, the differences between Indonesia and Singapore on the degree of support to be extended to U.S. air and naval capabilities in the region, not to mention the even greater differences separating ASEAN and Australia on preferred forms and levels of institutionalization and related questions of membership.

Systemic influences on Asia-Pacific regionalism were not confined to the geopolitical arena. The region could hardly remain immune to the globalizing impact of economic and technological change. Indeed, regionalism is in no small measure a response to the increasing globalization and deregulation of markets and the consequent erosion of national economic control. Global economic interdependence, precisely because it gives rise to global issues, networks, and institutions, makes it increasingly difficult for states and communities to pursue interests that are nationally or culturally specific. Greater regional coordination thus becomes one of the few remaining instruments that states can use as they navigate across the turbulent and relatively unfamiliar waters of globalization. For Asian countries the regional option has an added attraction in that economic and technological globalization—and its institutional expression across the OECD world—tends to assume a distinctively "Western" rather than Asian form and to exert a homogenizing influence over the ever expanding flows of values, knowledge, and ideas.

The problems arising from ever-deepening integration are not, in any case, always amenable to global solutions. A regional approach may be politically more viable to the extent that it can more effectively draw upon "commonality of culture, history, homogeneity of social systems and values, convergence of political and security interests," and to that extent make more acceptable "the necessary levels of intrusive management, both in terms of standard-setting and regulation" (Hurrell 1995, 56). Though such issues as environmental degradation, refugees, piracy, and the narcotics trade have an important global dimension, their effect may be more easily visible and the incentives needed to implement efficacious policy responses more readily available at the regional and subregional levels. This factor has significantly shaped the development of ASEAN and the South Pacific Forum and accounts for the emergence of such environment management schemes as the UNEP-sponsored Northwest Pacific Action Plan, the UNESCO-sponsored Intergovernmental Oceanographic Commission, the Northeast Asian Environmental Program, and the Sub-regional Technical Cooperation and Development Program (Hayes and Zarsky 1993).

Finally, it is worth noting in this context that economic globalization can also generate powerful pressures for mercantilist economic rivalry. Regional formations, including trading blocs of the kind spearheaded by the European Union and the North American Free Trade Agreement, may be interpreted as attempts to retain market share and especially competitiveness in important high-technology industries. These considerations have influenced the establishment of the ASEAN Free Trade Area and APEC, although a combination of internal and external influences has in each case ensured that neither institution operates as a closed trading bloc. Indeed, APEC, including as it does both Japan and the United States, may serve at least in part as a bridge between two of the world's three major centers of economic power. True enough, the East Asian Economic Caucus (a Malaysian proposal previously known as the East Asian Economic Grouping) is not without support and could gain considerable momentum should economic tensions escalate between the United States on the one hand and Japan, China, and the other rapidly industrializing economies of East Asia on the other. The evidence thus far suggests the APEC experiment and other subregional groupings are seeking to increase the intensity of trade and investment relations by taking advantage of geographical proximity and functional interdependencies but not in ways likely to sharpen interregional rivalries. In the foreseeable future at least, the continued dependence of the East Asian economies on the U.S. market, not to mention the continued preeminence of U.S. military power, will militate against the politics of closed regionalism.

Paralleling and at times reinforcing the systemic pressures acting on the Asia-Pacific region have been a number of subsystemic (i.e., regional or subregional) influences. Reference has already been made to the geographic concentration of production made possible by the emergence of technology complexes and subregional clusters, usually combining the mobility of finance and technology with ready access to raw materials, cheap labor, and especially favorable industrial and fiscal conditions. In all of this, Japanese capital, technology, and economic aid have played a key part in regional integration. Although what is often referred to as the complementary relationship between the Japanese economy and the economies of Asia and Oceania is a euphemism for structural economic dependencies that may in due course set limits to further economic or political integration. Though Asian regionalism has been largely market-induced, highly complex institutional relationships between business and government have been decisive in shaping regional patterns of trade and investment. These institutions include the progressive extension of Japan's vertical *keiretsu* structures linking major industrial operations and their supplies to various parts of Asia (Stern 1996, 72–83, 92–103; Machado 1996). Paralleling these developments, the Japanese government has over the last three decades sought with varying degrees of success to institutionalize the process of economic regionalization, hence the prominent role it has played in the establishment of the Asian Development Bank, the convening of the Ministerial Conference on Economic Development in Southeast Asia, the proposal for a Pacific Free Trade Area, and the formation of PBEC, PAFTAD, PECC, and most recently APEC. All of these structures have to a greater or lesser extent provided avenues for incorporating business interests into the emerging intergovernmental regime, thereby replicating at the regional level one of the most important features of Japan's political economy.

Another important factor contributing to regional economic integration has been the economic growth of "Greater China," to which reference has already been made. The complex web of ethnic, cultural, and economic linkages between the Chinese mainland and Taiwan, Hong Kong, Macau, Singapore, and the overseas Chinese (*China Quarterly* 1993) will in all probability assume even greater significance following the reestablishment of Chinese sovereignty over Hong Kong. According to one estimate, the Chinese diaspora, though it constitutes only 4 percent of the Chinese population finances, accounts for three-quarters of the 28,000 Chinese firms with significant foreign equity and has a hypothetical national income that is perhaps the equivalent of two-thirds of China's gross domestic product (Katzenstein 1996, 134).

No discussion of the regional influences bearing upon multilateral processes and institutions would be complete without reference to the continuing sources of regional tensions and instability, many of them predating the Cold War. Des Ball has listed more than thirty "simmering and potential conflicts involving competing sovereignty claims, challenges to government legitimacy, and territorial disputes" (Ball 1994, 160). Included among these are the competing Russo-Japanese claims to the Kuril Islands (referred to by the Japanese as the Northern Territories), Japan-Korea tensions, the division of Korea, the sovereignty dispute between China and Taiwan, the competing Japanese and Chinese claims to the Senkaku (Diaoyutai) Islands, the Spratlys dispute, the separatist movements in Tibet, Bougainville, East Timor, Aceh, and West Irian, the residual conflict in Cambodia, the political turmoil within Burma, not to mention numerous other insurgencies and boundary disputes between China and India, China and Vietnam, and between ASEAN members.

Complementing and reinforcing the potential for regional conflict was the widespread trend toward rising military expenditures and acquisitions of potentially destabilizing offensive weapons systems and platforms during the 1980s and early 1990s (Ball 1993/94, 79). During the greater part of the 1980s, military budgets in East Asia experienced much higher growth rates than in other parts of the world, including the Middle East. Between 1982 and 1991 Japan, South Korea, Taiwan, Singapore, and Thailand increased their military expenditures by between 34 percent and 100 percent in real terms (SIPRI 1991, 260; SIPRI 1992, 362, 367, 373). Several years later the end of the Cold War had still not yielded any peace dividend. Between 1986 and 1995 the same four countries continued the upward trend of their military spending by between 24 percent and 58 percent in real terms (SIPRI 1996, 367). A clear, though by no means uniform, connection appears to exist between the competitive dynamic of economic growth and that of military procurement and deployment. Increased defense spending in Indonesia, Malaysia, South Korea, Singapore, Thailand, and the Philippines has paralleled GNP growth, although there have been considerable variations between countries as to the timing and scale of military expenditures (Looney and Frederiksen 1990, 274; Camilleri 1993).

Side by side with the steady expansion of conventional capabilities is the impetus toward horizontal nuclear proliferation, which, though not as yet deeply entrenched, is nonetheless potent. Much recent attention has centered on North Korea's nuclear ambitions, but several other countries already have the capacity and may over time acquire the incentive to take up the nuclear option (e.g., Japan, South Korea, Taiwan). Set in the context of the many unresolved regional conflicts, China's steady expansion of its nuclear arsenal, India's and Pakistan's nuclear tests in May 1998, and the uncertainties surrounding North Korea's future intentions may well compound the insecurity of neighboring states and accelerate the dynamic of horizontal proliferation. The overt acquisition of nuclear capabilities may not, however, constitute the most disturbing trend, at least in the short to medium term. A government may choose instead to use the development of commercial or research capabilities to signal to a potential adversary that it could with relative ease and at relatively short notice acquire at least a rudimentary nuclear weapons capability. Japan's already large and still growing plutonium stocks, coupled with the possible development of new reprocessing capabilities in different parts of Asia, could escalate the already worrying level of nuclear ambiguity.

To complete this brief overview of the region's security environment, mention must be made of the developing scramble for resources and strategic advantage, fueled specifically by territorial disputes and the establishment of exclusive economic zones (EEZs), but more generally by the competitive dynamic underpinning rapid industrialization. Partly as a consequence of the provisions of the UN Convention on the Law of the Sea (UNCLOS), particularly in connection with EEZs and archipelagic waters, maritime issues have assumed increasing significance in recent years. Of the thirty or so potential flashpoints in the region listed by Des Ball, about a third involve disputed islands, continental shelf claims, EEZ boundaries, and other offshore issues (Ball 1994, 164). Recent attempts by China and other regional powers, including several ASEAN states, to develop their naval capabilities are closely related to these maritime rivalries. The Spratlys dispute is the most complex (with six states claiming partial or total jurisdiction over the islands) but also the most revealing of the challenges posed by the region's rapidly evolving geopolitical landscape (Tai To 1995; Valencia 1995).

In all of this, China is emerging as the focus of regional concerns. The modernization of its navy and a series of recent actions, most dramatically in the South China Sea, have been described as "a progressive militarization of its claims" (Acharya 1995, 182). According to this view, the Chinese navy's increased long-range deployments and exercises reflect a desire to enhance China's control capability over the major sea lanes of communication between Southeast Asia and Japan. Whatever the validity of this assessment, it is clear the next 10 to 20 years are likely to see a steady rise in China's economic and military power and with it an increasing challenge to American dominance of the region. The past few years constitute perhaps the early stages of a difficult transitional period likely to generate a good deal of friction and uncertainty and considerably tax the diplomatic skills and ingenuity of great and small powers alike.

At one level, the cumulative impact of the tendencies we have just outlined—the competitive dynamic of economic growth policies, ambitious military modernization programs, acquisition of offensive military capabilities, the potential for horizontal nuclear proliferation, the scramble for maritime resources, shifts in the regional configuration of power—is likely to exacerbate regional tensions and threat perceptions. To that extent, this may hamper the development of a normative and institutional regime based on notions of cooperative security. At another level, however, the very same tendencies are likely to generate interest in and support for the kind of regional institutionalization that might prevent actual and potential flashpoints from degenerating into armed hostilities. Aaron Friedberg has aptly described the process as "a race between the accelerating dynamics of multipolarity, which could increase the chances of conflict, and the growth of mitigating factors that should tend to dampen them and to improve the prospects for a continuing peace" (Friedberg 1993/94, 27–28). Though how this race will unfold is ultimately unpredictable, three distinct yet clearly connected forms of contestation are likely to have a decisive influence.

The first has to do with the global and regional balance of power, which is likely to remain in a state of considerable flux for some time to come. Though both Japan and China are rising powers, neither is likely to achieve a position of regional hegemony, either in political or structural, let alone ideological, terms. As for the United States, it has already abandoned its former role as "magnanimous economic mentor" in order to protect its own interests in a fiercely competitive world market and will be less and less attracted to the unilateral deployment of military force in Asia. This, then, is a transitional period in which three complex but contradictory processes will remain in uneasy coexistence: *residual U.S. hegemony, increasing regional and global interdependence, and intensifying economic competition and geopolitical rivalry.*

A second and closely related form of contestation is likely to dominate trade relations, most dramatically between the United States and the other East Asian economies. At the declaratory level, all governments remain firmly wedded to the principles of free trade, but at the operational level there is a marked tendency for many of them to focus on the failure of others to eliminate quantitative and qualitative barriers to free trade, while turning a blind eye or even justifying their own protectionist practices.

At first sight, the conclusions of the first five APEC Leaders' Meetings may be taken as evidence of rapid progress toward trade liberalization. Of particular importance in this regard is the 1994 summit, where the developed and developing APEC member economies set 2010 and 2020 respectively as the dates by which they would remove all restrictions to trade. Yet no sooner had the agreement been reached than individual governments began putting their own interpretation on it and even questioning its feasibility. Malaysia made it clear that it did not regard the Bogor commitments as legally binding, and therefore not amenable to any kind of enforcement. Moreover, it continued to advocate the need for an Asian forum that would assist its members to develop common positions on international trade negotiations, provide them with a useful counterweight to the world's major trading blocs (i.e., EU and NAFTA), and counter Western attempts to link trade and social issues, namely, human rights, labor conditions, and environmental protection. Though strongly opposed by the United States, Japan, and Australia, the Malaysian position was not without support in other parts of Asia. In any case, the United States has also made it clear that it is not prepared to place all its eggs in the basket of multilateral trade liberalization and that it reserves the right to apply, unilaterally if necessary, any number of punitive measures in a bid to open up Asian markets to American goods and services. Powerful transnational pressures, it is true, may help to keep open the doors of economic regions, but a good many states and some of the most influential interest groups they represent, including farmers and local manufacturers, may not be so easily persuaded to abandon the advantages of protection. The APEC commitment to open regionalism may yet prove more brittle than is often assumed, particularly in the aftermath of the East Asian crisis.

A third form of contestation is likely to arise in relation to issues of governance, with far-reaching implications for institution building at the regional level. In much of the Asia-Pacific region the state remains a fragile institution, which the centralization of power and authority can obscure but not remedy. The East Asian financial crisis has exposed that fragility in a number of countries, not least in Malaysia and Indonesia. In several states indigenous minorities, overseas communities, and ethnic separatist movements have continued to challenge either the legitimacy of existing political institutions or the meaning and substance of national identity. Periodic tensions in civil-military relations, leadership succession problems, regional inequalities in wealth and income distribution, and systematic violations of human rights have all contributed in different places and at different times to varying degrees of political instability. Relatively low levels of social and political cohesion have in turn tempted political elites to experiment with more authoritarian structures.

The centralization of authority has been justified, at least in the short term, as the only effective way of controlling ethnic tensions and pressing ahead with the priorities of economic development. In defense of their policies, governments have also appealed to Asia's cultural traditions and in particular to the Confucian ethic, notably the primacy of community and family values and the importance of states and authority relations. These centralist tendencies have not, however, gone unchallenged. A sizeable and rapidly growing middle class eager to taste the fruits of its newly found wealth and political influence and, more generally, an increasingly assertive civil society have given rise to powerful countervailing pressures. The collision of authoritarian and democratic impulses, dramatically demonstrated in the Tiananmen events of 1989, has become a distinguishing feature of political life in South Korea, Taiwan, Indonesia, Thailand, Burma, and most other parts of the region. The political awakening of civil society, for which the East Asian crisis has provided a powerful stimulus, promises to play a key role in shaping the pace and content of region-building, in part through the increasing regionalization of social flows, networks, movements, and organizations and less directly but no less effectively through its cumulative impact on the political apparatus of the state.

CHAPTER 4

Environmental Security and Sustainable Development in Asia Pacific

Teng Teng

The Asia-Pacific region includes a vast area and a huge population with great differences in natural conditions and level of economic development. In the economic sense, the Asia-Pacific region mainly refers to the countries in the eastern and southeastern parts of Asia along the Pacific Ocean and the various North and South American countries bordering the Pacific Ocean. It also includes major countries of Oceania. This region, especially the coastal areas along the western edge of the Pacific Ocean, has witnessed the most dynamic and rapid economic growth in the postwar era and has become a new growth point of the world economy. We should, however, also take notice that economic development in the Asia-Pacific region has come at a heavy environmental cost. Behind economic success, the environment has been destroyed, natural disasters take place frequently, and the fragile ecological environment seriously hinders further economic development. It is, therefore, urgent that we protect the environment to create happiness for mankind and our future generations. The key to properly handling the relationship between development and the environment is to deepen the understanding and implementation of the ideology of sustainable development.

Characteristics of the Asia-Pacific Region

There are great differences in historical and cultural backgrounds, social systems, and economic development levels among the many Asian and Pacific countries. There are the highly developed countries such as the United States and Japan, newly industrialized developing countries in East and Southeast Asia, and poverty-stricken underdeveloped countries such as Mongolia, Laos, Myanmar (Burma), and some Latin American countries. Such differences dictate that the nature of regional cooperation in the Asia-Pacific region will be different from the competitive regional cooperation of the European Union (EU) and the North American Free Trade Zone, but they may favor regional development if turned into complementary advantages. The development of Asia-Pacific Economic Cooperation (APEC), the biggest organization for economic cooperation in the Asia-Pacific region, provides a good example. At the Manila conference, President Jiang Zemin summed up the modes of cooperation within APEC: recognizing diversity and differences; stressing flexibility, incrementalism, and openness; adhering to the principle of mutual respect, mutual benefit, consultation, autonomy, and voluntarism; combining one-sided and multisided action. These approaches, based on regional diversity and differences, have promoted the development of APEC, and they will also advance cooperation in the Asia-Pacific region on a wider scale.

Population Concentrations

Another characteristic of the Asia-Pacific region is the coexistence of heavy and concentrated populations and a multiplicity of countries. The Asia and Pacific region accounts for more than 50 percent of the total world population. Enormous population pressure has brought about serious difficulties in reaching the take-off point for economic development. A large population base results in scarcity of per capita resources, cultivated land, and grain, surplus labor force, and other employment difficulties. With constant improvement of social and living conditions and with the prolonging of life expectancy, the elderly have come to constitute a large sector of society. Thus a social security system that takes into account the aging of the society needs to be perfected as soon as possible. China has been aware of the pressures its huge population poses and has made agriculture the priority in economic work so as to ensure grain self-sufficiency. Gaining control over population growth is, however, a long and hard process, and this large population is still an obstacle to social and economic development. In developing countries, economic development is relatively slow and backward and the cultural level of the populace is rather low, which no doubt further aggravates population problems. Many developing countries in Asia and the Pacific region, including China, are faced with the common problem of population inflation and the fact that the quality of the life of the population is to be enhanced. Therefore, getting out of the dilemma of population inflation and developing the economy are two tasks for the developing countries in this region.

Natural Disasters

Natural disasters take place frequently in the Asia-Pacific region. First of all, the area surrounding the Pacific Ocean and the Himalayan belt are the main distribution areas of earthquakes and volcanoes. Earthquakes taking place in the belt surrounding the Pacific Ocean make up 80 percent of the shallow-source earthquakes, 90 percent of the medium-source earthquakes, and almost all the deep-source earthquakes of the world. Some ten earthquakes measuring 8 on the Richter scale have taken place in the belt surrounding the Pacific Ocean in this century, and because of this, this belt is called a "seismic and calamity ring."

Sea waves, windstorms, floods, and large-scale landslides occur mainly in coastal areas and near sea areas in the middle and low latitudes. Therefore, Southeast Asian, Oceanic, and Central American areas located in Asia and the Pacific region are often plagued by such calamities, which can not be accurately predicted by the present level of science and technology. Even if they could be predicted, some natural disasters would still bring about great casualties and economic losses due to the heavy and concentrated population and developed economies in the Pacific Ocean region.

We are very concerned with such things as the El Nino phenomenon, which reflects the changes of the sea-water temperature in the Pacific Ocean. This phenomenon may cause grave calamities such as elevation of the sea level and affect the climate, but we cannot definitely point out their causes and regular patterns.

With population growth and with the increase of destructive utilization of resources, natural disasters in Asia and the Pacific region are marked by heavy casualties in wide areas. We should, consequently, carry out in-depth and meticulous studies of natural disasters so as to predict their patterns and protect ourselves. Many disasters are related to each other and have regional continuity, and therefore disaster prediction and alleviation activities may usefully strengthen regional links between disaster belts. The struggles of mankind against natural disasters are long-term and common responsibilities.

Destruction of the Environment

Natural disasters are frequent in Asia and the Pacific region, but man-made environmental destruction is even worse, especially environmental pollution. With population growth and development of industry and transportation in the region, pollutants discharged by various sources have increased, resulting in serious air pollution. For instance, from 1975 to 1989, the volume of SO_2 discharge in the Western Pacific Ocean area increased from 10 million tons to 29.14 million tons, and the increase of SO_2 in the air has led to an increase of acid rain. Since the 1980s, acid rain has been noticed to varying degrees in Tokyo, in the southeast coastal areas of Taiwan and the China mainland, in South Korea, in Malaysia, in Thailand, and in other countries and regions. Acid rain poses a threat not only to nature but also to the health of human beings.

Large quantities of waste water and solid waste materials resulting from rapid industrial development seriously pollute water resources. Many rivers in the United States, Japan, China, South Korea, Malaysia, Thailand, and elsewhere have been polluted to varying degrees.

The development of communications and transportation has brought about tail gas and noise, which again have done great harm to cities. Scientists generally hold that about three million to six million tons of oil are discharged each year into the sea. In 1985 alone, 34 accidents involving oil leakage of more than 1,000 tons took place, with a total oil leakage of 0.167 million tons.

In addition to environmental pollution, man-made environmental destruction is another important aspect of ecological destruction. Important among the many ecological disasters taking place is destruction of tropical forests. The forests are called the lungs of the earth. Tropical forests account for only 6 percent of the surface of the earth, but the species of organisms they host make up 50 to 90 percent of the total. Central and South America and Southeast Asia once boasted large areas of tropical forest, but much of the forest has been felled. In the coastal areas of Brazil 90 percent of the moist forest has disappeared, and 68 percent of the primitive forest in the areas from the eastern part of India to the Philippines and from the southernmost part of China to Indonesia has faded away. Altogether 40 percent of the tropical forest on earth has already vanished. Forests occupy an important position in the energy-exchange cycle of the biosphere. Their destruction would result not only in climate changes and disappearance of species but also in soil erosion, change of soil into sand, droughts, floods, and so on. The islands in the Pacific Ocean are especially vulnerable: 75 percent of the mammals and birds that have become extinct in modern times were species living on islands. It is therefore a big task for the various island countries in the Pacific Ocean area to protect wild animals.

Another culprit that poses a serious threat to the environment in Asia and the Pacific region is nuclear waste. Peaceful utilization of nuclear energy resources may remedy the shortage of energy resources and bring about enormous benefits and interests to industrial production and people's lives. However, nuclear waste will result in greater disasters to mankind if it is not properly dealt with. Such disasters have become a reality in some areas in Asia and the Pacific region. It is therefore imperative for those countries utilizing nuclear energy resources to ensure safe handling of nuclear waste while forbidding the shift of nuclear waste to other countries. The old Chinese saying of do not do to others what you do not want done to you is the most appropriate and reasonable request of nuclear countries because the happiness of people of one country cannot be built on the miseries of peoples of other countries.

Apart from these problems, the solution on a global scale of environmental problems such as the greenhouse effect and ozonosphere cavity also merits attention and cooperation in Asia and the Pacific region. In short, many developing countries in Asia and the Pacific region are heavily burdened with population problems and wait to be exploited and developed. They are, at the same time, countries with natural disasters and man-made environmental destruction. It is a common task in Asia and the Pacific region to face these problems squarely, to find solutions, and to improve the environment while seeking economic development.

Environmental Protection and Sustainable Development

Realization of sustainable development on a global scale is the only strategy for coordination between environment and development, because sustainable development has been put forward on the basis of awareness that environmental disasters have hindered the further development of mankind. Since the publication of the book *Our Common Future* by the World Committee on Environment and Development (WCED), the concept of sustainable development has gained currency in international discourse. Sustainable development advocates the economic view of sustainable growth on the basis of protection of the earth's natural system, the ecological view of harmony between mankind and nature, and the social view of fair distribution within the generation and between generations. Since its inception, sustainable development has become a common responsibility of the whole of mankind and become the criterion for common action by the international community. It is not limited to any one country or region.

Equitable Sustainable Development

The most common definition of sustainable development is: development that satisfies the needs of this generation but poses no threat to the ability of future generations to satisfy their needs. An important aim of sustainable development is to seek fairness: fair distribution of limited resources within and among generations. When people came to realize that environmental pollution and ecological destruction had brought about grave disasters to social development, they began to pay attention to environmental protection with the hope of leaving behind to their children an environment not worse than the present one. Thus theories of sustainable development stress fairness in distribution between generations. But fair distribution within the generation is not sufficiently emphasized. It is not practical to discuss giving rights and freedom to future generations without speaking of circumstances that prevent achieving fairness within the present generation. We have proposed the idea of equitable sustainable development to remedy this defect. We lay more stress on fairness among the present generation—fairness within a country and between countries.

Within a country, we hope that people may be rich together while on the world scale, we emphasize that each country has the equal right to development and distribution. The reality is, however, very cruel: the income of the richest 20 percent of the world population is 60 times more than that of the poorest 20 percent. People in developed countries account for 26 percent of the total world population and consume 80 percent of the earth's energy, iron, steel, and paper. Distribution of global resources and wealth is seriously unbalanced, gaps between the South and the North are widening, and poverty is a common phenomenon in developing countries. It is the same in Asia and the Pacific region. It is acknowledged by the PCED in *The Strategy Outline for the Sustainable Development in the United States* that rich countries are more advanced in utilizing resources, and developing countries have taken advantage of this long-standing knowledge to further their own economic growth. In the past, developed countries discharged and accumulated the largest part of the world's pollutants. But even today, when they have taken notice of environmental problems, they still account for a larger share of the yearly total volume of discharged waste. Furthermore, in places where the environment is being seriously damaged, developing countries are heavily burdened with the two tasks of developing their economies and protecting the environment. Natural resources have been excessively exploited, and the ecological system has been destroyed by those who were the first to get rich. It is therefore unreasonable and impractical to demand that both the rich and the poor shoulder this environmental responsibility equally. The poor indeed cannot attend to resources, the environment, and the existence of other living species while still struggling to make ends meet. The rich and the poor have common yet different responsibilities toward the environment.

Developed countries should give sufficient support to developing countries in the fields of economy and environmental science and technology and help them invest in improving the seriously damaged natural environment. They should not adopt the attitude of an outsider or make unrealistic demands on developing countries regarding environmental protection. Developing countries should squarely face their own environmental problems and try to enhance the efficiency of their use of energy resources, promote clean production, and improve the environment while developing their economies and enhancing the living standards of their people.

Another characteristic of sustainable development is its globalism. The environment is global and so is present world economic development. Therefore, a strategy of sustainable development that emphasizes both environment and development cannot be realized solely in any single country. It is understandable that developed countries want to develop further and that developing countries also wish to do so. Developing countries do not wish to develop at the expense of the global or other countries' environment. Developed countries should not blindly demand that developing countries already plagued with economic difficulties shoulder the same responsibilities as themselves while giving no assistance to the latter. The thinking of equitable sustainable development is to let people of the whole world together protect our common ecological environment and make concerted efforts to get rid of environmental pollution in the process of mutual assistance. We should increase our cooperation in the fields of science and technology and environmental protection on the basis of joint efforts by both developing and developed countries and promote the realization of the strategy of equitable sustainable development on a global scale.

Integration of Environmental Protection with Sustainable Development

The theory of sustainable development includes three aspects: ecological sustainability, economic sustainability, and social sustainability. Ecological sustainability is the base, economic sustainability is the condition, and social sustainability is the goal. Strengthening environmental protection is key to the realization of ecological sustainability and sustainable development. We can neither blindly seek development at the expense of the environment nor give up development to protect the environment statically and in isolation.

Development is the starting point of sustainable development that encourages, instead of excluding, economic growth. For developing countries in particular, economic growth can not only increase their comprehensive strength and total social assets and enhance the levels of people's material as well as cultural lives but also can increase their ability to do away with poverty and ecological degeneration. We cannot, however, blindly pursue development at the cost of high consumption of natural resources and high pollution of the natural environment nor can we take the road of "pollution first and handling later" of industrialized countries. Sustainable development should seek economic development and enhancement of efficiency through moderate and effective consumption of resources on the premise of not exceeding the bearing capacity of the environment.

Sustainable development was first put forward by Western ecologists upon realization of the deterioration of the environment. It can thus be seen that environmental protection was the original intention of sustainable development. The natural environment plays an indispensable role in the economic system and life-supporting system. The more developed human society becomes, the more it depends on natural resources and on the environment. With the deterioration of the environment and exhaustion of resources, the natural bearing capacity of the earth is decreasing, which will hinder and eventually restrain economic development and the improvement of the life of the people. Of course, while attaching importance to environmental protection, we cannot neglect economic and social development. The ecological environment cannot be more effectively protected and improved without economic development and progress in science and technology.

In sustainable development, economic development and environmental protection are considered an inseparable organic necessity. Economic development provides scientific, technological, and economic support to environmental protection on the basis of effective but low consumption of resources; an important part of social development, the improvement of the environment constitutes one of the objective standards for judging the quality, level, and degree of development.

Strengthening Cooperation in Environmental Protection

Traditional modes of economic growth and inappropriate models of production and consumption are among the reasons for environmental problems in Asia and the Pacific region. The economic development model that took industrial growth as the only standard for judging development has had disastrous environmental effects in developed countries in the past and in present-day developing countries. These include excessive consumption of resources and energy and sharp deterioration of the natural environment, leading eventually to a dire situation in which development cannot be sustained. In view of the huge population, wide area, frequent natural disasters, and serious environmental pollution in Asia and the Pacific region, solution of environmental problems merits the attention of various governments and sincere cooperation among the various countries as well as reliance on progress in science and technology.

Science and Technology

First of all, both environmental protection and development depend on scientific and technological progress. Environmental pollution is a special way of expressing the non-optimal transformation process and outcome of resources in modern material production. As production input factors, various kinds of resources are not transformed into the end products but are released into the environment as pernicious materials. Or, they are ineffectively and wastefully utilized instead of being most effectively and most economically used, thus resulting in pollution. To control pollution, the technological level of the means of harnessing pollution should be improved, and, more important, the technological level of production techniques should be enhanced. Improvements in the level of science and technology may render support to environmental protection and economic development in the three ways.

Progress in science and technology can promote the development of the energy industry. Of the many energy resources now in use, mineral energy still has the highest utility rate with the lowest cost, but the development of science and technology makes it possible to widen use of nuclear energy and renewable energy resources. Nuclear energy has not been widely used due to scientific and technological limitations as well as safety problems. Peaceful utilization of nuclear energy is, however, most favorable for replacing fossil energy resources if safety can be ensured. Besides nuclear energy, we may in the future also make use of renewable resources such as solar electric energy, solar thermal energy, wind energy, bio-energy, and geothermal energy. The application of these clean, renewable energy resources is still restricted by the present low level of science and technology and difficulties in exploitation, and consequently their benefits cannot be brought into full play. The progress of science and technology will therefore play an incalculable role in promoting the development of the energy industry.

Second, progress in science and technology can enhance the utility rate of energy resources. Utilization of energy resources, especially fossil energy resources, inevitably results in environmental pollution. The more energy resources we need, the more pollutants they produce. But the environmental bearing capacity of the earth is limited. Population growth and improved living standards have promoted quick growth of demand for energy resources, which conflicts with the increasing scarcity of energy resources. If we can increase the utility rate of energy resources, we may decrease, to some extent, the quantity of pollutants, reduce the use of energy resources, and remain within the environmental bearing capacity of the earth. In the efficient use of energy resources, the unit GNP energy consumption in many developing countries is much higher than in developed countries such as the United States and Japan. This inefficient use of energy resources is incompatible with the scarcity of energy resources. It is, therefore, an important task for developing countries to economize on energy resources and to improve energy utilization efficiency. The solution of this problem depends on progress in energy-utilization technologies.

Third, progress in science and technology is favorable to the development of environmental protection technologies. Developing environmental-protection technologies is the most effective way to solve the present environmental problems if we cannot fully exploit renewable energy resources in a short time and if we cannot enhance the utilization efficiency of energy resources quickly. The concept of clean production was proposed when people began to pay attention to environmental problems. Studies of the whole life cycle of a product from the utilization of raw materials to waste handling are beneficial to the reduction of environmental pollution in both production and in daily life. As a major fossil energy resource, coal will be an important energy source in various countries, particularly in developing countries, for some time to come. Coal is, nonetheless, a polluting energy, and so development of clean coal technologies will contribute greatly to the abatement of environmental pollution.

At present, clean coal technologies are being developed very rapidly in developed countries such as the Untied States and Japan, but developing countries are lagging behind, which is especially manifested in electric energy production and civilian use of coal. Of coal pollution, the most serious is air pollution. Sulfur dioxide in the air is the main source of acid rain and can bring about destruction of the environment of a country and even of a region. It is known to all that environmental problems in any country are regional and even global because of the extensive links of environmental pollution. In view of the grave environmental problems in Asia and the Pacific region, cooperation should be encouraged to develop environmental protection technologies. Developed countries with technology and capital should help developing countries to promote general improvement of the environment in Asia and the Pacific region.

Regional Cooperation

Strengthening regional cooperation is the most effective way to solve environmental problems in Asia and the Pacific region. The environmental problems in the various countries of the region are closely related. For instance, the frequent natural disasters have astonishing commonalities. Earthquakes, hurricanes, and the El Nino phenomenon are common in the Pacific Ocean region. In areas surrounding the Pacific Ocean, air and water are seriously polluted, tropical forests have vanished, and nuclear waste pollution is a critical problem. So, environmental protection calls for global cooperation, particularly among the countries in this region that have common environmental problems. As for the solution of these problems, developed countries should take care of their own problems. Shifting seriously polluting industries to developing countries so as to evade the strict environmental protection laws and regulations in their own countries will not only destroy the environment of developing countries but also affect whole regions and even the whole world. To achieve the goal of general improvement of the regional environment, developed countries should be aware of their own responsibilities for environmental protection and should provide developing countries with advanced environmental-protection technologies and environmental-management experiences and capital while changing their own unsustainable waste and consumption models. On the other hand, developing countries should make full use of these technologies and capital, realize the transformation of the development model from the extensive to the

...sive as early as possible, and try to solve their environmental ...oblems while seeking economic growth. Developing countries should not follow the industrialized countries' practice of "pollution first and handling later." The various countries in Asia and the Pacific region should also carry out joint research and monitor natural disasters so as to reduce casualties and economic losses.

Cleaner and more effective utilization of energy resources cannot be realized due to the current limitations of science and technology. Developed countries take the lead in energy-resource exploitation and utilization technologies, but their conservative science and technology policies do not favor the popularization of new energy-utilization technologies. Although there are different countries and regions on the earth, the resources of the planet are common and limited. It will be beneficial for the global energy industry if both developed and developing countries can work hand in hand to develop energy-resource application technologies.

To sum up, in the face of frequent natural disasters and serious environmental pollution problems in Asia and the Pacific region, we have become increasingly aware of the importance of environmental protection, of development of science and technology, and of formulation and implementation of the strategy of sustainable development. It is our sincere hope that a common and beautiful environment for the existence and development of mankind will be created in this region and that regional and global sustainable development eventually will be realized through our concerted efforts.

CHAPTER 5

APEC—A New Model for Regional Economic Cooperation

Wenrong Qian

The 18-member Asia-Pacific Economic Cooperation (APEC) has been very successful since its founding in 1989. It is generally held that APEC's development will not only have an enormous and far-reaching impact on the Asia-Pacific economy but also will contribute to peace and security in this region. This essay will focus on the characteristics of APEC as a new model for regional economic cooperation and its impact on regional development as well as peace and stability.

A Brief Review

The development of APEC since its founding can be divided into three stages. Efforts to propel Asia-Pacific regional economic cooperation had been going on for nearly 30 years by the time APEC entered its initial stage (1989–1990). Early explorations had led to the eventual affirmation of the term "open regionalism."

The first economic cooperative institution in the Pacific region was the Pacific Basin Economic Council (PBEC), founded in 1967. It was followed by the Pacific Trade and Development Conference (PAFTAD) in 1968 and the Pacific Economic Cooperation Council (PECC) in 1980. All three organizations are nongovernmental in nature. Nevertheless, they have reflected the growing desire for economic cooperation in the region and have laid sound groundwork for the establishment of APEC, an intergovernmental economic cooperation organization, which is now more influential than any other economic organization in the region.

The first APEC ministerial meeting was initiated by Australia in Canberra in November 1989 and declared the birth of the APEC organization, with 12 nations of the Asia-Pacific region as founding members (Australia, United States, Canada, Japan, New Zealand,

Republic of Korea, and six ASEAN nations). In its early days, APEC was a loose economic forum that operated mainly through the annual ministerial meeting. The first meeting set certain important objectives and principles for the organization, such as:

- APEC should be an increasingly open, multilateral trade regime, not a closed trading bloc;
- APEC is merely an economic forum which only discusses regional economic cooperation and its related problems with the aim of promoting trade liberalization;
- Regional economic cooperation should be gradually pushed forward through negotiations on an equal footing.

These objectives and principles defined the nature, goals, and working methods of this regional economic cooperative organization.

The second stage spanned 1991 to 1993. The 1991 Seoul meeting, a milestone in APEC's development, was marked by the admission of the People's Republic of China, Taiwan, and Hong Kong as new members. The Seoul Declaration emphasized that APEC should not evolve from a forum into an institutionalized structure.

The 1993 Seattle meeting became another turning point. The United States, in the capacity of host country, called the first informal summit meeting of APEC members, leading to a fundamental change in its organizational structure. As a result, a three-level decision-making structure, that is, the Senior Officials Meetings (SOM), ministerial meetings, and informal summit meetings, has taken shape. Since then, important APEC decisions have been left to the summit meetings, whose undertakings become a guarantee for implementing the decisions. This decision-making structure and pattern have made APEC a more authoritative organization, though it still remains a forum. The informal summit meetings have become an indispensable component of the annual APEC meetings, and four informal summit meetings have been held so far. The other important achievement of the Seattle meeting was the approval by the participating leaders of a definite goal for the cooperation process, namely, trade and investment liberalization and development cooperation to promote sustainable growth and reduce economic disparities in the region.

The third stage began with the 1994 Jakarta meeting in Indonesia to further APEC's development in depth. The most important achievement of the Jakarta meeting was the adoption of the Bogor Declaration, which set a timetable for achieving trade and investment liberalization, that is, no later than 2010 on the part of developed members and by 2020 for developing members. At the same time,

APEC leaders announced that the coordinated process of liberalization would begin the moment that their statement was made public. Thus, the Bogor Declaration has been regarded as the starting point for implementing trade and investment liberalization in the Asia-Pacific region.

Later, both the 1995 Osaka meeting in Japan and the 1996 Manila meeting in the Philippines were continuations of the Jakarta meeting. The Osaka meeting adopted an Action Agenda, which urges all members to make their own plans of action for implementation. As an expression of faith in the liberalization process, members proposed a program for first investment in implementing the trade liberalization of the Bogor Declaration. Then, at the Manila meeting, all 18 members presented their respective plans of action for implementation of the Action Agenda, promising to reduce tariff rates to 15 percent by the year 2000. The commitments undertaken by a number of members have exceeded the commitments they made in the agreement of the Uruguay Round. The Uruguay Round of negotiations lasted seven and a half years, whereas in the case of APEC liberalization, it only took two years from formulation of concept to implementation. Moreover, the Manila meeting, for the first time in APEC history, adopted a guiding document to promote economic and technical cooperation among members. This was another big achievement.

Characteristics of the Asia-Pacific Region and the APEC Approach

The postwar situation in the Asia-Pacific region has been quite different from that in Europe. It is widely recognized that the most distinguishing characteristic of the Asia-Pacific region is its diversity, manifested by imbalanced economic development, uneven distribution of population, a wide gap between the poor and the rich, different cultural backgrounds and religious beliefs of various nationalities, and different social and economic systems.

However, the diversity and heterogeneity do not exclude common interests and unanimity in certain fundamental aspects, including the common desire for economic development through regional cooperation. The Asia-Pacific countries are fully aware that, with the acceleration of the economic globalization, their development ambitions cannot be achieved without an outward-looking or trade-oriented approach to economic development strategies. But, "any realistic appraisal of international economic policy strategy for the

Pacific community has to accommodate the fact of heterogeneity and the divergent, even conflicting, interests" (Drysdale 1988, 18).

As economic cooperation based on diversity requires a proper policy to ensure common interests, it would be difficult to form a European-style exclusive economic union. An open and nondiscriminatory trade system is important for development of trade and economic cooperation in Asia-Pacific countries. The objective of economic cooperation is to formulate common and mutually complementary policies. The objective for developing regional economic cooperation and the objective for maintaining a global open system are the same. Regional action and global objective are not contradictory but complementary to each other.

Based on recognition of diversity and other practical conditions in the Asia-Pacific region, the APEC members have explored and developed a unique way of cooperation. Known as the "APEC approach," it features the following elements.

Mutual Respect and Equality

All members, big or small, rich or poor, appear as equal and mutually respectful participants in the deliberations and consultations in the APEC development process, as all of them are unanimous in respecting the diversity of the Asia-Pacific region. In view of the fact that different members find themselves in different phases of development, with different views, capabilities, and demands, mutual understanding is necessary in the cooperative process. In a diverse community there is a measure of equality among the members as they seek and settle upon common understandings and come to collective agreements. Only through consensus can things be done for APEC. When differences are great, it will prejudice the interests of the weak if the strongest economy is free to make decisions unilaterally. APEC cannot go on developing in this way. Therefore, relations among the members must be based on mutual respect and equality. As long as this principle is implemented, APEC will go forward.

Mutual Benefit

The two major goals of APEC are both mutually beneficial: trade and investment liberalization and economic and technical cooperation. Implementation of the former promotes smooth regional economic and trade activities and reduces cost, thereby increasing efficiency and benefiting all the members. The latter makes possible reasonable and more efficient use of various resources, technologies, and management expertise of the region and attains the common development of individual members and that of the region as a whole. Although members may get benefits in varying degrees, they ought to benefit in a proportionate and well-balanced manner. That is the prerequisite and foundation for the future development of APEC and the key for its continued development.

Open Regionalism and Nondiscrimination

From its start, APEC opposed creation of a closed trading bloc. The diversity among APEC members also limits the appeal of a European-style comprehensive and discriminatory economic union. An open and nondiscriminatory trading and economic system remains fundamental to the trade and development aspirations of the industrializing members within APEC. The U.S.-proposed establishment of an Asia-Pacific Community was abandoned in the face of objections. Members have reached consensus on implementing the principle of open regionalism. "Open regionalism" means that, first, the trade and investment liberalization within APEC is in principle also applicable to non-APEC members, and, second, APEC must contribute to promoting global trade liberalization not only by reducing trade and investment barriers within the APEC region but also by striving to diminish barriers beyond the region. In the process of developing, APEC has not transformed itself into an inward-looking and exclusive free-trade zone through multilateral agreements. Rather, it promotes regional liberalization of trade and investment by virtue of the motivation of market forces and strengthens the links between the APEC region and the entire world market.

Consensus and Voluntarism

The vitality of APEC lies in how it maintains consensus and voluntary participation in the forum as it develops and how the members honor the promises undertaken. Consensus does not contradict voluntary participation. And consensus is attainable through consultation on an equal footing and mutual benefit. Experience has already attested to the feasibility of advancing the APEC process by achieving consensus gradually through consultation at the Senior Officials' Meetings, ministerial meetings, and summit meetings. The APEC consultative mechanism is unique. It is true that the results of the consultation are nonbinding. That they appear in the undertaking and joint declaration of the heads of state, however, adds a high sense of moral responsibility and restraint. Normally, the promises undertaken will be implemented, and that is why people have high expectations for and confidence in APEC.

In terms of the Action Agenda, members are expected to be voluntary implementers, but supervision and coordination are needed to help realize the goal of liberalization through collective action, reviewing, and comparison. The mechanism of reviewing and supervision is sure to be strengthened when the plan of action gets underway. Meanwhile, APEC collective action is promoted through (voluntary) common participation and active initiatives. For instance, the building of the customs data bank, the training center, and the center of technological transfer is being done in this fashion. The achievements attained have been remarkable.

Combination of Unilateralism and Collectivism

The Osaka declaration stressed that APEC leaders had chosen the unique approach of concerted liberalization grounded in voluntarism and collective initiatives by its members as the key means for implementing the Action Agenda. This in effect constitutes the core of an Asia-Pacific liberalization, distinct from the European Economic Community and the North American Free Trade Agreement. Its most salient features are reliance on voluntary action by each member and the simultaneous beginning by all members but without signing any formal agreements.

In view of the versatility of the Asia-Pacific region, it is necessary for members to take unilateral action independently without resorting to forcible means. On the other hand, however, respecting diversity does not mean that certain members may go without honoring their commitments. In order to accelerate the liberalization process within the framework of APEC, it is imperative that APEC members coordinate their voluntary actions. Therefore, a two-track system that combines both unilateral and collective action has been adopted. In this system, individual practices grounded in voluntarism—for example, control and reduction of tariffs—are called off, whereas coordination of standards and simplification of standard procedures are handled collectively.

Gradualism

Given the significant disparity in levels of economic development and differences in political status and development priorities among members, realization of the goal of trade and investment liberalization cannot be simultaneous. It should proceed step by step in a gradual, pragmatic, phased, and prudent manner in order to achieve optimum results. Thus, the Bogor Declaration puts forth two timetables, that is, to liberalize individual members' trade and investment practices by 2010 for developed economies and by 2020 for developing ones, thereby giving member economies, the developing economies in particular, sufficient time to achieve liberalization and enabling them to determine priorities independently.

APEC's institutionalization must not be carried out with undue haste. It cannot, especially, evolve into an organization with legal functions. The United States and some other developed countries are eager to introduce the negotiation mechanism to accelerate the institutionalization process, while most developing members disagree with such a tendency and emphasize the necessity of advancing step by step. Thus, the whole process of liberalization is incremental: in 1996, implementing the first investment plan of the Osaka meeting; in 1997, beginning to implement the unilateral plan of action of the Manila meeting; and then a gradual, phased progress toward the goal. The important thing is that gradualism gives the members the flexibility to arrange their own priorities and the speed at which they will proceed. This flexibility conforms to the characteristic diversity in the level and structure of economic development across the Asia-Pacific region.

All six principles strike an optimal balance among the diverse interests and demands of APEC members.

China's Policy toward APEC

Since the founding of APEC, China has been an active and constructive voice in the forum, sparing no efforts to promote regional economic cooperation. President Jiang Zemin attended all informal APEC leadership meetings in the last four years and put forth a series of constructive proposals to enhance cooperation. China attaches great importance to APEC and gives its full support for several reasons.

First, China's main interests lie in the Asia-Pacific region. China conducts roughly 80 percent of its foreign trade with APEC members. Around 90 percent of foreign direct investment in China comes from this region. With the exception of Hong Kong, the United States and Japan are China's largest trading partners. The ASEAN countries and the Republic of Korea are its close neighbors and are ever-expanding economic and trade partners. It is thus natural that China attaches great importance to developing relations with the Asia-Pacific nations and with APEC members in particular.

Second, globalization and regionalization are the main trends in the development of the world economy. As the opening up of the Chinese economy expands and deepens, China fully realizes its vital interest in advancing internationalization and participation in regional economic cooperation. It is especially significant for China to take an active part in APEC at a time when the country is still unfairly and unreasonably barred from the World Trade Organization (WTO).

Third, China needs an international coordination institution to help settle its growing trade disputes with other countries. With the speedy expansion of exports, China has had an increasing number of trade disputes with the United States and other countries. China is in a very disadvantageous position as it is left out of the WTO. America's annual review of most-favored-nation trading status for China has caused much trouble. China hopes that the APEC mechanism can help diminish American pressure, especially by applying the principle of nondiscrimination. APEC's mechanism for settling trade disputes can help soften the contradiction.

Now, what is the Chinese policy toward APEC? Briefly speaking, it includes the following main points.

China has taken an active part in formulating and fully supports the above-mentioned principles, namely, recognition of diversity, emphasis on mutual respect and equality, mutual benefit, flexibility, gradual progress and openness, consensus through consultation, a voluntary approach, and a combination of individual and collective actions. China believes that only by abiding by these principles can APEC develop smoothly and keep its vitality.

China is active in trade and investment liberalization. At the Osaka meeting in November 1995, China declared that it would cut import tariffs on 4,000 commodities by an average 30 percent, thereby playing a positive role in the passage of the Osaka Action Agenda. As a matter of fact, the actual reduction of tariffs beginning in April 1996 exceeded China's declared target by 34 percent, lowering China's tariff rates from 35 percent to 23 percent. At the Manila meeting in November 1996, China once again announced that it will further cut its tariff rates to 15 percent by the year 2000. All this has testified to China's good faith in and its positive attitude toward APEC.

China attaches great importance to promoting economic and technical cooperation. Economic and technical cooperation is essential not only because developing-member economies demand speedier development but also because their liberalization efforts might hit snags in the absence of sufficient growth. China therefore disagrees with the view that emphasizes trade and investment liberalization only, while assigning a subordinate role to economic and technical cooperation. China believes that without fruitful economic and technical cooperation, trade and investment liberalization cannot make much headway. The basic objective of economic and technical cooperation is to reduce economic disparities among APEC members and turn diversity into complementarity in the economic development of all members so as to achieve common prosperity. Nevertheless, APEC economic and technical cooperation is quite different from development aid in the traditional sense, both in principle and in practice. It is reciprocal and based on equality, mutual benefit, and complementarity.

To this end, China proposed at the Manila meeting that a science and technology industrial parks network be set up within APEC with a view to promoting exchanges of experience and information in order to accelerate integration of science and technology with the economy. China also declared that it is ready to open some representative state-level industrial parks from among its total of 52 for expanding cooperation with other APEC members.

In addition, China hopes that APEC will help narrow the gaps among its members and achieve common prosperity. There are 2 billion people in the Asia-Pacific region; 1.5 billion have an annual per capita income below US$1,000. When regional economic cooperation is discussed, people should take account not only of the questions of opening markets and liberalizing trade but also of the needs of developing members. The gap in economic development among APEC members should be narrowed and common prosperity achieved. To achieve this goal, developed APEC members should open markets to the products of developing members. The prospect of more than 1 billion people being relieved from poverty and becoming prosperous will have an inestimably positive impact on efforts to expand markets for trade, increase investment opportunities, promote progress of science and technology, and reinforce economic cooperation in the Asia-Pacific region.

Conclusions

APEC is not a strictly institutionalized organization and makes no binding resolutions. It is a kind of voluntary community. The truth of the matter is that the strength of APEC lies precisely in its being a voluntary community. Both past and present experience tell us that "the economic development of the Asia-Pacific is propelled by the market, not by agreements or treaties; and the unilateral action of each economy is taken in accordance with the market demands, but not forced by any supranational authority" (Chen 1996, 6).

Practice has proved that the APEC approach is viable and effective. Several conclusions can be drawn from the APEC development process of the past eight years.

The APEC approach reflects the interests of all its members. This approach is neither a "Western Model" nor an "Asian Model." It is a unique model based on the diversity of the region and a cooperative development process assimilating the good points of both Western and Asian models.

This approach has guided APEC members in successfully identifying the road for trade and investment liberalization as well as economic and technical cooperation, because it has given full consideration to the significant disparity in levels of economic development and differences in political status and development priorities among members.

Any deviation from the APEC approach would bog APEC down in difficulties and cause sharp contradictions among members. But once the APEC approach is adhered to, many seemingly insurmountable barriers and difficulties can be removed and APEC can develop smoothly.

Consensus through consultation and commitment is an effective means. Unlike alliances such as the European Union and the North American Free Trade Zone, APEC rejects a supranational authority or a between-states agreement, adopting instead a "consensus through consultation" policy.

In the beginning, a number of people worried that any "declarations" and "Agenda of Action" made by consensus through consultation might become mere scraps of paper. The APEC approach produces no resolutions with binding force, relies only on verbal or written commitments, and lacks any punishment or sanction measures when commitments are not fulfilled. Now, practice has shown that the commitments made publicly by the leaders of APEC member states bear moral responsibility and reflect on the reputations of the members. APEC members implement their commitments not only on a voluntary basis but also under mutual supervision and restraint of moral responsibility and reputation.

Because of the much-talked-about diversity among APEC members and the fact that most of them are still in their early development stages, powers like the United States and Japan should not try to control the process. If those powers try to push their initiatives too strongly, developing economies may be forced to drop out. APEC then would be just a collection of ordinary bilateral trade and investment agreements between developed economies. The opportunity to integrate the most dynamic economies in the world would be lost.

The APEC model bears important practical significance and produces far-reaching influence. The Asia-Pacific area, East Asia in particular, is the fastest-growing region in the world economy. APEC comprises 40 percent of the world's population, its gross national product accounts for 50 percent of world GNP, and its trade accounts for 46 percent of the total world trade volume. APEC cooperation will promote fast and sustainable economic development of its members, narrow the gap between developed and developing economies and achieve common prosperity. It will also give impetus to the development of the North-South relationship and the establishment of a new international economic order.

Moreover, despite the fact that APEC confines its discussions to economic cooperation and does not take up political and security issues, the development of APEC in recent years has contributed to peace and security in the region. The closer economic ties and cooperation become, the more interdependent APEC members will be. The growing common economic interests certainly require better political relationships. The annual informal summit meetings especially have greatly enhanced understanding, friendship, and trust among the leaders of APEC members. This undoubtedly contributes to peace and stability in this region and the whole world as well.

Different civilizations can cooperate instead of clashing. Since Prof. Samuel Huntington's article "The Clash of Civilizations?" was published in *Foreign Affairs* in 1993, there has been a heated debate on this issue. I will not get involved in the debate here but will suggest that through APEC different civilizations can cooperate with each other. Professor Huntington argues in his article that "economic regionalism may succeed only when it is rooted in a common civilization" and cites the example of the European Community with its shared European culture and Western Christianity. Yet APEC comprises at least four civilizations: Buddhism, Islam, Christianity, and Confucianism. In terms of social systems, there are capitalist and socialist countries among the 18 members. The eight years of APEC development have proved that economic regionalism can succeed even if the grouping is composed of different civilizations. Therefore, we should not overemphasize cultural, religious, or other civilizational differences but pay more attention to the creative, constructive interaction and engagement between different civilizations. Philosophically, different civilizations are not inherently prone to conflict; they share certain common perspectives on relationships among human beings. As the world is entering the 21st century and globalization is becoming a main trend in the development of the world economy, the increasing interdependence of nations makes it more possible and practicable to cooperate across cultural boundaries.

CHAPTER 6

The ASEAN Model for Regional Cooperation

Johan Saravanamuttu

The state-centric perspective, backed by an effective three-centuries-old hegemonic Westphalian interstate system based on the sovereign state as the basic unit and actor in international relations, remains the dominant discourse informing political practice and international relations in the Asia-Pacific region.[1]

Postulations by writers such as James Rosenau (1990) that international relations have become "multi-centric" and have entered an era of "post-international politics" remain by and large unconvincing, especially in the light of recent events. To cite just one datum, the national state has multiplied from a mere 50 in 1945 to some 185 or more today with the prospect of more to come. A decentralized multistate system in which individuals, possibly through nongovernmental organizations (NGOs), have gained efficacy, much less hegemony, in world politics has largely not come to pass in the somewhat grandiose manner envisioned by Rosenau (Willets 1993, 25).

A rather more interesting view is that of Richard Falk, who sees national sovereignty as the basis for providing the "contexuality" to international relations while at the same time being itself increasingly subject to the expansion of the realm of "global civil society":

> Despite the erosions of territoriality as a consequence of globalization, it is definitely premature to cast traditional notions of sovereignty aside. Sovereignty retains a critical importance in contemporary thinking about world order, especially because of its instrumental connections with nationalism, still the most robust mobilizing ideology on the planet. (Falk 1995, 89)

Falk suggests that "Sovereignty, then, embodies contradictory features and induces ambivalence as to its role in the transition to geo-governance," that is to say,

- sovereignty remains an essential concept, yet its reality is being steadily and inevitably subverted;
- sovereignty can not be relinquished, but its invocation by strong states to justify disregard for international legal restraints on the use of force can be challenged;
- sovereignty, state, and territorial community remain a powerful, if variable and uneven, nexus of identity expressive of the old world order based on geopolitics; at the same time, sovereignty, peoples, and global civil society are emerging as an overlapping, alternative, and future-oriented secondary nexus of identity that is engaged in promoting the possibility of humane governance. (Falk 1995, 91)

The Falk statements provide in part the contours of an enlightened, alternative realist discourse[2] from the World Order Models Project (**WOMP**) with its notion of "geo-governance" and "humane governance" conceived as constructs outside of the traditional and hegemonic state system of "geopolitics." Wompists such as Falk, Mendlovitz, Kotharii, and Walker represent an intellectual discourse that attempts to reconstitute and re-present the peace perspective in the face of the major overhaul of the state system via a full-blown globalization process sweeping economies and states today.

Such an approach, I believe, has to be married with a Coxian appreciation that takes into account both the hegemonic and counterhegemonic forces—both statist and nonstatist—articulating within a capitalist global order. According to Cox, a so-called posthegemonic phase of world order may allow for both regionalist and globalist hegemonic systems or even different civilizational ontologies to coexist.[3] Indeed, I assume here that such a world order has emerged or at least is unfolding in the Asia-Pacific region. What is not adequately addressed empirically is a more mundane point, that is, the fact that hegemonic statist structures obtain in the current regional formations such as Asia-Pacific Economic Cooperation (**APEC**) and the Association of Southeast Asian Nations (**ASEAN**), but nonstate-centric actors from civil society are responding to such statist formations by projecting their own counterhegemonic agendas and visions of regional order.

If one may be allowed to restate recent history, a major (posthegemonic) break within the state-centric paradigm occurred with the end of the Cold War in 1990. The East-West, capitalist and anticapitalist state-centric discourse has been superseded by a post-Marxist, market-capitalism discourse anchored on the revival of neoclassical, neoliberal and neorealist discourses, which currently inform debate and practice by state actors. The set of "alternative" discourses that were prevalent in the Cold War period, especially in the peace studies and peace research community, which was informed by liberal, Marxist and neo-Marxist critiques of the conventional realist paradigm and Cold War strategic studies discourse, have lost considerable ground. Some would contend that they have tended to create mostly alternative intelligentsia and failed in generating an alternative "order" in the social and, especially, in the political-institutional senses. Liberal discourse pivoting around democracy and democratization, was partly responsible for the breakdown of the planned, socialist economies in Eastern Europe. Some peace researchers like Johan Galtung have claimed that the Eastern European collapse should be seen as a "victory" for peace research. More significantly, the "end of history" rather symbolized the ascendancy of the liberal and neoliberal perspective over the Marxist alternatives with their opposite ontological assumptions (Fukuyama 1992). In interstate relations, this "takeover" is almost complete, but social democratic praxis of the socialist variant still informs important elements in civil society and their civil discourse. A new discourse of "civilizational clash" (Huntington 1993) emanating from the traditional realist perspective can arguably replace the state-centric paradigm and refurbish the Westphalian order along larger regional groupings rather than states. This seems unlikely since dominance of the state unit remains paramount in both discourse and practice terms through a mobilization of bias and the prevalence of state power.

Two points should be noted about contemporary discourses on world order:

- It is important to recognize that much more plural civil societies now exist across the globe with vast variations between and within states. In some instances, especially in postcolonial social formations, there is grave doubt that civil societies have actually emerged, or rather, that the breakdown of traditional social orders have led to the emergence of modern civil societies.
- Contrariwise, in the NIEs, and would-be NIEs, the growth of new middle classes have begun to impact on the social and political character of civil society in a significant way. Globalization has led to parallel state-centric and people-oriented visions and missions for global and regional order.

In this essay I will attempt to unpack both sets of discourses in terms of their actual practices with a view to arriving at a better understanding of geo-governance in Southeast Asia, a region now dominated by the ASEAN formation. It is obvious to any astute observer that the people-centric vision(s) are by degrees much less developed than their interstate counterparts. The sheer mobilization of bias via the maintenance of the status quo through statist discourse and practice, now refurbished by neoliberal and neoclassical thinking a fortiori after the end of the Cold War, makes the task of operationalizing the alternative discourses and visions so much the more daunting.[4]

Security Cooperation in Southeast Asia:
ASEAN "Hegemony"

The ASEAN grouping has assumed an ascendancy and prominence that make it virtually the "hegemonic" regional organization in Southeast Asia and, as it turns out, it is providing the framework for security cooperation in the region as well. ASEAN has assumed this role by default and will continue to do so as long as the impasse of movement toward larger and more encompassing regional bodies obtains.[5]

ASEAN's development may be divided in two broad phases. During the earlier part of the Cold War era, the stage was set for regional stability among the noncommunist states of Southeast Asia after a turbulent period that saw Indonesia's Konfrontasi (war) against Malaysia because of the incorporation of Sarawak and Sabah into the new Malaysian Federation and the severing of diplomatic relations between the Philippines and Malaysia over the Sabah claim of the Philippines. Thus the Bangkok Declaration of 1967, which marked the emergence of ASEAN, also symbolized the end to political discord among these states. Until the mid-1970s, ASEAN had a rather unspectacular track record. There was a general cautiousness in undertaking genuine integrative measures, and most of the regional body's successes came by way of common political stances vis-à-vis third parties, especially the Communist bloc countries. By the early 1970s, there was a distinct shift toward nonalignment, the centerpiece of foreign policy being the Malaysian-initiated Zone of Peace, Freedom and Neutrality (ZOPFAN) declared in Kuala Lumpur in 1971.

Developments from the mid-1970s on were marked by the watershed Bali Accords, which I have argued elsewhere (Saravanamuttu 1984) provided the basis for the emergence of a Deutschian "pluralistic security community."[6] The two major Bali documents—the Declaration of ASEAN Concord and the Treaty of Amity and Cooperation—carried the ASEAN states, at least in theory, to a new plane of security cooperation and, in effect, operationalized that part of ZOPFAN which was to be underwritten by the ASEAN states themselves. In particular, the Amity Treaty was very much in the spirit of a nonaggression pact and one which paid particular attention to the UN Chapter VIII stipulation on pacific settlement of conflict by regional bodies.[7] Thus, under the treaty, the ASEAN members, as contracting parties in pursuit of "perpetual peace, everlasting amity and cooperation," agreed to abide by the principles of (Article 2):

- mutual respect for the independence, sovereignty, equality, territorial integrity, and national identity of all nations;
- the right of every state to lead its national existence free from external interference, subversion, or coercion;
- noninterference in internal affairs of one another;
- settlement of differences or disputes by peaceful means;
- renunciation of the threat or use of force; and
- effective cooperation among themselves.

All told, the Amity Treaty does stand as testimony of a group of states' providing the basis for a security community for themselves and the region. The treaty, which is open to the accession of other states, has since been acceded to by Brunei, ASEAN's sixth member, Vietnam, ASEAN's seventh member, and would-be members Laos, Cambodia, and Myanmar (Burma), who became members of the "ASEAN 10" in July 1997.

An aspect of security cooperation that has been pursued successfully by ASEAN is the quest for a nuclear-weapons-free zone with Southeast Asia-wide coverage. The treaty for a SEANWFZ was signed at the December 1995 Bangkok Summit, providing yet another measure of confidence-building among the ASEAN states.

In light of the recent "beefing up" of ASEAN, one is inclined to reject the views of some recent commentators that post–Cold War developments would reduce the efficacy of ASEAN and that regional cooperation on a wider front in the Asia-Pacific region may spell a diminution of the ASEAN role, if not its demise. Such a view is expressed by Ganesan (1994), who sees excessive state-centrism in ASEAN as a problem in coping with the new post-Cold War environment. More diffuse state sovereignty would empower individual member-states in ASEAN, but such empowerment would be to the detriment of ASEAN in two ways. First, the creation of multiple channels would leave ASEAN with a smaller agenda, which would in turn inhibit its institutional growth potential. Second, the consistent use of alternative institutional channels by member states might in time make ASEAN irrelevant (Ganesan 1994, 466).

It is clear that there are two diametrically opposed dynamics operating in Asia-Pacific regionalism today. They hinge on two major issue areas: security cooperation and economic cooperation. The question to be posed is how these dynamics will affect the scope and shape of regional organizations. I suggest that ASEAN, by virtue of historical precedence and political track record, will propel its version of a "pluralistic security community" throughout the whole of Southeast Asia. This is both a multitrack and a multilayered structure, albeit in a system that is profoundly state-centric. For ASEAN (and individual ASEAN member states) to move dynamically and meaningfully in this respect would mean discarding anachronistic Cold War structures and practices, which ASEAN is capable of effecting and to which it has already addressed itself. But for the ASEAN formation to be fully effective in instituting regional order, such statist maneuvers must be matched by an imaginative engagement on both the state-centric and non-state-centric planes of action and diplomacy.

Currently there are two main ASEAN state-centric tracks, one internal to the ASEAN structure and the other external to it. The internal mechanisms are somewhat weaker and hinge on the Treaty of Amity and Cooperation of the original five, signed in Bali in 1976. ASEAN's sixth member, Brunei, is today a signatory, and most recently Vietnam and Laos have agreed to accede to the treaty as a prelude to their entry into ASEAN. The treaty remains untested, however, and the mechanism for pacific settlement of conflicts through an ASEAN High Council is perhaps ineffectual for conflicts that involve member states, who will themselves have to sit on the council. Perhaps such is the case now with territorial claims between Malaysia and Indonesia and Malaysia and Singapore in which disputants apparently are more prepared to refer matters to the World Court.[8] The problem of the Sabah claim has never been referred to the pacific settlement process either, which suggests that the formal mechanisms of the Amity Treaty are window dressings rather than true instrumentalities for conflict resolution. Nonetheless, the treaty should be taken as a statement of intent to peacefully resolve conflict and as a nonaggression pact rather than as a legal-political structure to solve disputes. In this respect, the participation of Indochina and Myanmar is crucial for the emergence of the pluralist security order that the treaty can, in a general sense, provide for Southeast Asia, even if its conflict resolution mechanisms are flawed.

The external track of ASEAN diplomacy has been through "dialogue" relationships with nonmembers on both the economic and political fronts. The most important post–Cold War development on the political level was the setting up of the post-ministerial conference (PMC) held annually after the annual ASEAN foreign ministers' meeting involving the ASEAN dialogue partners and the formation of the ASEAN Regional Forum (ARF), which held its inaugural session in July 1994 in Bangkok. The ARF was apparently the brainchild of the strategic studies institutes, the ASEAN-ISIS and, as intimated by Jusuf Wanandi, was mooted in June 1991 as an "ASEAN-PMC plus" mechanism (Wanandi 1994). It is clear that today it will function as the governmental track in a two-track diplomatic system in the Asia-Pacific region. The other track is the Council for Security Cooperation in the Asia Pacific Region (CSCAP), launched in June 1993 in Kuala Lumpur. The CSCAP for the first two years will be served by ISIS Malaysia as secretariat, in Kuala Lumpur, with a Steering Committee co-chaired by the Pacific Forum/CSIS and CSIS Jakarta.[9]

The ASEAN states have moved with uncharacteristic alacrity in developing an ambitious framework for the ARF. In the concept paper presented at Bandar Seri Begawan in 1996, three stages or levels of ARF activities are outlined: confidence building, preventive diplomacy, and conflict resolution. Specific ideas to be explored include the setting up of a Regional Arms Register, Regional Risk Reduction Center, a subregional arrangement for nonproliferation and arms control, a Peacekeeping Center and an ASEAN Relief and Assistance Force and Maritime Safety Unit, among other things.

Another new development at Brunei was the proposed formation of the Asia-Europe Economic Meeting (ASEM). Again here, the exclusion of Australia and New Zealand by the ASEAN members became a bone of contention, with the Australian foreign minister arguing that both countries were in the "East Asian Hemisphere" and therefore qualified as members. Perhaps the very fact that Australia and New Zealand want to be part of these new ASEAN formations is testimony to the "hegemony" of ASEAN itself as a regional body.

People-Centered Discourses: The People's Plan for the 21st Century and ARENA PP21

In contrast to the state-centric discourse and the various visions and scenarios of peace building contained therein, the non-statist and people-centered discourse and missions for a peaceful regional order in Pacific Asia remain somewhat inchoate and weak, especially in operational or implementational terms—although they have been articulated with great conviction and fervor in various NGO forums throughout the region.

Civil society visions of the future shape of the Pacific-Asia region include PP21—the People's Plan for the 21st Century—which in some ways attempts to match and parallel the state-centric idea of the Pacific Century. We will describe some of the details of the PP21 since it emanates from the Asia-Pacific region and purports to provide an alternative discourse, vision, and practice to the statist discourse and as a concept has also demonstrated some continuity and longevity.

A Japanese people's alliance led by the Pacific-Asia Resource Center (PARC) in 1988 proposed the PP21 as a forward-looking, people-centered vision of an alternative Asian future to regional economic, political, and cultural integration by transnational corporations and international power elites (Serrano 1994, 87). PP21 proposes a model of development that measures social progress by the degree of equality, justice, dignity, and conviviality with nature. As Serrano puts it,

> Since the Vietnam war, there has been no Asia-wide people's movement of such ambition and magnitude. By 1989, PP21 had linked largely autonomous activities of grassroots and citizens' movements throughout Japan and Asia-Pacific. Farmers and fishers, indigenous peoples and ethnic minorities, workers, women working outside the home and housewives, consumers, and activists in cooperative, alternative trade, alternative aid, anti-nuke, peace, human rights; environmental and NGO movements all began to go beyond criticism of society to the assertion of a positive vision of the future. (Serrano 1994, 87)

In December 1992, some 500 Thai and other NGO participants representing regional and international peoples' movements and networks from 46 countries met in Bangkok to "reiterate and renew our commitment to build transborder alliances of peoples in struggle, solidarity and hope" and in the spirit of the Minamata Declaration (1989), which marked the birth of PP21.[10] The discourse behind PP21, as propounded in the 1992 Rajchadamnoem Pledge, was one of addressing "global domination" perpetrated by the "international capitalist system," which its drafters saw as being responsible for the marginalization of various groups in society and the mass poverty and exploitation of these same groups:

> Integral to this system of global domination is a whole pattern of national control and domination expressing itself in different facets of life. Most governments in the region are armed to the teeth with wide-ranging powers that are stifling the growth of civil society. Democracy has become a system of symbols and

rituals shorn of substance. The fundamental civil and political rights of our people continue to be denied. This denial is perhaps most blatant in societies under military rule, but is equally, if not more, destructive in societies where authoritarianism parades with a human mask. (Serrano 1994, 108)

Among some of the actions that peoples' struggles have successfully waged are the campaigns against military rule in Bangladesh and Nepal and the ongoing one in Myanmar and the closing down of U.S. military bases in the Philippines in September 1991:

> The significance of these struggles within the Asia-Pacific reality is that they emphasise a profound commitment to life. It is a commitment that has great meaning since Asia is the continent that has given birth to the world's major spiritual and moral traditions. At the same time these struggles also point out the relevance and significance of the traditions, cultures and values of the indigenous peoples of the Asia-Pacific region. Central to these traditions is the vision of life and living inspired by justice, love and compassion. Harnessing what is essential in them demands re-interpretation of the traditions. It is this re-interpretation which has a resonance in the struggles of the poor and the oppressed to reassert their humanity. (Serrano 1994, 109)

The following action plans were adopted at the Thai meeting:

- *Information exchange and dissemination* to be carried out especially with respect to the impact of biotechnology on agriculture; starting and sharing inventories of NGOs, respective skills, resources, and areas of concern; sex trade and industry; aid, trade, debt, and structural adjustment; environmental issues directly related to development and sustainability.
- *Lobbying, advocacy, and solidarity action* on issues including the right of free association, protection and promotion of human rights, and the right to self-determination.
- *South-South and South-North peoples' alliance building,* including initiatives such as: strengthening mutual-support networks for shelter, rescue, legal assistance, counseling, reintegration, and so forth; women forging alliances across gender, sectoral, cultural, and national lines to strongly condemn the violence perpetrated against women; the mobilization of national and international support for tribal and indigenous peoples to mark 1993 as the Year of Indigenous Peoples.

The idea of building alliances on liberative cultures to respect and enrich diversity amidst growing tendencies toward ethnic chauvinism, communalism, and racism was seen as the basis behind such initiatives.

The February–March 1996 "Third Convergence" at Katmandu of PP21 took the plan a step further by setting up:

- A PP21 council composed of two members each from the sub-regions of South Asia, Southeast Asia, East Asia, and the Pacific region;
- A coordinating committee; and
- A secretariat with a full-time staff.

I will not attempt to analyze in any systematic way the extent to which the visions and initiatives of PP21 are being promoted or implemented. Suffice it that we reflect on some of its major thrusts and overall effect in contrast to the clearly more dominant state-centric discourse and missions for regional order. But first, it will be interesting to look at another example of Asian civil society discourse by a typical cross-national research-oriented NGO. Let me take the example of Asian Exchange for New Alternatives (ARENA) mainly because of its well-defined vision and mission.

ARENA's Vision and Mission

ARENA was initiated in Bali, Indonesia, in the early 1980s "to bring and knot together scholars, intellectuals and action-oriented researchers as a community on the basis of common goals and mutual recognition of the varied intellectual efforts and orientations needed for human and social progress in Asia" (ARENA 1994). The ARENA Founding Consultation asserted that "the concerned Asian Scholar not only affirms the necessity of commitment to social change and liberation. More immediately, the concerned Asian scholar confronts and transform a whole tradition of conformism and elitism that has long immobilized the traditional scholar."

> Firstly, those who would constitute ARENA's constituency can be found every-where—in schools and universities, among NGOs and other voluntary organizations, research institutions, in social movements and popular organizations, political parties, government agencies, in international organizations, women's organizations, trade unions, peasants movements, urban poor groups, middle class groups, and the youth and student sector.
>
> Secondly, given the fact that the long practical experience of social movements in the transformative process in Asia has also produced the "organic intellectuals" that could render the conceptualizing process a universal activity, the term "concerned Asian scholar" must be redefined as referring to individuals in all sectors of society who are capable of undertaking theoretical, conceptualizing, academic, and abstractive work as direct participants or in support of struggles for social transformation in the interests of disadvantaged peoples. (ARENA 1994, 7)

In its vision to prod organic intellectuals to contribute to people's search for liberating alternatives for a more humane social order, ARENA continues to reaffirm its original mission to promote alternative paradigms and development strategies that contribute to improving the quality of life for Asia's underprivileged; preventing the marginalization of communities in the face of the incursions of modernizing and postmodernizing influences; strengthening of popular participation in public life as against authoritarian centralization; the promotion of constructive and harmonious relations with nature and ecosystems; and the capability to draw upon and strengthen aspects of traditional knowledge systems that relate to the agenda of social emancipation.

Space does not permit mentioning the whole range of projects in which this noteworthy organization has engaged or promoted over the years from its small office in Hong Kong with some half a dozen dedicated individuals. A broad range of themes, issues, and concerns include: social movements and modes of social transformation; the NIC phenomenon in Asia and alternatives; a critical appraisal of the voluntary sector; debt and structural adjustment programs; impact of market-oriented policies on people's livelihood; environment issues and conflicts over natural resources; gender issues, women's rights, and empowerment; ethnic conflicts and the search for identity; and alternative economic arrangements, for example, alternative trade.

Ongoing regional solidarity campaigns in which ARENA participates include the International Campaign for Justice in Bhopal (ICJIB), of which ARENA is a founding member, the Asian Victims Network for Hazard-Free Environment, and the Permanent People's Tribunal (PPT) sessions on industrial and environmental hazards and human rights. ARENA has also been one of the co-convenor groups for PP21 and has been involved in the Asian Task Force on NGOs (ATF), which organizes training workshops and dialogues.

Taken together, PP21 and the programs of regional NGOs such as ARENA provide the contours of a clear, alternative discursive point of departure for regional order broadly defined to encompass the full range of civil society inputs in such a project. Though utopian, these alternative agendas and visions do constitute important inputs for geo-governance in the region.

Geo-Governance: A New Realist Approach

As is evident from the foregoing presentation of statist and non-statist discourses and visions for regional order and peace in the Asia-Pacific region, the plethora of competing visions and missions, as well as their ontological plurality, leaves a daunting task for anyone who would presume to resolve their differences. The competing statist visions for regional order are anchored on the continued dominance of state action and participation, with its implicit exclusion of non-state actors and forces. The non-state visions, with their "alternative" perspectives, are ironically mirror images of their state-centric counterparts with paradigms verging on a total rejection of the dominant state order.

I contend that the parallel networks, institutions, and social formations that currently exist along both the state-centric and non-statist pathways are noninteractive and nondialogic and the overall vision for nonviolent and humane regional orders is not served by the current nonengagement of the two sides. Falk's "essential vision" of a ten-dimensional normative project to achieve humane governance, I also contend, cannot be brought to fruition unless a more interactive and dialogic process occurs between the various statist and non-statist discourses. A series of internal discourses that are "sovereign" unto themselves may lead to greater pluralism within global civil society (my assumption is that both statist and non-statist globalization processes have spawned such a civil society), but it will be a pluralism that is ultimately detrimental to *regional order*. Falk does indeed provide the overall frame for a dialogic process when he says:

> The normative project posits an imagined community for the whole of human-
> ity which overcomes the most problematic aspects of the present world scene:
> the part (whether as individual, group, nation, religion, civilization) and the
> whole (species, world universe) are connected; difference and uniformities across
> space and through time are subsumed beneath an overall commitment to world
> order values in the provisional shape of peace, economic well-being, social and
> political justice, and environmental sustainability. As such, the normative project
> partakes of shared values and aspirations, trends, fears and expectations about
> the future, rooted hopes, visions of the possible. The framing of the project
> acknowledges primarily the efforts of governments and peoples at the grassroots,
> but also takes note of the participation of prominent leaders, governments and
> other institutions, as well as the specificity of opportunities and challenges arising
> in the aftermath of the Cold War. (Falk 1995, 243)

The ten dimensions of the normative project are: taming war, abolishing war, making individuals accountable, collective security, rule of law, nonviolent revolutionary politics, human rights, stewardship of nature and positive citizenship, most of which have a ring of plausibility about them as universalistic agendas (although one could easily add to the list), but this still begs the question of "how" the interactive process of engagement between significant state and non-state forces can be brought about.

I take Serrano's point that older paradigms of social movements that valorize revolutionary discourse based on Marxist and socialist ontologies (Serrano 1994, 44ff) have become increasingly irrelevant and also the point that citizens' movements in the 1970s, 1980s, and 1990s have tended to be "multiclass" or "supraclass" in membership and leadership. In my own work on the middle class in Malaysia, I have found that strong elements within this class have been particularly active in the propagation of democratic norms and the rule of law in politics of dissent vis-à-vis an authoritarian state structure (Saravanamuttu 1992). Thus, in fashioning a discourse for interactive and dialogic intercourse between civil society and the statist structure in international relations, one needs to appreciate the changing climate and social conditions of social movements in today's world. The sheer plurality of forces, which are multiclass, ethnic, and often atavistic in their ontological stances and political orientations, makes the task of fashioning such discourse difficult, save for the fact that even in civil society once senses an overall ascendancy of the universally, ethically, politically "correct" and that such stances tend to be more convergent than divergent.

On the basis of the above arguments, I suggest that it is civil society with all its blemishes—and since it is the weaker of the two, state and non-state, forces—that has to build the bridges for the interactive dialogic process. This, perhaps, could be attained more effectively by a discourse procedure of moving out of *doxa* into *doxy*[11] without abandoning the substantial elements of its agendas. Taking as one example the project for "sustainable development," one can argue that in many ways the emergence of Agenda 21 at the 1992 UNCED Earth Summit represents the beginnings of an important dialogic process between forces of civil society and the state. Another area in which there is increasingly a dialogic approach is human rights, a high point of which was attained at the 1993 UN World Conference on Human Rights. Similarly, a high degree of dialogic interaction already exists on gender questions among statist and non-state forces participating in the UN Decade for Women 1985–1995, with their respective Nairobi and Beijing conferences. Time and space do not permit a discussion of these examples, but suffice it to say that many possibilities exist for a greater level of exchange and interaction on convergent agendas for peaceful, progressive, and humane change among state and non-state actors.

Another approach to a greater dialogic interaction with statist forces is in respect to the issue of violence and war, which Falk has touched upon. In the Asia-Pacific region, while competing structures exist for regional order, the move by the ASEAN states to establish the ASEAN Regional Forum could be taken advantage of by civil groups in the region insisting on participating as independent citizens' forums and alliances in the ARF to engage in issues such as greater transparency in defense policies and postures of Asia-Pacific states in light of the of the Cold War; enforcement of and citizens' engagement in nuclear-weapons-free zones, which are already agendas endorsed by the state actors; regional human rights issues; and environmental degradation.

In conclusion, I am proposing, albeit in the most rudimentary manner at this juncture, what may be termed an enlightened realist approach to an interactive, reflexive, and dialogic engagement of civil society with the states in order to negotiate more effectively realizable visions and agendas in the posthegemonic world order of the next millennium.

Notes

1. Various portions of this paper were presented as "Peace Building in the Asia Pacific: Alternative Realist Pathways to Non-Violent Regional Order" at the International Peace Research Association Conference, Brisbane, Australia, July 8–12, 1996.
2. The use of "realism" here is in a more considered and philosophical sense and not in the mold of the conventional Morgenthauian discourse of power politics nor other versions of realpolitik. Philosophical realism in my sense can be seen as a neoradical, critical discourse that takes into account objective reality while attempting through reflexive strategies to alter it for the general good. Cf. Giddens 1994, 1–21 and passim.
3. See Cox 1996, 151–153, and Gamble and Payne 1996, 16ff, for their commentary on Cox.
4. See Shaw (1994) for an attempt to deconstruct three different sets of contemporary social movements impacting upon international relations: women's movements, peace movements, and human rights and humanitarian movements. His argument that social movements need to be located within the wider context of civil society, which has varying effects on international relations, is one that is shared by this author. Such an analysis tends to lead to a more realist appreciation of their roles.
5. See Higgott and Stubbs (1995) for an analysis of the politics of Asia-Pacific regionalism.

6. A similar notion of an ASEAN "security complex" has been propounded by Barry Buzan. See, for example, its use by Ganesan (1994).
7. That is to say, "The Security Council shall encourage the pacific settlement of local disputes through such regional arrangements or by such regional agencies either on the initiative of the states concerned or by reference to the Security Council" (Article 52/3).
8. The case in point is the Malaysia-Singapore dispute over Pulau Batu Putih (Pedra Branca), an island situated 15 km from the coast of Johor, which is claimed by both countries. At a meeting of the Malaysian and Singapore prime ministers in Langkawi in September 1994, both countries agreed to refer the matter to the International Court of Justice. In Mid-June 1995, top officials of both countries met in Kuala Lumpur to work out the modalities of the dispute before submission to the World Court (*New Straits Times*, June 16, 1995). It appears that neither country has given even a moment's thought to resolving the dispute through the provisions of the ASEAN Amity Treaty.
9. In 1991, ASEAN-ISIS, the Pacific Forum in Honolulu, the Seoul Forum for International Affairs, the Japan Institute of International Affairs, and other research institutes began a two-year project on Security Cooperation in the Asia Pacific (SCAP). Following a series of conferences with participants from 17 countries, including scholars and officials, CSCAP was born in 1993, complete with a charter. See Ball 1994.
10. The Rajchadarnnoen Pledge, PP21 Thailand, cited in *Asian Exchange* (Hong Kong), May 1993, p. 107.
11. See Bourdieu (1977) for an explication of these concepts. Essentially "doxa" refers to a realm of discourse that is outside the thinkable, while "doxy," from whence come orthodoxy and heterodoxy, is the duly recognized realm of thinking.

CHAPTER 7

Regional Conflicts and Peacemaking in South Asia

Rohan Gunaratna

Global Context

The most violent conflicts in the Asia-Pacific region are the Afghan, Sri Lankan, and Kashmiri insurgencies. These conflicts were influenced by the sweeping changes of the 1990s that witnessed the collapse of the Soviet empire. The post–Cold War international system has seen a decrease in international conflicts and an increase in internal conflicts, which have greater spillover effects than Cold War conflicts. Thus in the first half of the 1990s there were only two international conflicts—in Peru and Ecuador and in Iraq and Kuwait—compared to 61 internal conflicts in 1994.[1]

A third of nation-states of the world experienced internal conflicts with the disintegration of the Soviet empire. Although the number of internal conflicts has declined from 61 to 47[2] during the past half decade, the level of violence in all conflicts has increased. Researchers seeking explanations of these conflicts focus on their causes and consequences. No grand theory to explain post–Cold War conflict behavior has emerged. Some speculate that globalization—a phenomenon that has enhanced the porosity of boundaries—heralded this predicament. Today there is greater migration, freer flow of information, and more access to lethal technology than ever before.

Unlike during the Cold War, today's non-state actors play a dominant role, often challenging the authority of the state. Almost all the internal conflicts are ethnic or religion-driven. Many of the substate actors have developed a transstate dimension. Ethnic or religion-based conflicts continue to produce mass migration, creating ethnic and diaspora networks that support political as well as militant struggles for greater autonomy in their homelands. Today, an insurgent group may raise funds in one theater, train and procure weapons from another theater, and fight in a third theater. Without cooperation and coordination at the global level, peace and stability cannot be achieved at the state, regional, and international levels.

The South-Asian Context

South Asia is vulnerable to conflict for multiple reasons.[3] The South Asian ethnopolitical, religious, and strategic landscape is more vulnerable to rebellion than that of sub-Saharan Africa.[4] Of the two poorest regions of the world, South Asia has greater opportunities to transform the region from poverty and war to prosperity and peace. Although South Asia had a poorer rate of growth between 1965 and 1980, today it is the fastest growing region in the world. During the past year more U.S. companies have invested in India than at any time since 1947. South Asia's gross domestic product was expected to grow by 6.6 percent in 1997 and 6.8 percent in 1998, with India leading the way at 7.0 percent and Nepal trailing at 4.5 percent (Asian Development Bank 1997).

Some comparisons provide insights into the strengths and weaknesses of the region. In South Asia, 43 percent of the population suffers absolute poverty, compared to 39.1 percent in sub-Saharan Africa and 23.5 percent in Latin America.[5] Although South Asia performed better than Africa in giving its people education, health, and nutrition, South Asia hosted more than half the malnourished children under the age of five in the world (i.e., 92.4 million of the 175 million total). The comparable figure for sub-Saharan Africa is 15 percent (Asian Development Bank 1997). In South Asia, 77 percent of the people have access to health services compared to 56 percent in sub-Saharan Africa. As a result, South Asian life expectancy is 60 years compared to 52 years in sub-Saharan Africa, and infant mortality in South Asia is 84 deaths per 1,000 live births compared to 93 in sub-Saharan Africa.

The rapid economic progress of South Asia has not adequately dampened the potential for conflict. There is no single explanation for this. The common thinking is that if South Asia is to be free of conflicts, their root causes must be addressed. These include dependency, unemployment, underemployment, low productivity, illiteracy, poverty, and malnutrition. Many speculate that relative deprivation, not poverty as such, makes communities vulnerable to ethnic and religion-triggered political unrest or terrorism. While state military action can buy time to implement political and economic solutions, only good governance and astute leadership can restore stability.

Conflict Spectrum

Many of the conflicts that plague South Asian states are both cross-border and interrelated. The post–Cold War threats to South Asian security can be classed into twelve categories:

1. Ethnicity. Ethnic groups transcend six of the seven borders of South Asian states. Tamils live in northern Sri Lanka and southern India. Punjabis live on both sides of the Indo-Pakistan border. Bengalis live on both sides of the Indo-Bangladesh border. Although minority Sri Lankan Tamils are only 12.5 percent of the total population of 18 million, the majority Sinhalese perceive the Tamils as a threat to their existence. This is because 60 million Tamils live in the South Indian state of Tamil Nadu. This is not the only case of double ethnicity in the region. Geography, history, politics, and more particularly the resurgence of ethnicity and religiosity have complicated South Asian security.

2. Religiosity. In South Asia, there is no ethic against the use or abuse of identity to advance political goals. As a consequence, both ethnicity and religion have been effective politicizing and mobilizing tools. With the escalation of the Kashmir insurgency, tension between the Hindu and Islamic groups throughout the subcontinent has increased. The rise of Hindu and Islamic fundamentalism has empowered political representation on communal lines, strategically weakening the overall and the long-term stability of a secular India.

3. Terrorism. Transstate ideological, financial, and technological linkages have made terrorism a major destabilizing force within the region and a potent source of destruction extraregionally. Kashmir militants are linked to the Islamic Brotherhood–Jamaat-i-Islami network that supports the campaigns in Chechnya, Afghanistan, Algeria, Egypt, Saudi Arabia, Sudan, and until recently in Bosnia in former Yugoslavia and in Mindanao in the Philippines. Groups with such linkages receive, procure, and exchange weapons from diverse sources, thereby contravening established international arms-control conventions and agreements. There is recent evidence to suggest that the suicide bomb technology has been transferred—copied or emulated—from the Liberation Tigers of Tamil Eelam (LTTE) to the Kurdish PKK, Algerian FIS, and Punjabi Sikh militants. The Hamas and Hezbollah suicide technology is rudimentary compared to the South Asian counterpart technologies.[6] Organized crime and terrorism are closely linked.

4. Nuclearization. Exactly a decade after China carried out its first nuclear test in 1964, India exploded a 15-kiloton plutonium device. By 1990, both India and Pakistan were classified by Western intelligence and security agencies as undeclared nuclear powers. Should the current campaign in Kashmir graduate into a conventional war between India and Pakistan, the threat of nuclear war in South Asia will become a reality.

5. Illicit weapon transfers. Although South Asia is moving heavily toward militarization, to date 90 percent of the weapons in the region originated from outside. Markets in West, Central, and Southeast Asia, the Middle East, and Europe provide conventional weapons to non-state actors. The arms pipeline of the semicovert multinational anti-Soviet Afghan campaign leaked profusely and continues to feed South Asia. Although the U.S. and Soviet intelligence agencies have scaled down their operations in the region, domestic agencies have stepped up their activities.

6. Migration. The level of migration has dramatically increased within and outside the region.[7] Of the 2.2 million Sri Lankan Tamils, some 550,000 live overseas. The Tamil diaspora has enabled the LTTE to establish offices and cells in 40 states to generate funds, operate bases beyond the jurisdiction of Sri Lanka, and manage a fleet of seagoing ships for trafficking in armaments and narcotics. Substantial segments of the Kashmir and Sikh diaspora too advance their militant goals by lobbying foreign governments against aid to India and by providing direct assisance to militants.

7. Refugees. The displacement of more than 800,000 Bengalis from East Pakistan in 1971 provided an excuse for Indian intervention. Similarly, the displacement of about half a million Sri Lankan Tamils, including the movement of 100,000 refugees to Tamil Nadu, created an opportunity for India to intervene in Sri Lanka. Militants and refugees figure in the agendas of states to advance their geopolitical designs in the region. Even today, refugees across Bhutan and Nepal, India and Bangladesh, and Pakistan and India have become political tools. Re-infiltration into Bhutan of ethnic Nepal refugees from Eastern Nepal, who were originally expelled by Bhutan, affected both the landlocked states. The flow of refugees across state borders complicates state as well as regional security.

8. Narcotics. Heroin from the Golden Crescent and the Golden Triangle feeds South Asia, a region with major transit routes to the West. Some 80 percent of the heroin found in the United

States originates in Myanmar, a state sharing a common border with India. In addition to the increase in consumption within the region, narcotic trafficking is a major source of revenue for South Asian militants, particularly groups with a transstate reach.[8]

9. Territorial borders. Border disputes exist between India and several of its neighbors, notably China, Pakistan, and Bangladesh. India has fought wars with China and Pakistan over disputed borders. In the recent past, there have been concerns in Tamil Nadu over Kachchtivu and in the Maldives over Malikku (Minicoy). History and politics play a critical role in determining the level and timing of the conflict.

10. Sharing of common resources. A durable solution to the disputes over the sharing of the Ganges water between Nepal, India, and Bangladesh can only be reached through bilateral or multilateral agreements. Ironically India and Pakistan reached an agreement on the sharing of Indus water in September 1960. In the past, water has been used as political leverage against Bangladesh, a land vulnerable both to floods and desertification.

11. Organized crime. Since the collapse of the Soviet Union, organized crime has increased and assumed a new vigor. There are organized crime networks operating in India, Pakistan, Sri Lanka, and Bangladesh. None of the networks originate in the region, but the vulnerability of the region has made South Asia a lucrative ground for operation. Illicit weapon transfers, organized crime, terrorism, narcotics, and corruption are closely linked.

12. Corruption. South Asian societies are riddled with corruption, preventing the people from benefiting from the full potential of their economic achievements. In Pakistan, for instance, the public has great faith in the military because almost all the other branches of government are corrupt. In India, key political leaders have been accused of corruption.[9] In Sri Lanka and in Bangladesh, the issue of corruption has not been adequately addressed and is depriving the state of both economic prosperity and committed leadership. Corruption at higher levels has compromised state security and generated political instability, thereby strengthening the role of the military, as in Pakistan.

Many of these security concerns can be addressed by developing multidimensional solutions. For instance, the questions of illicit weapon transfers and narcotic trafficking, as well as nuclearization and territorial borders—at least in the case of India and Pakistan and India and China—are inextricably linked. When addressing any of these issues in the South Asian conflict spectrum, both the interrelated issues as well as the geopolitical and strategic imperatives should be taken into consideration. The dominant geopolitical and strategic imperatives shaping South Asian security perceptions range from the Kashmir conflict (Indians and Pakistanis) to the role of India as a regional power (almost all South Asians) and the rise of Islamic and Hindu fundamentalisms (Muslim vs. non-Muslims of India). Therefore security issues can be understood and resolved only by addressing them through the South Asian geopolitical and strategic framework.

Intraregional Rivalry

South Asian states have gradually developed their capacity to wage war by proxy. This became more evident after India and Pakistan assumed a nuclear dimension in 1990. Today, the international community will neither tolerate interstate aggression nor a confrontation that could graduate into nuclear status. Therefore, waging war by proxy, by empowering dissident groups of inimical states or unfriendly regimes, is becoming an increasingly "acceptable" method of advancing the foreign-policy objectives of states. This often entails a state's providing sanctuary, finance, training, and weapons to a non-state actor.

In South Asia, three states—India, Pakistan, and Sri Lanka—have provided assistance to militants. Two others—Nepal and Bhutan— have been used by militants for sanctuary. In the case of Bangladesh, militant groups have sought sanctuary. There are indications of military assistance, directly or indirectly, from the Bangladeshi state.

Bangladesh: An insurgency between the government and the Shanti Bahini guerrillas in the Chittagong hill tracts has raged since 1974. The insurgency was supported by the Research and Analysis Wing (RAW), India's foreign-intelligence agency. At least four anti-Indian groups have sought refuge in Bangladesh—ULFA from Assam, Tripura Volunteer Force, two factions of the Nagas, and the Mizos.

India: Insurgencies between the government and several non-state actors have raged since the independence of India in 1947. Among the most-dominant actors in 1997 were the Bodo Security Force, Bodo Liberation Tigers Front, People's Liberation Army of Manipur, National Socialist Council of Nagaland, and several Sikh and Kashmiri militant groups. They were supported by Inter-Services-Intelligence (ISI), Pakistan's foreign-intelligence agency.

Pakistan: The violence between the government and the Mohajir Quami Movement (MQM) continues in 1997. The MQM leader Altaf Hussain resides in the United Kingdom. MQM procures weapons from Sindh with financing provided by RAW. Pakistan is also witnessing Shia and Sunni clashes.

Sri Lanka: The insurgency between the security forces of the government and the Liberation Tigers of Tamil Eelam (LTTE) has assumed mid- to high-intensity proportions. It was supported by RAW from 1983 to 1987. LTTE cadres procure war-related equipment from India with the assistance of Indian Tamil political and militant groups in South India and simultaneously from markets outside the region.

Nepal: In 1996–1997, the insurgency and counterinsurgency between the government and the Maoist insurgents claimed more than 200 lives.[10] The insurgents of Nepal, with training from their north Indian counterparts, are demanding abrogation of the monarchy and a change in the constitution.[11] The insurgency is in the sparrow-tactics phase—the environment is favorable for its escalation. From time to time, militants of the Gurkha National Liberation Front (GNLF)—campaigning for an independent Guruka state in West Bengal—sought refuge in Nepal. Relations deteriorated between India and Nepal when India accused Nepal of providing sanctuary to the GNLF. The operation of GNLF militants from Nepal into India as well as Nepal's procuring antiaircraft and other weapons from China antagonized New Delhi. In mid-1988, Indian personnel violated Nepalese territory by raiding suspected GNLF hideouts along the border.

Bhutan: ULFA militants from Assam have sought refuge in Bhutan. Indian troops violated the Bhutan border in an attempt to apprehend ULFA militants.

As much as political and militant activities within South Asian states have implications for neighbors of South Asia, spillover effects from Central Asia and Southeast Asia also affect South Asian stability and security.

Bordering States

The conflicts in two states bordering South Asia have serious implications for South Asian security. They are the conflicts in Afghanistan and Myanmar. Other conflicts, such as the continued Chinese-occupation of Tibet and the initial signs of rebellion in Xingjing, have implications for South Asia, but they are not as serious as the Afghan and Myanmar conflicts.

Afghanistan

The spillover effects of the semicovert multinational anti-Soviet insurgency in Afghanistan, supported primarily by the United States and Chinese governments prior to Soviet withdrawal from

Afghanistan in February 1989, threaten domestic and international security. Afghanistan continues to be a source of trained militants for campaigns in Mindanao in the Philippines, Chechnya, Tajikistan, Kashmir, Bosnia, Egypt, Algeria, Nagorno-Karabakh, Bahrain, Israel, Lebanon, Sudan, and Turkey. Further, Afghanistan continues to be a major source of weapons for South Asian as well as other insurgent groups. The LTTE in Sri Lanka and several Kashmiri groups continue to benefit from the weapon pipeline of the anti-Soviet Afghan-Mujahidin campaign. Insurgent cooperation across states, strengthened by Indo-Pakistan rivalry, has led to the transfer of insurgent technology. With the introduction of the rank and file of the Indian Peace Keeping Force (IPKF) that fought the LTTE in Sri Lanka to Kashmir, a group of LTTE instructors trained Kashmiri and other foreign Mujahidin fighting in Kashmir in training camps in Afghanistan.[12] With Taliban, a fundamentalist group backed by ISI entering the Afghan theater, Pakistan's control over developments in Afghanistan (the gateway to Soviet Central Asia) increased but strained Pakistani-Iran relations. Since the mid-1990s India and Iran have developed close political and military relations. The population of Afghanistan, estimated at 18 million in 1995, has suffered heavy social and economic losses due to continuous war. There are six million Afghan refugees in Pakistan and Iran and another six million internally displaced persons. The war has killed, widowed, maimed, and displaced half the Afghan population.

Afghanistan overtook Myanmar as the world's leading producer of opium in 1994. Afghanistan produced 3,270 tons of opium in 1994, and since 1990 the land area in poppy cultivation has increased by 50 percent. Illicit drug trade between Afghanistan and Pakistan is estimated at Pakistani Rs 50 billion in 1994 (Rafferty 1996, 66).

Myanmar (Burma)

The core of most ethnic militias at war with the Myanmar ruling military junta—the State Law and Order Restoration Council (SLORC)—broke away from the Communist Party of Burma (CPB). Until 1984, the CPB developed militarily with covert Chinese assistance and was politically supported by the China-based secret radio transmitter, Voice of the People of Burma. Thereafter, the CPB traded in narcotics from Vietnam and Laos and procured Soviet weapons with the proceeds. With the steady disintegration of the CPB, many joined the ethnic militias. The most prominent were the Was,

Shans, Konkang Chinese, and the Kachins. The National Coalition Government of the Union of Burma (NCGUB), the precursor of the Democratic Alliance of Burma, was formed in 1990 by 21 ethnic rebel forces to wage war against the SLORC and establish democracy. Through dialogue and autonomy arrangements, the SLORC has been able to reach agreements with many of the regional ethnic militias of the NCGUB, who finance their economies both through nongovernmental-organization assistance from Canada, Switzerland, and Norway and through opium. Among the ethnic militias were the Mong Tai Army (Shan United Army) of Khun Sa (Chang Chi Fu), the opium warlord controlling the Golden Triangle and the Karen National Union and its military wing, the Kayin National Liberation Army. Many of these groups, particularly the Kachin Independent Organization and its military wing, the Kachin Independent Army, had links with several South Asian insurgent groups for both training and procurement.[13] Further, corrupt Cambodian military generals sold SAM-7 missiles to the Mong Tai Army as well as to the South Asian insurgent group LTTE. By mid-1997, there were only two groups fighting the SLORC.

The SLORC regime is perceived by the West as pro-Chinese and undemocratic. In late 1989, the Myanmar military junta (SLORC) began resettling Buddhists in the predominantly Muslim areas of Rakhine (Arakan) state. In April 1991, the Rohingya Muslims fled and joined an earlier wave of 200,000 refugees that came to Bangladesh between 1976 and 1978. Some of these refugees received military training in Bangladesh. In late 1992, with UNHCR assistance, many of the 288,000 refugees were repatriated to Myanmar. India, critical of human rights violations by the SLORC and supportive of the prodemocratic party National League for Democracy of Daw Aung San Suu Kyi (Nobel peace laureate in 1991), developed relations with Myanmar to challenge the growing Chinese influence there. In March 1993, India signed bilateral agreements on the suppression of separatist movements and drug-trafficking along the common border and even conducted joint military offensives against Naga militants, operating on both Indian and Myanmar soil. The United States, which had suspended economic aid following SLORC brutality in suppressing the prodemocracy movements, resumed its antinarcotics assistance program to the Myanmar junta in 1995 because 80 percent of the heroin found in the United States originated from Myanmar. In May 1997, the United States isolated Myanmar, in an attempt to declare it a pariah state, because it failed to take action against its drug warlords.

Kashmir and Sri Lanka

During the last decade of the 20th century, the conflicts in Afghanistan, Sri Lanka, and Kashmir produced more violence than any other conflicts in the Asia-Pacific region. The conflicts produced regional and international implications that could neither be predicted nor reactively controlled. The protracted insurgencies in the predominantly Muslim Kashmir valley and the predominantly Tamil northeastern Sri Lanka are South Asia's most violent conflicts. While the Kashmiri insurgency is an international conflict between South Asia's most-powerful military contenders, India and Pakistan, the Tamil insurgency is an internal conflict between the minority Tamils and the majority Sinhalese in Sri Lanka. Both Indian and Sri Lankan states are cautious of inviting external intervention to resolve their domestic problems, primarily because of the limitations of diplomatic and military intervention as a tool to reach a solution. India has attempted to project Kashmir as an internal conflict. Similarly, Sri Lanka—with the exception of a British-initiated bipartisan agreement between the two most powerful political groups—has shunned international mediation.

The inability and unwillingness of the international community to resolve both the Kashmiri and the Sri Lankan conflicts reduces the prospect of resolution. The continuity of the Indo-Pakistan subcontinental "Cold Peace" over the Kashmiri conflict poses serious regional and international security implications. India and Pakistan destabilize each other by (a) providing covert military and financial assistance to dissident groups, (b) engaging in heavy militarization, and (c) developing their clandestine nuclear programs. In the case of the Sri Lankan Tamil insurgents, they have developed into an organization with global reach. A study of the international operations of the Sri Lankan Tamil insurgents provides invaluable insight into the problems for domestic and host-state security posed by non-state actors with a transnational reach. Just as governments cooperate, South Asian militant groups too cooperate ideologically, financially, or technologically. Many of the South Indian groups have established links with northern Sri Lankan groups. Many of the northeast Indian groups have established links with Southeast Asian groups. Many of the north Indian groups have established links with Pakistan and Afghanistan groups. Landmine technology and explosive- and arms-sharing agreements are common among some of these groups (Gunaratna 1997). Sri Lankan Tamil militants have established links with Indian Tamil, Mizo, Naga, Assam, Tripura, Punjabi Sikhs, and Kashmiri groups engaged in insurgency. Among the other groups are Naxalite and communist groups operating throughout the subcontinent. For instance, the Maoist insurgents of Nepal have been trained both by retired military men and by communist insurgents of northeastern India.[14] Groups from outside the region, notably the Afghan Mujahidin and the Myanmar Rohingya Muslims, have established links with South Asian groups. Hezbul Mujahidin and Harkatul Ansar, two Kashmiri groups, trained the Myanmar Muslims on the Bangladesh border.[15]

These non-state actors move in search of new opportunities to amass political strength, economic wealth, and military power. Although the bulk of the world's narcotics are grown in Central Asia and in Southeast Asia bordering South Asia, many non-state South Asian actors traffic in narcotics.[16] New routes are both through China to the United States and by ship around Africa to Europe and then to the United States.[17] To facilitate the transportation of narcotics as well as weapons, many militant groups manage offices and cells in world capitals. For instance, the LTTE maintains a state-of-the-art transstate propaganda, fundraising, procurement, and transshipment network, including an international secretariat in London and some 40 offices throughout the world. Although the Kashmiri Mujahidin has offices and cells in at least 15 states, it is less active than the Sikh militants. Naga militants have political cells in Switzerland, Thailand, and the United Kingdom. The more-educated ULFA militants have a wider distribution, although not as widespread as the LTTE, Kashmirs, or the Sikhs.

Trends and Patterns

Several impressive studies identify processes and conjunctures that create insurgencies.[18] The forces that work interactively to reach this stage are declining state resources relative to expenses and the resources of adversaries, increasing elite alienation and disunity, and growing popular grievances and autonomy. The Kashmiri and Sri Lankan Tamil cases fits into the theoretical model of revolutionary situations leading to the breakdown of state law and order. There are certain unique features, however, that distinguish the Kashmiri, Sri Lankan Tamil, and other contemporary insurgencies from earlier insurgencies. During the Cold War many scholars and analysts claimed that the pattern of insurgency was "never deadly." Due to globalization, the force structures of post–Cold War insurgent movements will pose a threat comparable to a conventional force. This is because an insurgent group, if allowed to grow unchecked, can develop the ability to fight at least as a semiconventional army. Although in the past insurgents have fought in different forms to maximize their impact, globalization has enhanced their role as force multipliers.

The Kashmiri Mujahidin has not yet reached the sophistication of the LTTE but is moving in that direction. Today, the LTTE fights (a) conventionally when the LTTE force levels are high and in the densely Tamil-populated, familiar, built-up terrain supportive of the LTTE; (b) unconventionally when the security forces strength is high and the open-country terrain is conducive to the LTTE operating in relatively low strength in "hit and run" (guerrilla) warfare; and (c) ultrasecretly in the capital city of Colombo and overseas by engaging in long-range reconnaissance followed by successful strikes by deep-penetrating male/female suicide and small-team high-explosive vehicle bomb squads. Considering the successes of the LTTE in overrunning military camps, assassinating military and political leaders, and bombing public places, it is clear that the impact of insurgent groups on national security has dramatically changed the traditional concepts of insurgency.[19]

Despite the prevailing myths in the West, there is no satisfactory explanation for the appearance, development, or chances of success of any guerrilla group in any Third World state. An examination of the Kashmiri and Tamil insurgencies clearly indicates that there are common causes leading to the emergence, sustenance, and exacerbation of insurgencies. Neighboring states respond to insurgencies by strengthening their forces, accommodating hundreds of thousands of refugees, fighting border wars either with the insurgents or with neighboring states, accommodating insurgent bases, or taking part in the fighting. Both the Kashmiri and Tamil insurgencies demonstrate the changing dynamics and spell out other regional and international security implications.

Toward Resolution

In light of the Palestinian, Irish, and the South African conflicts, there is some hope for Kashmir and Sri Lanka. Examining the Kashmiri and Tamil insurgencies suggests a number of lessons that are applicable in resolving similar conflicts.

First, there are no permanent military solutions to political problems. Persisting in enforcing a military solution to a political problem can exacerbate the conflict.

Second, a mediator cannot be a participant in a conflict. However, a mediator with a direct or indirect interest in the conflict may make his or her contribution and commitment to the resolution of the conflict far greater.

Third, all the actors involved in the conflict must be parties to the agreement leading to the resolution of the conflict. Further, the success of any agreement lies in the details of the agreement.[20]

Unless, India and Pakistan agree to resolve the Kashmiri dispute by dialogue, the insurgency will continue. After a few years, even without external assistance, the Mujahidin will be sufficiently motivated and militarily developed to sustain its campaign. Today, the LTTE in Sri Lanka has reached that stage. The main supply of weapons to the LTTE comes from the Sri Lankan security forces.[21] It will be in the interests of India and Pakistan to resolve the Kasmiri dispute as early as possible. Only a trilateral dialogue can resolve both conflicts. The principal actors can be: The Kashmiri insurgents, the Indian and Pakistani governments, under UN or U.S. mediation initiative, and the Tamil groups, the Sri Lankan and Indian governments, under a South Asian, UN, or Western mediation initiative. To demonstrate neutrality, particularly in the Kashmiri conflict, a UN initiative will be preferred to a U.S. initiative, or the United States under the banner of the UN. Today, the Pakistanis feel, as does the Mujahidin, that the United States is becoming a stronger ally of India. In 1993, the U.S. State Department threatened to place Pakistan on the terrorist watch list when it was public knowledge that India too was financing, training, and arming anti-Pakistani youth. The 1995 visit of U.S. Defense Secretary William Perry to India led to greater military-military and civilian-civilian cooperation in the defense spheres of policy, research, and production while U.S.-Pakistan cooperation was limited to a meeting of the consultative group.[22]

There have been a number of initiatives by third parties to resolve the Kashmir dispute.[23] The Pakistan and Indian positions on Kashmir, however, have remained unchanged. There have been suggestions that India and Pakistan come together and resolve their other differences, such as the Siachen glacier dispute, but Pakistan has avoided this as it will take the heat off the Kashmiri issue. The Siachen glacier is the highest battleground in the world. Indian and Pakistani troops have fought each other at 6,000 meters since India occupied the area in 1984. In late 1993, when Benazir Bhutto agreed to discuss the Kashmir dispute, the strongest opposition came from her parliamentary opponent, Nawaz Sharief. Thereafter Benazir adopted a tougher approach. Although the Kashmir issue is more an international issue, it evokes an equally strong domestic reaction.

In the Tamil conflict, it is likely that the United States will not interfere as it has no large interests at stake, but as a gesture of goodwill a European or a North American state may offer its good offices as a mediator. Although there will be no military component, this may prove to be effective because there are about 550,000 Tamils living in the West, and the LTTE continues to maintain offices and cells in the West to raise funds and disseminate propaganda. The LTTE is likely to maintain the goodwill of the Western states provided a power-sharing arrangement can be worked out between Colombo and Mulativu.[24] Although the Indian government ceased to be a genuine mediator and became a participant in the ethnic conflict in Sri Lanka after August 1983 (as it began to covertly arm the Sri Lankan Tamil youth), the good offices of the Indian government continued to be used by Sri Lankan Tamil groups until the LTTE assassinated Rajiv Gandhi in May 1991.

Indian threat perception vis-à-vis Sri Lanka is precarious. If the LTTE and the government of Sri Lanka enter into a negotiated settlement, the question of India "sabotaging" it remains a concern of the Sri Lankan political and security establishment. If the LTTE emerges as a formidable force, even a political force, India perceives that as a threat to Indian security. The current New Delhi position is that India will not support a negotiated settlement with the LTTE as empowering the LTTE as the legitimate rulers of northern and eastern Sri Lanka will pose a serious threat to South Indian security. The hawks in New Delhi believe that the LTTE will use northern Sri Lanka as a staging post to create a greater Tamil identity by encompassing the Tamil Nadu State of Southern India. RAW has been covertly given the responsibility to kill the LTTE leadership responsible for declaring war against the IPKF and assassinating Gandhi. New Delhi does not wish to reintroduce Indian security forces to Sri Lanka as they fear a repetition of the IPKF episode. RAW did not cease activities in Sri Lanka after the removal of the IPKF.[25]

Conclusion

After decades of violence, there is little hope that the international community will pressure developing states experiencing high levels of violence to resolve their conflicts through negotiation. There is also little hope that the international community will intervene in internal conflicts unless the level of violence reaches extraordinarily high levels. It is likely that the Kashmiri and the Tamil insurgencies will continue at least in the foreseeable future.

India strongly believes that parting with Kashmir will lead to the breakup of the other volatile states. Pakistani hawks believe that they will be able to "do another Afghanistan" to the Indian army in the Kashmir valley. After two decades of fighting Tamil insurgency, Sri Lanka has concluded that militarily it is nearly impossible to annihilate the Tamil guerrillas. Despite wiping out rival militant and political leaders, the northern military high command, including the minister of state for defense, the president of Sri Lanka, and several senior officials, the LTTE failed to break the government's commitment to a unitary state. Both in the Kashmir valley and in northern and eastern Sri Lanka, there may be periods of cease-fires, cessation of hostilities, negotiations, and even amnesties, but until and unless the government of India and the government of Sri Lanka compromise their traditional concepts of sovereignty, the two insurgencies will continue. No political party, whether in New Delhi or in Colombo, will agree to such a move because it will mean not only an end to the career of the political leader but political suicide for that party. Today, the question of an independent Kashmir or Tamil Eelam is non-negotiable.

Five distinct conclusions emerge from a comparative study of the Kashmiri and Tamil insurgencies.

First, without externalization and internationalization, the two conflicts could have been easily resolved or controlled. The Kashmiri link with Pakistan, the relationship between the Kashmiris in Indian-controlled and Pakistan-controlled Kashmir, and the connection between the subcontinental Kashmiris and the Kashmiri diaspora have made the Kashmir issue an international concern. In the aftermath of the 1983 ethnic riots, the Tamils who left Sri Lanka form the economic backbone of the current insurgency. It is these refugees who suffered or witnessed the ethnic violence that began to materially and politically support the war for an independent Tamil state. At one point, India accommodated more than 20,000 insurgents and from mid-1983 to mid-1987 actively supported violence in Sri Lanka. The Indian objective was neither to assist the minority Tamils nor to support Tamil insurgents, but to further India's own geopolitical interests in the region at a time when India was pro-USSR and Sri Lanka was pro-West. The two struggles were motivated and fueled by assistance provided by the intelligence agencies of Pakistan and India, by the Kashmiri and Tamil diaspora, and by the international environment that supported concepts of self-determination and advocated human rights. While India is determined to handle the Kashmir dispute as a domestic issue, Pakistan has placed it on the international agenda by giving it the nuclear trigger.

Second, policy makers make use of conflict to further their interests. Often they allow a conflict to take its own course without controlling it from the beginning. After a certain point, even if they want to manage the conflict, it becomes difficult and socially and economically costly. Conflicts should be transformed, diffused, or settled early. Once a conflict matures, the probability of resolution dramatically diminishes as the cost of the conflict dramatically escalates. Conflicts steadily escalate over a period of time. Elections by the governments of India and Sri Lanka in Kashmir and in northern and eastern provinces respectively yielded less than 10 percent of votes. Once insurgency takes root, even if the government teams up with the surviving or marginalized politicians, the election results may not be valid, legitimate, or acceptable by the public. Politically, militarily, economically, and legally, very little that can be done to fight externally assisted insurgency. Often, governments find it hard to interlock all these components into an integrated strategy. Most often, the doctrines of militaries are to fight conventional wars and they are unable to adjust to fight guerrilla wars within a reasonable time.

Third, states prefer to avoid international war and fight enemy states by proxy. This is indicative of a future trend, particularly because manipulation of political, ethnic, linguistic, and religious groups is less costly and highly effective. Further, such conflicts can be fought at low-intensity rather than at high-intensity levels. The Kashmiri and Tamil insurgencies could lead to conventional wars but not nuclear wars. However, a conventional war can directly lead to a nuclear confrontation. There is a greater safeguard fighting proxy wars than fighting conventional wars. This has been an operational tool of foreign policy developed gradually since the 1960s into an effective strategy to keep other states under pressure. It cannot be kept secret for too long, nor does it produce the desired effect, and often it becomes a liability. Today, the JKLF and a few Mujahidin groups are not fully under the control of ISI. If the Kashmiris are given a mandate to decide, many of the Pakistan-supported Mujahidin groups are likely to campaign for self-rule. Similarly, from mid-1983 to mid-1987, the Sri Lankan Tamil insurgent groups operating out of South India were not fully cooperating with RAW. The entry of the LTTE into war with the IPKF is indicative of the loss of the control RAW had on the LTTE. This became more apparent with the LTTE killing of Rajiv Gandhi.[26] A state could overtly or covertly retaliate against a neighbor engaging in covert action. But, often, a state's decision to do so is dependent on relative strength, the opportunities available, and domestic and international compulsions. In the case of Pakistan, India has retaliated by stepping up assistance to the anti-Pakistan dissident groups, particularly to the Mohajir Quami movement in Pakistan. Sri Lanka was too small to retaliate against giant India. However, most Sri Lankans have no sympathy for India and have silently encouraged Pakistan to step up assistance to the Mujahidin. Very rarely would India's neighbors willingly support India against the course of action Pakistan has resorted to vis-à-vis Kashmir.

Fourth, insurgencies may temporarily tilt but rarely do they permanently shift the balance of power. Even if externally assisted, insurgencies take more time and resources than conventional wars, but often they do not culminate in victory or defeat. They continue unabated, expending resources, human and material, without reaching their goal. They have a contagious effect—the Tamil insurgency originating in the mid-1970s was inspired by the JVP insurgency of 1971, and the continuity of the Tamil insurgency prompted the JVP insurgency of 1987–1990. The White Shark movement of the Maldives learned the JVP tactics, and many of the Tamil separatist groups of India learned from the Tamil insurgency of Sri Lanka. Like the security and intelligence agencies of governments, insurgent groups too cooperate and coordinate their efforts, share expertise, exchange technology, and learn from each others' experience. The Kashmiri militants perfected their knowledge of landmine warfare by training with the Sri Lankan Tamil militants who developed it by trial and error. Similarly, the art of the suicide vehicle bomb technology was developed in the Middle East in the early 1980s but was perfected and modified into a human bomb in the early 1990s in Sri Lanka. The Middle Eastern groups have since borrowed the hitherto unknown, daring, and highly innovative suicide body suit from the LTTE.

Fifth, the trend for globalization of domestic conflict is on the rise. Therefore, the ability of governments to play the leading role in resolving domestic disputes is diminishing, and the acceptance of third parties (foreign governments, regional and international organizations) is increasing. Unlike in the past, it is not the voice of a single government but international public opinion that controls international action. The current international environment favors rebellion. Legally, there are international norms protecting dissenting people, and geographically, boundaries have become porous and both weapons and people move unhindered. Increases in bilateral as well as multilateral cooperation, international traffic, and the communication revolution have favored the airing of minority grievances. The emergence of transnational organizations has complicated the traditional concept of security, and no single government can protect the territory of its state without the cooperation of the neighboring states. Regional and international collective and cooperative security structures are the keys to retaining stability and ensuring peace in the future. The lack of commitment and resources will constrain both the United Nations and the United States from playing the role of global policemen. However, both the United Nations and the United States can empower and help develop the capabilities and force structures required for regional organizations to intervene in and resolve disputes or at least keep combatants at bay.

Notes

1. International conflicts are interstate and internal conflicts are intrastate. Statistics compiled by International Alert (IA), UK, Dr. Kumar Rupesinghe, secretary general, IA, London, personal communication, 1994.
2. King 1997, 84–87. King lists 47 conflicts, which he defines as civil wars, unresolved internal disputes, and areas of major unrest.
3. Dennis Pluchinsky, Office of Threat Assessment and Terrorism, Bureau of Diplomatic Security, U.S. State Department, Washington D.C., personal communication, May 1997. The United States in 1997 assessed the regions most vulnerable to conflict to be, in order of declining vulnerability, the Baltic states, the former USSR, and South Asia.
4. Studies on vulnerability of geographic regions by Gurr and Wallenstein, two respected social scientists, confirm the greater vulnerability of South Asia than other regions. Gurr and Wallenstein maintain state-of-the-art databases.
5. For the poor, purchasing power per person per day falls bellow US$1 (Asian Development Bank, 1997).
6. The U.S. State Department's 1997 Annual Global Terrorism Report lists the suicide bombing of the Central Bank building in the heart of Sri Lanka by the LTTE as the world's worst international bombing in 1996.
7. Weiner (1996, 5–42) provides an excellent analysis, highlighting the security implications of refugee flows.
8. In Manipur, there were 600 addicts in 1988. In 1996, there were 30,000–40,000 addicts, of whom many were infected with the AIDS virus (Lintner 1996, 16). In the 1980s, there were as many as 400 Sri Lankan Tamils languishing in the jails of Italy alone. Dushmantha Ranatunge, researcher on the LTTE, UK, personal communication, May 1997

9. In 1997, the Central Bureau of Investigations (CBI) of the Indian central government listed former Indian premier Rajiv Gandhi as an accused in the Bofors arms deal.

10. Pradhan, inspector general of police, Nepal, personal communication, May 1997.

11. Amod Gurung, head, Counter-Terrorism, Nepal, personal communication, May 1997.

12. Chris Smith, Centre for Defence Studies, Kings College, University of London, personal communication, April 1997.

13. The Golden Triangle is the world's major opium producing region where the borders of Myanmar, Laos and Thailand meet.

14. Amod Gurung, head, Counter-Insurgency Unit, Police Headquarters, Nepal, personal communication, May 1997.

15. Anand, Minister, Political, Indian High Commission, Thailand, May 1997, personal communication.

16. Latin America is the only other region that produces comparable quantities of narcotics. Both cocaine and heroin have been produced and transshipped out of Colombia since 1994.

17. *Washington Post*, July 26, 1996, A 29; *Asiaweek*, June 6, 1997.

18. Jack A. Goldstone, Michael Radu, Ted Gurr, George Lopez, and Martha Cranshaw are among the leading theoreticians in this field.

19. The JVP, the Sinhala counterpart of the LTTE, brought the government to its knees during 1971 and 1987–1989.

20. Ted Robert Gurr, professor, Center for International Development and Conflict Management, University of Maryland, College Park, personal communication, 1995.

21. LTTE International Procurement, Ministry of Defense, Sri Lanka, Secret, 1996.

22. Ronald Dean Lorton, director, India, Bhutan, Maldives, Nepal, and Sri Lanka Affairs, U.S. Department of State, Washington, D.C., personal communication, 1995.

23. The most outstanding research into this area has been conducted by Professor Moonis Ahmer at the Office of Arms Control, Disarmament and International Security, University of Illinois at Champaign-Urbana.

24. Since early 1995, the LTTE leadership has shifted from Jaffna to Mulativu, the LTTE jungle base complex originally established in late 1987.

25. Recent evidence shows that a number of refugees repatriated from India to Sri Lanka have been provided with specialized training, particularly in the art of handling explosives, by RAW. Similarly, RAW continues to develop its relations with anti-LTTE Tamil militant groups, including the Eelam People's Democratic Party, which had no relations with India during the IPKF episode.

26. Rajiv Gandhi only continued his mother's policy of spawning terrorism in neighboring Sri Lanka for geopolitical compulsions. Soon he realized that it was a flawed policy, but by that time RAW had lost tight control of the LTTE.

CHAPTER 8

Regional Conflicts and Cross-border Ethnonationalism in Southwest Asia

Amin Saikal

Transborder ethnic nationalism, ethnonationalist conflicts, and major-power exploitation of these conflicts are now dominant features of the changing geopolitics of Southwest Asia—the region comprising Pakistan, Afghanistan, and Iran, as well as the Central Asian republics.[1] These developments have caused a cycle of instability and redefined the limits of what constitutes a sovereign state and the meaning of nationalism in its classic sense in the region.[2] At the center of this development lies the Afghanistan crisis, which has rapidly been transformed from a Cold War superpower-driven confrontation in the 1980s into a post–Cold War regional struggle in the 1990s, backed by major-power strategic interests. While reflecting the multi-ethnic makeup of Afghanistan, the transformation is fueled by a number of outside actors, who have found it increasingly convenient to focus their individual national and strategic interests on the Afghan conflict. Placed in the wider regional picture—which is characterized by a number of other potential or active interstate disputes and conflicts, with the Indo-Pakistan dispute over Kashmir heading the list—this has polarized not only the Afghans along ethnic lines, with Pashtuns opposed to non-Pashtun groups, but also the external actors. Pakistan and Saudi Arabia, with some degree of U.S. acquiescence, have credibly been identified as supporting the Pashtun, ultrafundamentalist Islamic Taliban militia, while Iran, some Central Asian republics (especially Uzbekistan and Tajikistan), Russia, and India have deemed it essential to back the non-Pashtun anti-Taliban groups.

This chapter has three objectives. The first is to look at the processes by which the Cold War Afghan crisis has been transformed into a post–Cold War ethnonationalist conflict. The second is to assess the role of outside powers in fueling this transformation, giving rise to competing cross-border armed ethnonationalist movements in the region. The third is to examine the regional landscape in relation to the question of how ethnonationalist conflicts have altered the classical notion of nationalism and given rise to cross-border ethnic clientelism as a formidable post–Cold War obstacle to achieving a regime of collective peace and security in Southwest Asia.[3]

A central feature of the Afghan conflict when it commenced in the late 1970s was that it predominantly emerged as a clash of two opposing ideologies: Marxism-Leninism, as expounded by the successful pro-Soviet coup makers of April 1978 and reinforced by the Soviet invasion of Afghanistan 20 months later, and Islam, the religion of almost all Afghans, who rejected communist atheism as repugnant to their faith (Roy 1986, chs. 2, 5–7; Saikal and Maley 1991, chs. 2–4). This ideological polarization was critical to the failure of the Communists to gain popular legitimacy and to the success of the Afghan Islamic resistance forces, the Mujahideen, in securing widespread domestic support and attracting international backing for their cause. Although the resistance rapidly split into various groups, the overall ideological schism between the Mujahideen and the Communists facilitated a degree of intergroup mobility and cooperation and national consciousness within the resistance. This proved to be instrumental in enabling the resistance to maintain sufficient operational cohesion, if not at the level of leadership (which was marred by growing personal rivalries), then at least at the level of field commanders and their followers inside Afghanistan.

Two factors, more than anything else, eventually changed the character of the resistance from being loosely national to becoming fragmented along the lines dictated by the mosaic nature of Afghanistan as a state made up of a collection of microsocieties.[4] One was the Soviet policy of brutal pacification, which resulted in the breakdown of the carefully crafted national framework in which the precommunist Afghan governments had delicately placed Afghanistan's social complexities—a framework that enabled the country to enjoy the longest period of peace and stability in its modern history between 1929 and 1978. The Soviets and their surrogates destructured Afghanistan politically, socially, and economically, altering the boundaries and patterns of power, authority, and loyalty within each microsociety and among them. Yet they could build no substitute (Saikal and Maley 1991, ch. 8; Rubin 1995b, pt. 2). Another was the way in which the international actors conducted their counterinterventionist support for the resistance. The most important of these actors were: Iran, Pakistan, Saudi Arabia, and the United States. Although rhetorically all the actors proclaimed a single goal—the liberation of Afghanistan—in practice they varied in their objectives, the nature and extent of assistance, and the method of distribution of assistance.

The Iranian Shi'ite Islamic regime of Ayatollah Khomeini, deeply preoccupied with its own domestic consolidation and opposed to involvement in any scheme that could make it appear as cooperating with its arch adversaries—the United States and Washington's regional friends, especially Saudi Arabia—decided to channel a limited amount of aid, but in a manner that would enhance its own regional interests. It pursued a sectarian line in its approach, selecting only those groups of Mujahideen whom it regarded as receptive and vulnerable to Iran's influence. As a result, Tehran threw its weight largely behind three Shi'ite groups which represented a segment of Afghanistan's 15–20 percent Shi'ite population. It continued on this path until the early 1990s, when it homogenized its clients into a single Shi'ite group—Hezb-i Wahdat (Party of Unity). It refrained from providing any substantial support even to probably the largest Mujahideen group, Jamiati Islami Afghanistan (Islamic Society of Afghanistan), composed mainly of ethnic Tajiks, with whom the Iranians have much in common culturally and linguistically. It is important to note that the Tajiks, who are divided into a number of subgroups and who populate much of north and western Afghanistan as well as Kabul, have historically formed the second largest Sunni ethnic group, after the Pashtuns, in Afghanistan (or 30–35 percent of the country's 15–17 million population), and provided the bulk of the Afghan intelligentsia. It was also the famous Jamiat commander, Ahmad Shah Massoud—a member of the Panjshiri subgroup of Tajiks—who led the Mujahideen to take over power from the Soviet-installed but crumbling government of Najibullah in late April 1992, resulting in Jamiat under its political leader, Burhannudin Rabbani, soon assuming dominance in the Mujahideen Islamic government in Kabul—a dominance that persisted for the next four years. At any rate, the Iranian assistance was not of a volume sufficient to influence the overall direction or operational capacity of the Mujahideen in any decisive manner (Roy 1986, ch. 9).

Pakistan assumed a far greater role than Iran in the Afghan crisis.

Its support of the Mujahideen proved to be both critical and discriminatory. As a predominantly Sunni state, with a sizeable Pashtun population of its own concentrated mostly in its Northwest Province on the border with Afghanistan, Pakistan in general favored the main Sunni Mujahideen groups, which represented the majority of the Afghan people, but in particular promoted only one as most conducive to its own objectives.[5] The country's military dictator, President Zia al-Haq (1977–1988), who was known for his politics of public deception and divide and rule, with a zeal to transform Pakistan into a powerful player in the region, premised his policy behavior toward the Afghanistan crisis on achieving three main objectives.

The first was to put an end once and for all to a long-standing Afghan claim over the Pashtun areas of Pakistan in order to create a theoretically independent but in practice Afghanistan-linked entity of "Pashtunistan" (Saikal 1980, 171–172; Haqshenas 1984, 366–380; Ghaus 1988, 109–147). The Afghan aim was to alter substantially the Afghan-Pakistan border—a border that the British had arbitrarily drawn toward the end of the 19th century, but to which the Afghans had never agreed. In the wake of the Soviet invasion, General Zia now appeared to have a unique opportunity to counter the precommunist Afghan Pashtunism with a strategy to bring all the Pashtuns in the region under the sway of Pakistan. He favored a relinkage of Pashtuns on both sides of the 2,400-kilometer Afghan-Pakistan border as a means to create a transterritorial ethnic enclave, which Pakistan could use as leverage not only to influence the direction of the Afghan resistance but also, if necessary, to be in a position to treat the Hindu Kush ranges, which bisect Afghanistan from northeast to southwest, as a natural barrier between Pakistan and the Soviet imperial domain to the north. The second was to secure the repatriation of what quickly built up to be a population of more than three million Afghan refugees in Pakistan, a majority of whom were Pashtuns, who had fled the Soviets' intense bombardment of their territories in the south and east of Afghanistan on the border with Pakistan. The third was to build, under the cover of countering the Soviet invasion, a strong protégé Afghan political-military force as a necessary means to achieve his goals in the medium to long run.

Hence Pakistan's military intelligence (ISI), which General Zia had entrusted with the conduct of Pakistan's Afghanistan policy, began the task of promoting Gulbuddin Hekmatyar—a Ghilzai Pashtun and extreme Islamist who had fled to Pakistan in the early

1970s following his implication in the murder of a fellow student at Kabul University—as the most prominent Mujahideen leader. Although publicly Islamabad proclaimed a commitment to the Afghan resistance as a whole and denied any interference in Afghan affairs, the ISI from the beginning channeled the bulk of Pakistan's and outside, especially American, assistance to Hekmatyar and his radical Mujahideen group, Hezbi Islami Afghanistan (the Islamic Party of Afghanistan) (Yousaf and Adkin 1992, 9–10; Rubin 1995a, 214). In so doing, it essentially embarked on a policy of politicization of Pashtun ethnicity and at the same time ethnicization of the Afghan resistance.

The Saudi Arabian and American approach to the Afghanistan crisis basically reinforced the Pakistani agenda. The Saudis, who substantially bankrolled the Afghan resistance and Pakistan's efforts in support of it, paid little attention to what Pakistan wanted to achieve out of the crisis, so long as Islamabad's activities fostered a situation whereby the Saudis could realize some of their own objectives. The Saudis wanted not only to appear as the defender of Islam against communism but also to be able to export their brand of traditionalist, Sunni Wahabi Islam to Afghanistan and to ensure that their main regional and Shi'ite rival, the Iranian Islamic regime, was denied the opportunity to make any sectarian/political gains in Afghanistan. Given this and their historically close friendship with Pakistan, which among other things had provided Saudi Arabia in the 1970s and 1980s with a military contingent to perform a "special mission," most likely that of protecting the Saudi royal family, the Saudis were happy to allow the ISI to channel most of their assistance to the Mujahideen in whatever manner it saw fit. As such, they shared, wittingly or unwittingly, Pakistan's preference for the Pashtun Mujahideen groups and viewed the latter's non-Pashtun counterparts as potentially vulnerable to Iranian influence.

The United States, leading the Western support for the Afghan resistance, also failed to show any major sign of concern about Pakistan's approach. While closely cooperating with the ISI as the conduit for supply of American arms to the Mujahideen, what Washington, or more specifically the CIA, wanted was to make sure that Pakistan remained firm as a frontline ally against Soviet communism, so that America could achieve its own wider goals. These were to turn the Afghanistan adventure into a costly and humiliating operation for the Soviet Union; to prevent the Khomeini regime from exploiting the Afghan crisis to its advantage; to reassure America's allies that the U.S. post-Vietnam isolationism was coming to an end and that it was ready to stand by them; and to rebuild American influence in the region, which had been shattered in the wake of the fall of the Shah and, before that, America's defeat in Indo-China (Hammond 1984, 120–124). As long as Pakistan's behavior supported these goals, Washington remained oblivious to what Pakistan's own specific objectives might have been in Afghanistan and to how and on what basis the ISI managed the distribution of American assistance to the Mujahideen, and to what the implications might be for the welfare of the Afghan people in the long run.

As a consequence, by the time the Gorbachev leadership pulled Soviet troops out of Afghanistan in early 1989, the policy approaches adopted by the international supporters of the Afghan resistance, most importantly Pakistan, had strongly encouraged the development of a politics of ethnicity within the politics of the Mujahideen, with a salient emphasis placed on the importance of Pashtun ethnic nationalism. Although General Zia, the architect of this development, died in a mysterious air crash and Prime Minister Benazir Bhutto assumed power with a return to a quasi-democratic system in Pakistan in late 1988, two new developments gave greater urgency to the cause of Pashtunists in the Pakistani ruling circles, even after Ms. Bhutto was replaced as prime minister by Nawaz Sharif in 1990. They were the end of Soviet support for the protégé government of Najibullah in Kabul and the emergence of the Central Asian Muslim republics as sovereign independent states, opening up to the outside world a new but resource-rich region with the potential for close geographical, ethnic, and cultural ties with the Middle East and West Asia.

The first development led to the collapse of the Najibullah government but brought no joy to Pakistan, and the second made Pakistan ambitious about finding access to the newly emerging markets and resources of Central Asia, for which Afghanistan was viewed as the country providing the best corridor. Contrary to Islamabad's expectation, the resistance leader who led the Mujahideen to Kabul was not Hekmatyar but his Tajik rival Ahmed Shah Massoud. In an initial alliance with a disillusioned communist Uzbek warlord from the north, Abdul Rashid Dostam, Massoud succeeded in taking over the reins of power in the capital and invited the Pakistan-based Mujahideen leaders to set up the first Islamic government in Afghanistan. Pakistan publicly called for a negotiated internal settlement and supported the Peshawar Agreement of April 1992, concluded under Nawaz Sharif's influence between the

Pakistan-based Mujahideen leaders, which allocated the presidency, for the first two months, to a minor Mujahideen leader, Sibqatullah Mujadiddi, and then to Rabbani and the subordinate position of prime minister to the Hezbi Islami, with the expectation that its leader, Hekmatyar, would fill it. But ultimately, Pakistan could not embrace Tajik domination of the new Rabbani-led Islamic government, with Massoud as its strongman, at the cost of the defeat of its Pashtunist policy. For this reason it did not attempt to stop Hezbi Islami from refusing to honor its commitment under the Peshawar Agreement (Saikal 1996).

The ISI continued its buildup of logistical and armed support for Hekmatyar, who within a few months of Rabbani's takeover exploited Dostam's and Hezb-i Wahdat's discontent with the Rabbani-Massoud leadership, which had not granted them a greater share in the power structure than their respective ethnic strength could permit, and commenced a campaign of sustained rocketing and bombardment of Kabul. The ferocity and intensity of this campaign, resulting in the deaths of more than 25,000 inhabitants of Kabul and the destruction of half of the city over the next two years, could not have been sustained without extensive Pakistani aid to Hekmatyar (Rashid 1995). The longer this situation continued, the less the Rabbani government was able to consolidate and to negotiate internal settlements in order to bring more than a couple of Pashtun Mujahideen leaders into its administration and thus to broaden its power base. In the end, however, Hekmatyar's failure to dislodge the Rabbani government confronted the ISI and indeed Pakistan's political leadership with serious dilemmas. It now faced the need either to abandon its Pashtunist efforts or to opt for deeper ethnicization of the Afghan conflict.

It opted for the latter (Ahmed 1996). Heading the Pashtunist elements within Benazir Bhutto's government, Interior Minister Nasseerullah Babar, who was a retired army general with excellent links to the ISI and considerable skills in dealing with Pashtuns through a policy of "divide and rule" in the region, decided to abandon Hekmatyar. He set out to craft a fresh Pashtunist force, the ultrafundamentalist Islamic militia, the Taliban.[6] Although mystery still shrouds the Taliban leadership, it is now clear that only some of the leaders came from among those puritanical Islamic elements of the Afghan southern provinces of Kandahar and Uruzgan who had become disillusioned with the intra-Mujahideen power struggle. As for their fighters, they were mostly raised from amongst Afghan and Pakistani Pashtuns, some of whom were studying in religious schools in Pakistan, knew little of Afghanistan or the wider world, and were urged to fight for the cause of a highly eccentric and discriminatory Sunni Islam. It is reported that the militia also drew support from the Pashtun officers of the former Afghan Khalqi communist regime and members of an irredentist Pashtun nationalist party, the Afghan Millat (the Afghan Nation), who have disguised themselves as Islamists.[7]

To all appearances, the militia was created purely as a fighting force, with a fairly decentralized and faceless leadership, although a Mullah Mohammed Omer, who comes from Kandahar and is based there, has been promoted as its supreme political-spiritual leader. This was a deliberate attempt not only to prevent the militia from becoming embroiled in personality-driven power struggles for leadership, which had marred the Mujahideen, but also to enable Pakistan to make changes at the leadership level as it deemed necessary. The militia's application of Islamic extremism to impose a theocratic order, forbidding women to work or even be publicly educated, and its deployment of draconian measures to punish those who violate their form of Islamic practices and values, is aimed at enabling them to claim wider and deeper ideological legitimacy than the Mujahideen, and to Islamize the imposition of a dictatorship of a kind which Afghanistan had not experienced in its modern history. While initially Pakistan's Interior Ministry was largely responsible for creating, training and equipping the original units of the Taliban, as a retired general, Babar was soon able to persuade the ISI and the Bhutto government as a whole to shift support from Hekmatyar to the Taliban.

As the Taliban's initial operations proved successful, leading to its takeover of Afghanistan's largest southern city of Kandahar by late 1994 and a year later the non-Pashtun western province of Herat on the border with Iran, the militia assumed wider marketability. The Saudis found it attractive to finance the Taliban as an anti-Iranian force, while there is a view that the United States perceived it as useful not only for enforcing the American containment of Iran but also for providing it with a new niche for securing ideological leverage against the anti-American political forces of Islam in the region and for expanding America's access to Central Asian resources. At least two international consortia, one led by UNOCAL of the United States and Delta Oil of Saudi Arabia and another comprising the energy independent Bridas of Argentina, found the Taliban beneficial for their bid to construct a pipeline across Afghanistan, at the cost of some $2.5 billion[8] to export gas from Turkmenistan to South Asia. At the same time, drug traffickers quickly embraced the Taliban for its liberal approach to the cultivation of the poppy and the production of heroin, estimated to account for 30 percent of world production in 1997 (Rashid 1997a) despite the militia's emphasis on being clean and incorruptible.

The Taliban rapidly became an unstoppable force as the Saudis pumped millions of dollars into its budget, once again mostly through the ISI; as American officials, as officially admitted, established regular contacts with the militia leaders; as international consortia promised major financial spin-offs to help it expand its territorial control of Afghanistan; and as the drug traffickers made lucrative deals with it. It was able to buy support and suborn vulnerable opponents as a significant means to expand the militia's territorial control of Afghanistan (Burns 1995). Although originally Massoud's forces were able to repulse several Taliban attempts to take over Kabul, ultimately divisions within the Rabbani government, together with the Taliban's numerical, financial, and military strength, proved overwhelming. In late September 1996, the Rabbani government found itself with little choice but to flee to the Tajiks' main territory in the north, allowing the Taliban forces, with backing from Pakistanis, some of whom were captured by Massoud forces and interviewed by Western journalists, to enter Kabul without much fighting (Barnes 1996).[9]

The Taliban takeover of Kabul was a watershed in the process of the Pakistan-driven ethnicization of the Afghan conflict. It clearly changed the Afghan conflict into an interethnic power struggle: Pashtuns versus non-Pashtuns, with the Tajik, Uzbek, and Shi'ite Hazara peoples of Afghanistan forming a loose alliance to defend their traditional territories in northern and central Afghanistan, especially in the face of the Taliban's acts of ethnic cleansing of the Tajiks in the areas it had overrun north of Kabul. Even more so, it widened the transterritorial ethnic dimension of the conflict, as it brought other neighbors of Afghanistan face to face with the necessity to dwell on their cross-border ethnocultural ties to anti-Taliban non-Pashtun opposition groups.

While alarmed by the Taliban's ideological and geopolitical challenge as part of a perceived wider American–Saudi–Pakistani strategy to tighten a circle of containment around Iran, Tehran now found it necessary to augment its support not only for the Afghan Shi'ites but for the anti-Taliban alliance as a whole. In this, it came to share a common interest with Afghanistan's Central Asian neighbors, especially Uzbekistan and Tajikistan, whose recycled communist leaderships felt deeply threatened by the Taliban's brand of fundamentalist Islam. At the same time, given Russia's strategic interest in maintaining a strong position in Central Asia and close ties with Iran, it could not sit idle either. To stem the tide of a perceived Taliban threat, Russia too began not only to shore up the defenses of the Central Asian republics but also to provide some help to the Afghan anti-Taliban alliance (Mehrotra 1997). In a similar vein, India—Pakistan's traditional arch enemy—could not feel comfortable with any strategic gains by Islamabad in the region.

However, the assistance from these quarters proved to be too little and too late. It could not ultimately halt personal rivalries between, and within, the diverse groups in the anti-Taliban alliance. Given the long-standing rivalries between Massoud and Dostam—as the former could not trust the self-proclaimed Islamic credentials of the latter as a former Communist—as well as the rivalries within Dostam's Uzbek camp, the alliance failed to develop a coherent anti-Taliban strategy, making the alliance increasingly vulnerable to manipulation by the Taliban and Pakistan. The crunch came in late May 1997, when a key commander of Dostam, Abdul Malik Pahlavan, bent on revenge against Dostam for killing his brother and one of his close allies, was reportedly persuaded during a trip to Islamabad to come over to the Taliban side with a promise of appointment to a key position in the Taliban administration and autonomous control over northern Afghanistan. His defection caused Dostam to flee to Turkey and changed the balance of forces dramatically, opening the way for the Taliban to attempt to overrun Dostam's territory and placing the militia closer than ever to proclaiming control over most of Afghanistan.

The apparent successes of the Taliban led Pakistan to accord prompt formal recognition to the militia as the legitimate force to rule Afghanistan—an act that was followed by Saudi Arabia and the United Arab Emirates (UAE)—despite the fact that the Taliban had not formed either a legally constituted or structurally recognizable government (Thomas 1997). Yet this, at the same time, enhanced the respective quest of various non-Pashtun Afghan microsocieties for ethnic survival and placed greater pressure on Iran and the Central Asian republics to take greater care of their diverse national security interests. As the Taliban's unholy alliance with Abdul Malik Pahlavan quickly broke down, the opposition forces inflicted a humiliating defeat on the Taliban, chasing it out of most of the territories it had recently captured in the north. In the process, there were four important developments.

The first was that Pahlavan and his Wahdat allies killed hundreds of Taliban fighters and captured several thousand of them, including not only many senior Taliban officials and commanders (with at least one of them, Abdul Razaq, the Taliban nominee to be governor of Mazari-Sharif, turning out to be the former Khalqi deputy minister of planning in the first communist government of Afghanistan) but also several Pakistani officials, including the newly appointed Pakistani ambassador to Kabul (*Hindustan Times,* 2 June 1997). Of the captured Taliban members, 2,000 were subsequently massacred by Malik—a contemptible act that tarnished Malik's image badly and was widely condemned inside and outside Afghanistan.

The second was that Massoud was able to come out of hiding in the Panjshir Valley to make territorial gains north of Kabul, blocking the Salang Pass and entrapping an expeditionary Taliban force of some 3,000 in the north of Hindu Kush. Massoud has retained his territorial gains to date, with his forces setting about 15 miles north of Kabul.

The third was that these events provided irrefutable evidence of the deep involvement of Pakistan and former Afghan Khalqi communists in support of the Taliban and served as a unifying and morale-boosting factor for the anti-Taliban opposition. They also helped to stiffen the resolve of their outside supporters to widen their involvement against the Taliban.

The fourth was that Washington began to refocus its attention on Afghanistan, especially the Taliban's behavior and Pakistan's involvement in support of the militia. So far, the American understanding of and attitude toward the Taliban had been very much influenced by the assistant secretary for South Asia, Robin Raphel, who had special sympathy for Pakistan and had met Taliban leaders (Jennings 1996), apparently in the belief that the militia constituted a force that, under Pakistan's control, could serve the interests of the United States in the region. This view was also supported by certain elements within the CIA, an organization with close links to ISI. However, an American reassessment of the Taliban and Pakistan revealed alarming anomalies in American policy.

It became clear to the Clinton administration, especially following the replacement of Raphel by Karl F. Inderfurth and the appointment of Thomas Pickering as under secretary of state in early 1997, that the Taliban was a force the United States could not comfortably embrace either politically or ideologically. It found the Taliban's treatment of women to be draconian, its rule-enforcement measures in massive violation of human rights, and its involvement in opium production abhorrent. Further, it realized that the Taliban would not be able to unite and govern Afghanistan on its own. This marked the beginning of a shift in American attitudes, with a policy objective of creating "an Afghan government that is multi-ethnic, broad-based, and that observes international norms of behaviour." This shift culminated in Secretary of State Madeleine Albright's openly deploring the Taliban as a backward and regressive force during a visit to Pakistan in mid-November 1997. She stated: "I think it is clear why we are opposed to the Taliban. Because of their approach to human rights, their despicable treatment of women and children and their general lack of respect for human dignity." She also said that the United States believed that the Taliban was not "in a position" to occupy all of Afghanistan. "There are other parties," she went on, "who need to be recognised and there needs to be a government that is composed of them" (Reuters, 18 Nov. 1997; Voice of America, 18 Nov. 1997). Albright's message, which was to be repeated by First Lady Hilary Clinton and the secretary of state herself in the White House during International Women's Day in March 1998, was certainly very unsettling for Pakistani leaders. Foreign Minister Gohar Ayoub Khan—a Pashtun who had taken up the mantle of Babar as the most significant supporter of the Taliban in the Nawaz Sharif government following the fall of the Bhutto government, was visibly uncomfortable and subsequently critical of the shift in the American approach.

These developments, together with the European Community's persistently strong criticism of the Taliban and Pakistan's backing for the militia, proved to be critical in deterring any countries other than Pakistan, Saudi Arabia, and the UAE from according recognition to the Taliban and in enabling the Rabbani government to retain the Afghan seat at the UN as well as most of the Afghan embassies abroad. They were also important in helping the anti-Taliban forces to regain their composure to some extent. However, nothing could ultimately stop the Taliban and Pakistan from pursuing their main goal: a military conquest of all of Afghanistan. Despite repeated assurances that Islamabad gave to Tehran that it favored a negotiated settlement of the Afghan conflict, the Taliban, reportedly backed by Pakistani regulars and air force, unleashed a decisive fresh offensive in July 1998. Within the next two months, it not only defeated Dostam (who after his flight a year earlier had returned and reclaimed control of his territory in the north) and conquered the last major city under opposition control—that is, Mazari-Sharif—but also routed the Wahadat forces and captured the stronghold of the Shi'ite militia: the city of Bomyan in Central Afghanistan. In the process, the Taliban killed thousands of Shi'ites in Mazari-Sharif, as confirmed by the UN and Amnesty International, as well as seven Iranian diplomats at the Iranian consulate in Mazari-Sharif, to show their detestation for Shi'ites and Iranian support for the anti-Taliban forces. The only opposition group that was able to hold out was that of Massoud, who continues to control four northeastern provinces with a capacity to target Kabul whenever necessary, but he is at the same time very much isolated and under siege. These developments resulted in two further major developments.

First, they infuriated Tehran, which publicly denounced the Taliban as an unacceptable force, condemned the militia and Pakistan for the murder of its diplomats, and demanded from the Taliban not only an apology, the handing over of the killers of its diplomats for trial, and the release of some 50 more Iranian prisoners but also a halt to their massacre of Shi'ites. Tehran also requested that the Taliban accede to the need for the formation of a broad-based multi-ethnic government in Afghanistan. In a show of strength, Iran amassed some 270,000 troops along the border with Afghanistan for possible direct punitive measures if necessary and gained widespread international support (inside and outside the UN) against the Taliban over the latter's killing of its diplomats.

Second, the developments alarmed the international community, prompting the UN to convene on 22 September 1998 a meeting of six of Afghanistan's neighbors, plus the United States and Russia, to find a resolution to the Afghan conflict. The meeting, attended by foreign ministers of the participants, with the exception of Iran, which was represented by one of its deputy foreign ministers, condemned the Taliban's killing of the Iranian diplomats in particular and its human-rights violations in general; called for the formation of a broad-based government in Afghanistan; and asked the UN secretary general to dispatch a fact-finding mission to investigate the alleged Taliban massacre of its opponents and to send his special representative for Afghanistan to the region to mediate a negotiated settlement of the Afghan conflict.

The crisis also prompted the United States to refine further its stand in relation to the Taliban and Saudi Arabia to reassess its policy toward the militia. As Washington felt frustrated over the Taliban's refusal to hand over the Saudi dissident Osama Bin Laden for allegedly masterminding the bombing of American embassies in Nairobi and Dar es Salaam in August 1998, Riyadh could no longer feel comfortable with its support of the Taliban. Whereas in the past its support of the Taliban may have been conditional upon the militia's controlling Bin Laden, Riyadh now deemed that the militia had gone too far in its protection of Bin Laden. When the Taliban reportedly rebuffed a Saudi request for the extradition of Bin Laden, Riyadh realized that it had helped to create a force that was now in a position not only to defy it but also to cause strain in its relations with its superpower ally, the United States, and to poison its recently improved ties with Tehran. As a consequence, Riyadh abruptly announced on 23 September a freeze in its diplomatic relationship with the Taliban, expelling the latter's chargé d'affaires and recalling its own from Kabul. This constituted a serious blow to the militia and to Pakistan, which had been campaigning vigorously to obtain wider international recognition for its client force.

Tehran's concerns about the Taliban have been shared by Afghanistan's Central Asian neighbors and Russia, which has proclaimed the borders of its former Central Asian republics with Afghanistan as the common borders of the Commonwealth of Independent States (CIS) and has taken on the responsibility to defend these borders against any threat. The bordering Central Asian republics, which are individually riddled with ethnic-cultural divisions—some of them as much as Afghanistan—have become deeply concerned about the fate of their cross-border ethnic Uzbeks and Tajiks in Afghanistan under Taliban rule and their own security. To counter this, while Russia has beefed up its border guards and adopted contingency measures to act whenever necessary to alleviate the security concerns of its Central Asian allies, the latter have grown very vigilant and nervous about the implications of a Pakistan-backed Taliban-dominated Afghanistan.

However, even if the Taliban succeed in subordinating all of Afghanistan and obtaining international recognition as the legitimate government of the country, the internal ethnic features and the international strategic dimension of the Afghan conflict are not likely to disappear in the foreseeable future. In the first instance, the ethnic Pashtuns, on behalf of whom the Taliban claims representation, are themselves not homogeneous but rather divided along tribal, clan, and family lines. With the leadership of the Taliban centered in Kandahar, the Pashtuns of southeastern and eastern Afghanistan would not ultimately find the militia an acceptable force to rule them. This has already become evident in frequent armed challenges that the Nangarhari and Kunara Pashtuns have mounted to the militia and in the former head of the Mujahideen Governing Council of

Nangarhar joining the opposition alliance. Even if the unity of the Taliban continues for longer than expected, in the worst-case scenario for the non-Pashtun groups, their leadership will simply cross the border into neighboring countries and use these territories as a launching pad against the Taliban just in the same way as the Mujahideen used Pakistani territory against the Soviets. This too has already been happening to some extent, with Massoud reportedly using bases in Tajikistan.

What has so far transpired is the growth of transterritorial ethnic conquests inside Afghanistan and transborder nationalist tendencies in relation to Afghanistan. This means that conflicting ethnonationalist trends for diverse purposes appear to be gathering momentum in southwest Asia, seriously hampering the growth of interstate cooperation in the region. Even if the regional states are interested in promoting economic cooperation among themselves in the direction of building a common market, for which they have established the Economic Cooperation Organisation (ECO), the chances of such cooperation occurring remain very much in doubt. For as long as the Afghan conflict is not settled on a viable basis, involving the establishment of a multi-ethnic rather than monoethnic government in Afghanistan, and Pakistan does not forego its strategy of transforming Afghanistan into its transborder ethnic enclave, no neighboring country can afford to be trustful of, and cooperative with, either the Taliban or Pakistan. For this reason, it is highly premature for multinational companies to plan construction of cross-regional projects with certainty and with the firm knowledge that they will prove beneficial to them—a fact that UNOCAL has recently recognized, as a result shelving its pipeline plan for the time being. A Taliban-dominated Afghanistan will not end the conflict in that country. Nor will it reduce tension in the region.

Meanwhile, it is not certain that the Taliban, with a change in overall regional circumstances, might not achieve the position of being able to defy its Pakistani patrons and extend its Islamic extremism beyond the borders of Afghanistan, especially into Pakistan itself. Many among the popular supporters of the militia in Pakistan have already publicly identified Pakistan as the next, but most vulnerable target, given the country's own deep ethnic and social divisions, economic difficulties, and problems of law and order (Rashid 1998). In fact, this has already begun to happen to some extent. The support that the Taliban has reportedly provided to some extreme Sunni groups against their Shi'ite counterparts in Pakistan and the serious military clash that occurred in mid-March 1998 between the Taliban and Pakistan border guards in relation to a dispute over border crossing may be signs of wider and more disturbing developments to come. Furthermore, the success of the Taliban carries with it the risk of further galvanizing the separatists in Jammu and Kashmir, who are also guided and supported by the ISI, in pursuit of independence from India. Several Taliban leaders have already identified the separatists' cause as their own and vowed to "liberate" Kashmir in the same way they claim to have liberated Afghanistan. In this case, the triumph of the militia in Afghanistan would create wider regional instability, with serious implications for global order.

The current transborder ethnonationalist developments raise serious questions about the future of the nation-state and state sovereignty in Southwest Asia. The pressure arising from these developments could well change the nature of sovereignty, encouraging more and more moves in the direction of ethnicized and tribalized cross-border entanglements in the region. Given the fact that one of the fundamental features of all the states in the region is multi-ethnicity and confused national identity, there is no certainty that cross-border ethnicization of the Afghan situation will not have an inspiring and radicalizing effect on forces which will tribalize and fragment the neighboring states. And no state is more vulnerable than Pakistan itself in this respect. As a matter of fact, the predominantly Pashtun legislators of Pakistan's Northwest Frontier Province (NWFP) have already found it expedient to pass a bill in late 1997 to change the name of NWFP to Pakhtunkhwa (Pashtunist) province—a development that has also encouraged many elements in Pakistan's neighboring Baluchistan province to call for the expulsion of Pashtuns from their province. This has caused much consternation in the province's relationship with the federal government in Islamabad, which has opposed any kind of move that could stimulate a secessionist movement in the province.

Moreover, the Afghan phenomenon has caused much confusion for the political forces of Islam, deepening the split within the Muslim world between those supporting the Taliban (such as Pakistan and Saudi Arabia, notwithstanding its recent downgrading of its diplomatic relations with the Taliban) and those opposing the Taliban (such as Iran and many radical Islamist movements in the Arab world). At the same time, the Taliban's puritanical Islam plays right into the hands of those adversaries who have deliberately sought to discredit the political forces of Islam as incapable of achieving a social-political transformation of their societies independent of Western interests and values. It enables them to present the Taliban's brand of Islam as repugnant to civilized existence and to continue their policy of geopolitical exclusion of Islam and yet to promote a "clash of civilizations" thesis in world politics in particular.

It is time the Afghan conflict was addressed comprehensively and effectively. The way forward is for the United States to attach greater saliency to finding a viable resolution to the conflict. It needs to tackle the problem in conjunction with support from the United Nations, the European Union, and the Organisation of Islamic Conference (OIC). In the first instance, Pakistan will have to be pressured to hold back its support of the Taliban as the best way to prompt the Afghan (not Pakistani) elements of the militia's leadership to recognize that they have no other alternative than to work for a political resolution of the problem. It will have to negotiate with the opposition forces for a cease-fire and the creation of a transitional, regionalized federative government, whereby the powers and structure of the central authority would be proportional to the need of different ethnic groups to have a reasonable degree of autonomy in their traditional areas of concentration. This would have to be managed as a prelude to constructing a viable political order in Afghanistan in the long run. In the meantime, the United States will have to reach a clear understanding with Iran and Russia on the issue. Any degree of rapprochement that could eventuate between Washington and the moderate Islamist government of President Mohammed Khatami in Iran could prove very beneficial in this respect. If Washington provides decisive leadership, the UN, OIC, and EC could usefully help with the details and implementation of the peace process. The alternative is a continuation of the Afghan conflict, with further devastating consequences not only for the Afghan people, but also for regional stability, for the foreseeable future.

Notes

1. For a good discussion of what constitutes ethnic nationalism and ethnonationalist conflicts in the post–Cold War era in general, see Brown (1993) and Smith (1993).
2. For a discussion of different meanings of "nationalism" and its applications, see Guibernau (1996).
3. On ethnic identity and nationalism, see Brass (1991) and Rex (1995).
4. On the social composition of Afghanistan, where state has traditionally been weak but society strong, see Tapper (1983) and Banuazizi and Weiner (1986).

5. For a detailed discussion of the role and objectives of Pakistan, Saudi Arabia, and the United States, see Yousaf and Adkin (1992) and Khan (1991).

6. This point was recently admitted by Nasseerullah Babar himself. See "Babar Admits Training Taliban in 1994," electronic document posted on 8 September 1998 to afghanistan@hypermail.com. Also see Arkady Dubnov, "Kabul: The Fate of Cathago?" *New Times*, December 1996, p. 55.

7. For a detailed account, see Sreedhar et al. (1997), chapters 1–3.

8. For details, see Rashid (1997b).

9. For a detailed analysis of the weaknesses of Rabbani's government, see Saikal (1998).

CHAPTER 9

The Lessons of the Philippine Peace Process

Florangel Rosario-Braid

The quest for peace and the search for solutions to local and global problems in human security and governance must be conducted within a comprehensive development framework. As the Toda Institute framework states,

> global perspectives must be constructed bottom-up, from the synthesis of the local views on the human problems facing communities. . . . The concept of human security is premised on the need to assess security concerns on the basis of well-being of people rather than the physical security of states. The traditional paradigm of political and state-controlled decision-making in peace and security matters is no longer viable in today's society where non-state actors are assuming an ascending role.

Past approaches to conflict resolution have often followed a competitive or win-lose strategy, which has ultimately led to further escalation of conflict. Lately, however, there has been a growing acceptance of peaceful strategies such as formal dialogues and negotiations as preferred modes in settling conflict. This analysis will focus on culture and communication and the active participation of civil society in the peace process in the Philippines.

The Philippine Situation: A Case Study on Peace Making

The country's struggle for freedom and democracy has been marked by violence and conflict, resulting in considerable loss of lives and property. On the positive side, it has given the people strength and clarity of vision to continue to preserve their democratic gains.

The peace movement started as a struggle against exploitation, inequalities in the distribution of resources, and violations of human rights. Over the years, the advocacy of people's organizations provided the impetus in awakening general consciousness. To a large extent, they have helped shape the direction of government initiatives in future peace processes.

The celebration of the centennial of the revolution against Spain has brought into focus historical accounts of armed conflict and a growing recognition of the need to emphasize peaceful struggles. For example, in the centennial's information and advocacy programs, there is a conscious effort to demonstrate that Muslims, women, and indigenous peoples actively participated in the struggle for freedom. This is to rectify historical accounts, which primarily centered on activities in Northern and Central Luzon. Documentation of local history likewise encourages the presentation of women, minorities, writers, artists, and development workers as "peaceful" players in the revolution. Global movements focusing on human rights, gender and children's rights, sustainable development, and social development issues have underscored peaceful social transformation strategies and continue to emphasize values of trust, mutuality, cooperation, sharing, compassion, and respect for other cultures.

The peaceful people's revolution at EDSA in 1986, which brought down the Marcos dictatorship, was followed by eight years of peaceful transition to democracy. As Abueva (1992) noted, "the government's success in suppressing coup attempts, reversing the communist insurgency and in containing the Moro secessionist threats in Mindanao was a clear demonstration to the people that peaceful change is possible."

The consensus in several peace conferences was that all armed combatants must be brought to the negotiating table. Continuing social mobilization of people at all levels was undertaken to build a peace constituency. Among the peace advocates and activists who constitute the nation's emerging peace constituency are leaders and members of churches and associations of religious leaders of both Christian and Muslim faith, peace advocacy networks, human rights advocates, environmental advocacy groups, labor and agrarian reformers, people's councils, and organizations of the urban poor. The outcome of major peace initiatives of the National Peace Conference and the Multi-Sectoral Peace Advocates was a declaration, "Towards a National Vision for Peace," drafted after President Aquino declared the Decade of Peace in January 1990. More than 100 nongovernment and people's organizations representing 17 sectors worked for more than a year to craft the vision of peace which "perhaps best captures the spirit and movements of people's participation in the peace process today. . . . This vision statement reflects the belief that peace is both a process and a pledge; the conviction that involves resolving conflicts as well as building possible futures" (Garcia 1988).

The peace process in Mindanao did not happen overnight. It is the consequence of vigilance expressed in overt and active social action over the years by concerned citizens' groups. The National Peace Conference was headed by former Supreme Court Justice Cecilia Munoz Palma, and the National Unification Commission was chaired by human rights lawyer Haydee Yorac. While the principal negotiators came from government, their authority was derived from continuing consultations with the peace constituency coming from various sectors.

The Mindanao Process: Lessons in Communication

On 2 September 1996, the historic peace agreement between the government of the Republic of the Philippines (GRP) and the Moro National Liberation Front (MNLF) was signed with the participation of the Organization of Islamic Conference (OIC) Ministerial Committee and its secretary-general. The quest for peace seemed like a "Mission Impossible," according to Pres. Fidel V. Ramos, who considered the comprehensive peace process framework as one of the most important hallmarks of his administration. The key actors were Chairman Nur Misuari of the MNLF and Amb. Manuel T. Yan, chairman of the GRP panel. It had taken about 19 years from 1972 to 1991 for the administration of former Presidents Ferdinand E. Marcos and Corazon C. Aquino to seek a solution to the conflict in the Southern Philippines that would be acceptable by all sides.

The strategy in the peace negotiations, which lasted all of four years, highlighted the communication approach and the use of information. Communication in its broadest definition includes such dynamics as the amount and quality of dialogue between the protagonists; media coverage; institutional or administrative communication; and use of information and informal networks.

Of the 16 lessons learned, as noted by President Ramos in his analysis of the Mindanao peace process (Ramos 1996), at least 11 were specifically communication strategies while the other five depended on effective use of communication. They are: use of constructive rather than adversarial encounters; emphasis in messages on commonalities rather than disagreements; exploration of the multifaceted angles of a simple idea; good administrative communication through aide-mémoire and continuing public information campaigns; use of broad consultations with various groups; use of "third party facilitation," or mediators, a culturally appropriate mechanism; use of informal communication in informal venues; appropriate choice of principal negotiators; sensitivity to difficult situations and ability to adjust to communication situations; effective coordination through communication during crisis situations; and finally, use of candor and straightforwardness instead of innuendoes to generate trust.

The general perception was that the public media contributed to delays in achieving consensus. The media had their own prejudices, which were quite evident, especially in the reporting of outcomes of the accord, the basis of the peace agreement. Informal surveys and content analysis of print and broadcast media reporting indicated that the media tended to deal with contentious issues— stories that pitted protagonists against each other rather than on areas of mutual agreement. This demonstrated the media's orientation to sensationalism, conflict, personalities, and one-sided presentations. Content analysis of news during the peace process showed that military briefings in the region or in Manila remained a significant source of news about terrorist attacks or bombings in Mindanao. But these briefings, according to the study done by the Center for Media Freedom and Responsibility in 1994 (De Jesus 1996), did not include a civilian perspective, carrying little news about the rest of the area, about schools or business, with little mention of efforts to bring relief to victims of attacks or to those displaced by war. De Jesus (1996) further observes: "It is typical of media's blind spot that citizen and NGO peace efforts receive so little attention as news. . . . Perhaps greater exposure (of journalists to community events) will develop a new sensitivity among journalists, a greater interest in news about communities healing themselves of past wars, who rise above the hostilities which have set them apart."

Field research to map positions of various sectors in Mindanao on the creation of the Southern Philippines Council for Peace and Development (SPCPD) showed a dearth of information on the SPCPD. The usual source of information cited was the mass media, but reports, particularly those of the views of dissenters and provisions in the agreement, were found to be distorted.

It may be recalled that the breakdown of the North-South dialogue during the historic Cancun summit in the early 1970s was attributed to the rigid stance of the protagonists, who brought inflexible agendas to the negotiating table. The countries in the West, or the North, had their own interests to protect, and the South, or the developing societies, had their own demands. A lesson learned during that summit is the importance of openness and willingness to listen to the other's point of view. Communicators describe this as the art of human dialogue—the presence of trust, authenticity, transparency, love, and an orientation toward "win-win" strategies.

Peace advocates suggest examples of successful indigenous peace processes—the *bodong* in the Cordillera, where consensus is arrived at within the context of dialogue and trust accompanied of course by the usual rituals. In the Mindanao peace process, the principals noted the use of what they describe as the ASEAN approach of *Musjawarah* (consultation) and *Mufakat* (consensus). The establishment of peace zones in certain areas of the country and the establishment of mechanisms for regular dialogues between Christians and Muslims are some of the examples of nongovernmental groups' initiatives.

Historical Antecedents of the Mindanao Conflict

The conflict in the South is not merely a Muslim problem but is in fact a Christian problem—a legacy of the Spanish era, according to Fortunato Abat (1997), a retired general and now the chairman of the government's peace panel for Mindanao. The MNLF rebellion, which broke out in 1972, was the result of benign neglect by Christian leaders who failed to recognize the worth of Muslim Filipinos. Even Jose Rizal, the national hero, regarded the Muslims as part of the Filipino nation, and in the statutes of La Liga Filipina, drafted in 1892, he proposed to unite the archipelago into one "compact, vigorous and homogenous body." Emilio Aguinaldo, the first president of the short-lived republic, sought the establishment of a special political system for non-Christian communities in conformity with traditional customs. However, the Christian delegates to the Malolos Congress, who were influenced by the Spaniards, were unable to appreciate Aguinaldo's call for unity. Spain's crusading spirit inculcated fear and hatred of Muslims.

In 1973, MNLF military might was demonstrated in the first Muslim rebellion. The response of government was military action—the organization of the Central Mindanao Command (CEMCOM), based in Cotabato under the leadership of Abat. The population ratio of Muslims to Christians at that time was 1:6. At present, the MNLF constitutes a minority and is perceived to be fanatic in its goal of establishing an "Islamic state." Its strength lies in its political and military structures in the controlled areas.

Ambassador Yan, chair of the government panel in the peace negotiations, attributes success to such factors as mutual respect, transparency, and sincerity, which helped in building confidence.

Yan, a soft-spoken senior diplomat and former army general, played a role that no one in Mindanao could have filled, as he was able to strike rapport with the scholar-activist Misuari, who perhaps saw in him a father figure worthy of emulation. The four-year negotiation process may be characterized as a series of collective-bargaining dialogues. It was a gradual granting of concessions to Nur Misuari after confidence-building measures were installed. But the panel's initial timetable of one and a half years was not realistic. Delays were caused by the absence of Misuari, who was abroad, and because the latter wanted to have talks held outside the Philippines. During the first 18 months, the negotiations were held in Jakarta. Most of the time, both panels stayed in the same hotel, which enabled them to hold a number of informal talks in coffee shops. Rapport was established, and Misuari, convinced of the sincerity and political will of the government, was eventually persuaded to come home. Talks were held every year, and during the third round, the government panel proposed Misuari's being elected governor of the Autonomous Region of Muslim Mindanao (ARMM) and that a council known as the Southern Philippines Council for Peace and Development be set up with Misuari as head. The council would be tasked with peace building through the implementation of social and economic reforms. In March 1996, 123 issues were resolved. But negotiations ended in a stalemate over three contentious issues, namely, the setting up of an autonomous provisional government; integration of the MNLF into the armed forces of the Philippines (AFP) and the Philippine National Police (PNP); and differences in perceptions of the implications of autonomy. The Philippine constitution requires a plebiscite, but Misuari was not agreeable as 75 percent of the people in the region are Christian. The peace agreement finally provided for integration into the AFP and the PNP of 7,500 MNLF members.

Further consultations were made by the GRP panel with sectors such as the Senate, the Integrated Bar of the Philippines, and the Philippine Constitutional Association. The consultations revealed what was already known—that the ARMM had already implemented the Tripoli Agreement.[1] Misuari and his group did not find it adequate, as it was set up by the Philippine government without the participation of the OIC, led by Khadafi of Libya and President Suharto of Indonesia. The decision was to set up the SPCPD as an interim body. Special Islamic ministerial meetings in Jakarta clarified the role of SPCPD, and at the mixed committee meeting in June 1996, the two negotiating panels arrived at what is known as the Davao Accord. This agreement defined the objectives and structure of SPCPD: it would be established without a plebiscite; the chairman would come from the MNLF; and a 70-member consultative assembly, with 41 members from the MNLF, would be created.

The common objection to the SPCPD[2] was that it gave the MNLF considerable power as the majority came from the Muslim group. But Yan felt that the Muslims gave up more, as their original intent was secession—to set up the Bangsa Moro Republic. Misuari wanted the SPCPD to last 10 years but in the end compromised with the GRP panel's recommendation of three years. Shortly after the Davao Accord, the Office of the Presidential Adviser on the Peace Process (OPAPP) implemented a Communication Plan partly to counteract the media's negative reporting and to inform various sectors of the progress in the negotiations. The cabinet and the Senate divided into teams, held press conferences and media interviews, and conducted hearings. A majority of the Muslims were on the government side; a majority of the objectors represented the Christian faith. A positive outcome of the communication campaign was public awareness that the *lumads,* or indigenous people, consisting of several millions, and not the Muslims, actually dominated Mindanao. The *lumads* acquired a status that they did not have before the public information campaigns.

Abat (1997) notes the views of observers who are concerned with the need to establish mechanisms to sustain the gains already made. The latter have raised questions such as: Will the grant of autonomy to the Muslims dissipate the secessionist movement? Now that autonomy is granted, what will prevent them from demanding independence later? What can be done to motivate them to stay within the Republic of the Philippines? How can we reduce the influence of the Islamic countries in what is purely an internal problem? Will economic development reverse the move toward secession or accelerate it? As scholars of contemporary Muslim affairs know, the MNLF, being the most militant, has received the highest and continued attention and the support of the OIC and the Muslim world.

To answer these questions, one must view them within a comprehensive framework of development. Such a framework considers the need to give equal importance to social, cultural, political, environmental, and economic concerns. The cultural issue is important in peace-building efforts as there are vast differences in the cultures of the Muslims and the Christians which need to be reconciled. The Muslims belong to the Islamic religion, have a high illiteracy rate, are traditionally water-bound, and live in dire poverty due to a high percentage of landlessness. To aggravate the problem, there is considerable political conflict among the Muslims themselves—the Tausugs, the Maguindanaoans, the Maranaws. One of the positive developments has been the ongoing peace talks between the MNLF and the more militant Moro Islamic Liberation Front (MILF). It is expected that a peace agreement will soon be forged between these two groups.

A study by Nunez (1997) showed that the lack of understanding of Islam which encompasses ideology, religion, and culture by both government and the Christians was a principal source of conflict. Using Gurr's theory of relative deprivation, Nunez, who was mayor of General Santos City in Mindanao, explains that conflict can result from a group's perceived discrepancy between what it seeks or what it values and what it actually attains. In her survey of a sample group from both the Muslim and Christian population, she found that although Muslims had high status expectations, they felt that their level of achievement was low because of lack of support from the external environment. The Muslims felt that Christians and the national government did not understand or give due recognition to Islam. Christians, on the other hand, felt that the conflict was primarily due to Muslims' desire to control Mindanao even if they were in the minority. In terms of attitudes toward the other, Muslims rated the Christians positively except for two negative attributes. The Christians, however, rated the Muslims negatively on nine out of fourteen attributes. The author therefor concludes that Christians had stronger biases and prejudices against Muslims than Muslims had against Christians. The ethnic factor is an important dimension in understanding Mindanao conflict, and thus the agreement signed in 1996 may just be a respite, according to critics, who also noted that efforts to solve the problem of ethnic separatism either through socioeconomic programs or military action are doomed to failure.

Toward a Comprehensive Development Framework

A comprehensive development framework encompasses the interaction of development processes, local and national institutions and infrastructures, movements, and regional and global alliances and blocs. The peace process is supported by processes such as decentralization, devolution, democratization, grassroots mobilization, and advocacy, all of which require dynamic information and communication support.

The institutional and infrastructure component consists of media, information technology, social and cultural institutions (specifically, education and human resource institutions), and social reform institutions. Popular movements include women's and children's rights (gender), green (environment), cooperatives, religious and spiritual, human rights, and literacy and educational movements. Regional and global alliances and blocs include the Brunei, Indonesia, Malaysia, Philippines–East ASEAN Growth Area (BIMP-EAGA), APEC, ASEAN, and the OIC.

The principal root of conflict is poverty, an outcome of social and economic inequities. The search for consensus in a free and open society requires an understanding of shared values with communication as a main resource to further cement the ties that bind people culturally. There is also the task of reconciling priorities of central with local governments, and subsequently with that of capital (business) and of civil society. A stable society is one where government, capital, and the civil society are in continuing dialogue. Peace goals must be shown within a framework that emphasizes not merely quantities or numbers of structures but also the quality of information, strategy in timing, relationships, approaches and methodologies as well as socioculturally appropriate perspectives and strategies.[3]

Decentralization, Autonomy, and the Role of Popular Movements

The peace accord was signed within a favorable policy environment in support of decentralization and local autonomy. The 1987 Philippine constitution provided the impetus for such a shift when it declared that the period of centralized governance was over and mandated the Philippine Congress to enact separate organic acts for autonomous regions in Muslim Mindanao and the Cordilleras. Both the Aquino and Ramos governments adhered to the principles of decentralization, devolution, and local autonomy.[4] The Local Government Code law transferred authority and responsibility to local government units. The Ramos administration adopted "people empowerment" as one of its pillars in governance to emphasize popular participation in nation-building.

During the four-year peace negotiations, the discussions centered on the factors perceived to be the root causes of armed conflict and discontent. The National Unification Commission (NUC) convened regional public consultations nationwide, perhaps the first opportunity for a truly multisectoral discussion. It helped in the realization that there can be honest differences of opinion as to the appropriate resolution of a single perceived problem. Bishop

Francisco Claver, a regional convenor, noted that the voices heard were not those of the traditional opinion makers—experts, political analysts, politicians, commentators—but ordinary men and women from all walks of life speaking from the guts of society. With or without government and rebel groups' initiatives, popular movements and nongovernmental organizations (NGOs) would have pursued peace through community-based activities like cooperatives, livelihood projects, and literacy classes where Muslims, Christians, and *lumads* could work together and learn to appreciate their religious and cultural differences.

A number of peace advocates served as "pressure groups." Their tasks included monitoring the progress of peace negotiations, convening fora for dialogue, developing peace agendas for various groups, and conducting peace education. They set up peace zones, particularly in areas of armed conflict between government soldiers and rebel forces. Peace zones are geographical areas where armed conflict could no longer be waged and where the entry and safekeeping of firearms, whether by residents or outsiders, is prohibited. The peace zones are creative alternatives to the armed conflict that traumatized the communities. The long and festering experience of violence from continued hostilities became a catalytic agent that moved the people to declare their communities as zones of peace.

Basic Christian Communities (BCCs), a Latin American pastoral innovation transplanted into the Philippines at the height of the Marcos regime in the mid 1970s, are voluntary organizations rooted in basic Christian values of social justice and equity. They are mostly found in the rural areas, and many of those involved in peacekeeping are found in Mindanao. They are engaged not only in religious activities but also in projects that address endemic poverty. Like the BCCs, Women in Enterprise Development was set up to provide literacy, entrepreneurship training, and credit assistance for poor Muslim women. Through structured learning experiences, the project has been able to promote peace and understanding among marginalized women belonging to both Christian and Muslim faiths. The Islamo-Christian Silsilah Dialogue movement provides an appropriate venue for communication by establishing a center that conducts courses on Islamic and Christian religions and culture. These are voluntary grassroots initiatives that continue to monitor the peace situation in Mindanao.

The peace process is a communication process. It starts with intrapersonal communication as the individual reflects on his values and attitudes toward peace, such as developing respect, acceptance, and appreciation of the views, ideas, beliefs, culture, and traditions of others. This is fostered by openness, active listening, and education. The communication media have played a critical role in facilitating free and open discussion, disseminating information on agreements on vital issues, creating an ambiance of cooperation, promoting hope and congeniality rather than despair. On the other hand, they have also created dissension and have contributed to further misunderstanding through use of negative stereotypes of ethnic groups, women, and foreigners.

An analysis of the gains made over the past decade since the country became free after 14 years of martial law shows a checkered balanced sheet in the area of peace and order. The signing of the peace agreement in the South was merely a beginning. Peace-building efforts are now being threatened by local and global developments. Unemployment, underemployment, continuing exploitation of the environment, children, and women, violation of human rights as well as crime and violence in the streets and in the media are among the threats that must be confronted with appropriate government policies and social-action programs by nongovernment organizations. Delivery of social services was delayed, and opposition groups within the government and the private sector continue to criticize the creation of the Southern Philippines Council for Peace and Development. These critics believe that the peace accord will not kill the desire of the Bangsa Moro people to pursue autonomy. Opportunities come in the form of a more socially and politically active citizenry. Cooperatives and NGOs working in the areas of social credit, literacy, and small economic enterprises have demonstrated that economic productivity can be achieved while at the same time building networks of solidarity, cooperation, and collective action.

The government's Social Reform Agenda (SRA), adopted as its antipoverty flagship program, may be considered an enabling intervention. It addresses three areas of inequity: access to quality basic services; access to economic opportunities and productive resources; and effective participation in economic and political governance. The SRA's main goal is the achievement of a just and lasting peace through literacy education, establishment of micro enterprises, and livelihood opportunities in 20 priority provinces. Five of the 20—Sulu, Tawi-Tawi, Surigao del Sur, Agusan del Sur, and Basilan—are in Mindanao. This program is however hampered by poor legislative support and slow implementation.

In terms of infrastructure support, the advent of new information and communication technology has expanded communication channels, thus facilitating the communication process, broadening the peace constituency, and creating a sense of national community. Peace negotiators are no longer limited to "across the table" dialogue but are now able to sustain discussions even after formal meetings through modern technologies. Consultations with the principals are facilitated by "hotlines." The CPP-NDF[5] maintains an Internet website, which provides the group's positions on certain issues. Broadcast stations compete for live or taped interviews via satellite with CPP-NDF leaders based in Europe for comments on late-breaking issues and events. Chairman Nur Misuari is regularly interviewed by Manila broadcast stations for recent developments in Mindanao.

Until recently, the lack of access to services by the people of Mindanao and other rural communities could be attributed to the lack of information technology and media infrastructures. Up to the early 1980s, some provinces in Mindanao, such as Sulu and Tawi-Tawi, were isolated. The only accessible radio programs were those aired from Malaysia and Indonesia. This reinforced the affinity of Filipino Muslims with the Muslim community outside the country.[6]

Global and Regional Influences

Interdependence in the global community necessitates the integration of geopolitical and economic concerns in today's national peace agenda. Hardline positions on economic sovereignty must now be seen in the light of regional economic blocs such as the setting up of the World Trade Organization. Cultural integrity is allegedly "threatened" by transborder data flow facilitated by information technology and satellite communication. In short, global and regional trends are creating new areas of conflict and adding new topics to the list of "talking points."

A recent development in the Asia Pacific Economic Cooperation (APEC) agenda is the desire on the part of the Philippines and other member countries to consider, along with the economic agenda of trade and investment liberalization, environment and political security issues (e.g., "strategic relationship between Asia and North America in a new era"). The environmental issue has become a priority concern as political analysts and futurists predict that conflict among nations in the next century will be abetted by competition for scarce natural resources. Food security is threatened by anticipated depletion of energy and water supplies.

At the recent forum, Alternative Security Systems in Asia Pacific, held in Bangkok, Richard Falk (1997) stated that the region shows all the features of potential degradation of security in an area where there is only a poorly developed regional cooperation system while there is a growing external geopolitical threat largely led by the United States. Other participants see the pursuit of high-speed industrialization with limited natural resources as a source of conflict. Disputes over territory (Spratly Islands) and conflicts over water resources, as well as potential rivalries over mineral exploitation, will surely affect the security of the region.

In the case of the Philippine government–MNLF relations, the Association of Southeast Asian Nations (ASEAN), particularly Indonesia, has played a critical role in facilitating the peace agreement. ASEAN emphasized respect for Philippine sovereignty and independence as a framework for settling the issue. On the other hand, the Organization of Islamic Countries may have served both as a political pressure group to both sides and as an "economic" pressure group as it represents oil-producing countries (on which the Philippines is dependent for oil and financial support for the MNLF). The challenge is one of maintaining a healthy balance so that the autonomous region of Mindanao does not become overdependent on the OIC.

Agenda for the Future

A response to the ongoing tensions and hostilities is a government–private sector partnership that seeks to mobilize a Mindanao-wide advocacy for unity and nonviolence. Building on shared concerns of citizens, a Mindanao Agenda for Peace and Development (MAPD) was drafted. It embodies a vision of the people of Mindanao—the need for sustainable and equitable development; transparent and accountable governance; a relevant, equitable, and culturally sensitive system of education, justice, and law enforcement; community-based mechanisms for dialogues and conflict resolution; and respect for the cultural integrity of indigenous people. The continuing consensus-building process includes information dissemination and advocacy for the MAPD, mobilization of peace-advocacy groups and communities, establishing a network of Peace Centers, and mediation initiatives in areas identified as "flash points" for violent conflicts (Mercado 1995).

It appears that the factors behind the Mindanao conflict support Huntington's "clash of civilizations" thesis.[7] Peace advocates are, however, optimistic that a sincere commitment to the search for commonalities among diverse cultures and developing creative responses such as innovative mechanisms for continuing dialogue may still avert the "clash" scenario. The Second International Conference on the Culture of Peace sponsored by UNESCO and the Philippine government in 1995 further stressed the central role of education and research in developing governance and empowerment for a culture of peace. Access to literacy and schooling and peace and human rights education in schools and in continuing education for civil servants, defense and security forces, and political leaders are recommended. Alternative participatory and anthropological research methods will enable documentation of local and grassroots stories of empowerment and strengthening of civil society.

If the government's intent to provide 30 percent of the total infrastructure budget for 1998 becomes a reality, the prospect of Mindanao's becoming a stable economy in 15 years is realizable. Mindanao's regional economy would further benefit from its interaction with the neighboring areas in the Brunei Darrusalam–Indonesia–Malaysia–Philippines East Association of Southeast Asian Nations (BIMP-EAGA).

Future strategies in peacekeeping must likewise consider Philippine National Unification Commission recommendations, which emphasize six institutional paths. They are: the pursuit of social, economic, and political reforms which deal with the root causes of insurgency and social unrest; consensus building and empowerment for peace; peace talks with the different rebel groups aimed at final negotiated settlements; reconciliation, reintegration into society, and rehabilitation of rebels; protection of civilians and the deescalation of conflicts, which includes protection of human rights; and building a positive climate for peace, which includes confidence-building measures, peace advocacy, and education.

Futurists and development scholars (Kennedy 1993; Brzezinski 1993; Talisayon 1996; Boulding 1993; Korten 1990; Club of Rome 1991) stress the importance of the moral, ethical, and spiritual dimension in our quest for peace as well as a new humanism. Boulding (1993) believes that a viable peace culture has to happen at the grassroots. Negotiation and accommodation and integrative behavior in peace building have to become personal habits in the family and the community. Korten describes the 1990s as the decade of voluntarism. As we move into the 21st century, the principle of global interdependence will apply not only to nation-states but also to NGOs and people's organizations. Korten noted the important role of NGOs in aiding the development of democratic organizations and movements particularly in authoritarian or newly democratizing countries.

Peace initiatives, whether taken at the formal negotiating table or in various informal settings, provide added knowledge on dynamics needed for effective governance. The search for commonalities despite cultural differences, the will to establish creative mechanisms for conflict resolution and to forge partnerships, alliances, and networks with various groups with similar goals are strategies that have proven to be successful. Peace building requires continuing vigilance, dialogue, and consensus on what is truly a balanced, just, and humane governance for our times.

Appendix

*The International Forum on the Culture of Peace (The Manila Forum)
26–30 November 1995, Manila, Philippines Summation of the Forum*

Five signposts:

1. Consensus that the process of conflict management resolution, healing and reconciliation are complex, requiring a participative and self-critical approach.
2. The development and economic rehabilitation are central to a culture of peace building. Development progress must be just and people-centered as well as being sustainable in an age of ecological crisis.
3. A culture of peace is built on process of empowerment and the strengthening of civil society. Governance needs to be defined as participative, inclusive, plural, and cognizant of the rule of law. It must respond to rights of all sectors especially marginalized people and groups including women, minorities, children, rural and urban poor and indigenous people. Transparency and accountability are essential and leadership must be transformational.
4. Education includes schools, media, family socialization, toys, sports, recreation, and religious and other social institutions. Education for peace must draw on appropriate and empowering pedagogies.
5. Solidarity must be developed between and among governments, nongovernmental institutions, the private sector and the components of civil society.

Principles in Building a Culture of Peace

●   Peace is a holistic concept. It is not merely the absence of war but a commitment to build a just, equitable, compassionate, multicultural, pluralistic and sustainable society.

- Building a culture of peace requires enactment and implementation of societal, international, and global reforms that meaningfully and democratically address the root causes of conflict.
- A culture of peace must be underpinned by values, knowledge, and practices of environmental care and ecological sustainability.
- A culture of peace is sustained by a process that is evolving, participative, reflective, critical and dynamic.
- The peace process must seek a principled and nonviolent resolution of armed and all other forms of conflict based on reconciliation, justice, and dignity for all.
- The peace process must be community-based reflecting the sentiments, values and principles important to all sectors of society. It must therefore be built on dialogue, negotiations, consensus-building and cooperation among government and civil society.
- The culture of peace seeks to prevent social exclusion. It thus involves governmental accountability and the empowerment of social sectors, particularly the poor and the marginalized, so that they may fully participate in defining, designing and implementing all aspects of peace-building. It thus also means that a strong civil society will ensure authentic participation in monitoring of the process.
- The transformation towards the culture of peace requires parallel and complementary development of values, knowledge and skills at both the individual and institutional or structural levels.
- It must also draw on the inherent strengths of local and indigenous knowledge, beliefs and practices for building and sustaining peaceful and just societies. In particular, the expertise, perspectives and rights of women and indigenous peoples must be recognized and integrated in peace-building.
- Building and nurturing a culture of peace is enhanced by the infusion of spiritual, moral, and ethical values in all aspects of individual, national, international, and global conduct and relationships.
- It thus also requires solidarity among peoples, ethnocultural communities, states, international organizations and all other actors in civil society to address and overcome common problems and obstacles to peace-building. Global and local problems of violence and conflict are so intertwined that their resolution calls for a mutual sharing of resources and strategies.

Notes

1. The Tripoli Agreement signed in 1976 by representatives of the Philippine government, the MNLF, and the Libyan government with the participation of the OIC was intended to end the armed conflict and provided for the establishment of autonomy in the Southern Philippines within the realm of the sovereignty and territorial integrity of the Republic of the Philippines.
2. The establishment of the SPCPD is also regarded as a violation of democratic principles and processes and an undue exposure of the Christian majority to expected Muslim retaliation for past offenses. The Muslim opposition was anchored on the argument that the council was giving less than expected. These are the perspectives of contemporary realities. The other perspective is that of history. The concept of *kaadilan* (social justice), which is to rectify historical oppression, and *gausbaugbug* (the geopolitical context of social justice), which is implied by "ancestral land," are factors that should be taken into account, according to the University of the Philippines Center for Integrative and Development Studies (1996).
3. The present leadership uses the cooking of *bibingka* (rice cake) as an appropriate analogy. It is cooked with coal embers placed on top and at the bottom. A perfect *bibingka* is the outcome of adequate and appropriate mobilization of political will (legislation, policies) from the top and a continuing bottom-up mobilization of collective groups working together toward common goals.
4. Decentralization is defined as the transfer of powers and authority from a central institution to local levels of a government system. Devolution, a form of decentralization, is the transfer of political power and is geographic or territorial. Local autonomy involves the transfer of authority, responsibilities, and resources by the national government to its constituent units so that these become more self-reliant.
5. The Communist–National Democratic Front leadership and the government panel are now engaged in another round of peace negotiations after more than a decade of peace talks. The Communist movement, like the MNLF conflict, has claimed a heavy toll as the estimated cost per rebel in a protracted counterinsurgency campaign is P21 million.
6. The restoration of the democratic space after the 1986 EDSA Revolution and the liberalization of telecommunications in the early 1990s have resulted in exponential growth in mass media and telecommunications, including in the countryside. Many trimedia establishments also set up news bureaus in Mindanao and other regions throughout the country.

7. According to Huntington, the fault lines in our new, post–Cold War world do not flow from politics or ideology but from culture. When large masses of people join in common purpose, the primary link between them will increasingly be their shared heritage of language, history, tradition, and religion—that is, civilization. And when they stonily face each other across the divide, the unbridgeable gap between them will be the lack of just such a shared civilization.

CHAPTER 10

Sovereignty and Security for the First Nations

Haunani-Kay Trask

I greet you as an indigenous woman of these Hawaiian Islands. In our culture, ancestry is paramount. Therefore, I tell you my genealogy. I am descended of the Pi'ilani line of Maui through my mother and the Kahakumakaliua line of Kaua'i through my father. I was reared in Kane'ohe, on the Ko'olau side of this island of O'ahu, where I now reside.

Hawaiians, the Natives of this archipelago, are the First Nation people of these islands. The term First Nations is often heard in North America, despite the more commonly used identifications of *indigenous* and *Native*. But for our purposes today, First Nations is the preferable term because it denotes political self-determination and sovereignty for aboriginal peoples.

A little history. Hawaiians lived in these islands for millennia until the coming of foreigners, called haole, in 1778. As in the case of most other Native peoples, the result of Western contact for Hawaiians was unrelenting violence: the violence of mass death due to introduced diseases, the violence of Christian missionizing, the violence of cultural destruction, including the institutionalization of private property and Western schooling, and, at the end of the 19th century, the violence of American military invasion, occupation, and overthrow of our government. By 1900, Hawai'i was a colony of the United States. Our language had been banned, our ruling chiefs imprisoned, and our people subjugated to an all-haole planter oligarchy.

Because of the American-engineered overthrow and annexation, Hawaiian control and Hawaiian citizenship were replaced with American control and American citizenship. Our nation suffered a unilateral redefinition of our homeland and our people. In the language of human rights instruments, like the United Nations Draft

Declaration on the Rights of Indigenous Peoples, Hawaiians suffered arbitrary deprivations of our nationality and our lands and a denial of our right to self-determination as a people, including aboriginal rights to our traditional practices, properties, and natural resources.

Taken together, these deprivations violate Articles 15, 17, and 21 of the Universal Declaration of Human Rights, as well as the American Convention on Human Rights. In these instruments, and others, citizenship, nationality, property, and identity are considered human rights, that is, rights that inhere in the condition of being human and that should, therefore, apply to all peoples. Moreover, in the Universal Declaration, Article 21 proclaims that the will of the people should be the basis of the authority of government.

In the case of my people and nation, it was the will of white foreigners, primarily Americans, that constituted the authority of both the short-lived and misnamed Republic of Hawai'i—really an oligarchy of white thugs aided by the American military—as well as the long territorial period from 1900 to 1959 and then the subsequent appearance of the state of Hawai'i which followed.

Today, modern Hawai'i, like its colonial parent the United States, is a settler society, that is, a society in which the indigenous culture and people have been murdered, suppressed, or marginalized for the benefit of settlers who now dominate the islands. Economically and politically, Hawai'i is an occupied tourist/military outpost of the American empire. Our magnificent archipelago has become a militarized zone with the largest portage of nuclear submarines in the world. Our beaches and bays are home to seven million tourists a year, which means 30 tourists for every Native Hawaiian. Our people are institutionalized in the prisons and military, marginalized economically, and identified by legally binding blood-quantum definitions that are both racist and divisive. Thus, Native Hawaiians are categorized in American federal law as those Hawaiians of 50 percent blood quantum. Our people unable to prove their blood quantum are officially not Native for purposes of land rights. Tragically, on every level of collective and individual experience, in every category of legal and cultural definition, my people have suffered egregious violations of our humanity because of the presence of the United States, indeed, because of all things American.

As personally and culturally humiliating as this situation has been, it is not unique in the Pacific Basin, nor under the American imperium, nor, indeed, in the world at large. Everywhere on mother earth, indigenous nations are invaded, removed, terminated, and disappeared. From the radiation of the people of the Marshall

Islands, to the removal of tribal peoples in Nagaland, to the dispossession of the Hopi and Navaho, to the extermination of the East Timorese and the West Papuans, to the invasion of Tibet, to the subjugation of the Saami and Inuit peoples of the circumpolar regions, indigenous peoples are under ferocious assault. Indeed, for most of us, genocide is the official settler policy, practice, and result.

Genocide: a term out of the horrors of the Second World War but applicable to Native nations today. According to the United Nations Convention on the Prevention and Punishment of the Crime of Genocide, any act committed with intent to destroy, in whole or in part, a national, ethnical, racial, or religious group, such as killing members of the group; causing serious bodily or mental harm to members of the group; deliberately inflicting on the group conditions of life calculated to bring about its physical destruction in whole or in part; imposing measures intended to prevent births within the group; and forcibly transferring children of the group to another group constitute *genocide*. In this definition, then, nuclear testing is not only a security issue but a genocide issue, especially in areas like the Pacific Basin, or for that matter, wherever indigenous nations are subjugated to imperialist countries.

For First Nation peoples, the greatest security issue today involves our physical and cultural survival as Native peoples. We are fighting our systematic, planned disappearance through all manner of removal, relocation, and eventual extinction. In this sense, the assertions of Native sovereignty all over the world—from the Indians of the Americas to the Aborigines of Australia—reflect the most basic of security issues: how to survive as indigenous peoples.

In the United Nations draft Declaration on the Rights of Indigenous Peoples, we find many categories of what are defined as concerns with security. Everywhere in the Declaration, for example, security issues appear as assertions of the right of protection from deprivations of collective integrity as distinct societies; or from forced assimilation into non-Native dominant societies; or from dispossession of lands, resources, family or tribal structures, even self-identity and languages.

In these human-rights instruments, two characteristics should be noted. First, security is defined collectively; that is, security involves survival of the group as a distinct collective. Thus, Euro-American nuclear testing in the South Pacific was a violation of the security of Pacific Islanders not only because of radiation and testing damage but also because the people were torn asunder, removed in some instances, or consigned to a slow and painful death.

Nuclear-waste storage and transshipment across the Pacific is also a violation of our security, of our claim to be free from First World predations. Additionally and rather obviously, these are clearly violations of our sovereignty.

Native sovereignty, as both goal and idea, has occupied center stage throughout the Pacific, including Hawai'i, for the past 15 years. As one of the last places on earth to decolonize, the Pacific Basin has witnessed a welcome assertion by its indigenous people to various claims of self-government.

In the words of the largest sovereignty initiative here, Ka Lahui Hawai'i, sovereignty is defined as the ability of a people who share a common culture, religion, language, value system, and land base to exercise control over their lands and lives, independent of other nations.

Founded in 1987, Ka Lahui now has more than 20,000 citizens. We support an end to the status of wardship that we now endure under United States law, and, among other strategies, we support reinscription of Hawai'i on the United Nations list of non-self-governing territories.

But we believe, with other indigenous peoples, that security is an attribute of sovereignty. In political terms, security issues almost always imply military issues. For Pacific Islanders, Euro-American colonization and militarization has been the largest security issue in our personal and collective lives.

In other words, the New/Old World Order of capitalism and imperialism means our cultural and physical disappearance. The question that remains is how, and even if, we, as Native peoples, can resist the New World Order and our planned disappearance.

My personal yet political answer is: probably not. The state of the world gives us little hope. Native resistance can be and has been crushed. As indigenous nations die out, our peoples reach a point of irreparable harm. We cannot sustain our numbers, our cultures, our stewardship of the earth. Even while they plan our demise, First World countries memorialize our passing.

The choices are clear. As indigenous peoples, we fight for the land even as she, and we, are dying.

But where do people in the industrial countries draw their battle lines? On the side of mother earth? On the side of rapacious consumption? On the side of First World nationalism?

If human beings, Native and non-Native alike, are to create an alternative to the planned New/Old World Order, then those who live in the First World must change their culture, not just their leaders.

Who, then, bears primary responsibility? Who carries the burden of obligation? Who will protect mother earth and her First Nation

CHAPTER 11

An Asian Philosophy of Peace and Human Security

Dayle Bethel

The scholarly writings of Tsunesaburo Makiguchi, the founder of Soka Gakkai, provide a unique perception of industrial society from the viewpoint of one who lived and worked in Japan during the early years of the 20th century. Makiguchi was enamored with modernization. He shared the high expectations of industrialism and the potential abundance it promised that were prevalent throughout much of the world at that time.

Like his American contemporaries, Lewis Mumford and John Dewey, however, Makiguchi foresaw the dangers and tragic consequences of the social and educational policies taking shape in industrial societies. He warned against tendencies he observed developing in his own society: reckless disregard for the environment, the sacrifice of traditional values in pursuit of profits, the isolating of children and young people day after day in schools, severing their ties with the natural environment as well as with their families and communities and forcing them to learn masses of fragmented, unrelated bits of information.

Makiguchi feared that the ultimate outcome of such policies would be disastrous for Japan. He worked tirelessly during the first four decades of the century, both through education and through his writing and, in his later years, through religion, in formulating and promoting what he believed was a more constructive and sustainable approach to industrial development.

The provocative ideas and proposals contained in Makiguchi's writings bring into focus some interesting questions. "Were the conditions we now observe in the world inevitable?" or perhaps the question should rather be: "Was industrial society inevitable?" "Will the 21st century be better from the standpoint of human well-being than the 20th century?" "Will we human beings have some part in consciously determining what kinds of society will characterize the 21st century, and if so, what kinds of society will we shape?" "Or will we simply be swept along by a tide of humanly uncontrollable cultural change?"

As people around the world take stock of the century that is now coming to an end, they are increasingly raising such questions. They are also seeking new information, new insights, and new intellectual tools with which to carry on a constructive yet critical analysis of the human situation and an exploration of the prospects for a more humane society in the next century. It is my purpose in this essay to summarize insights and understandings contained in Makiguchi's writings that can inform such inquiry and sociohistorical analysis.

An Overview

The earth, for Makiguchi, was a miracle. Life was a miracle, and he saw life vibrating and pulsating through all phenomena. A major goal that began to motivate him early in his professional career was to call his fellows, particularly young people, to an awareness of and appreciation for the earth and for the life pulsating through it. Thus, in *A Geography of Human Life*, his first major work, published in 1903, we are confronted with what to Makiguchi was the ultimate question: "How, then, can we observe our surroundings? How can we make contact with the earth? We are born of the earth; we are inspired by the earth; we die on the earth; the earth is our home" (Makiguchi 1971, 45). In our interaction with our environment, we should

> . . . regard people, animals, trees, rivers, rocks, or stones in the same light as ourselves and realize that we have much in common with them all. Such interaction causes us to feel, if not consciously think, "if I were in their (or its) place, what would I feel . . . or do?" Sympathetic interactions occur, therefore, when you regard or feel another person or object that you are in contact with as a part of yourself or as one of your kind. You share experience with that person or object and are able to place yourself in the position of that person or object.[1] (Makiguchi 1971, 55–56)

Again,

> . . . it is our nature as human beings to form societies. No one can live totally alone. It is through association in society that we can provide not only for our basic needs and security, but for everything that makes our lives fulfilling and rewarding. This realization leads to the universalization of sympathetic feelings which were initially toward a specific individual or object. Growing awareness of our indebtedness to our society gives rise to feelings of appreciation and a sense of social responsibility within us. Beginning in our very personal

> relationships . . . our sympathetic concern and appreciation expands to include the larger society and, ultimately, the whole world. (Makiguchi 1971, 60–61)

Perhaps more than any thing else, it was this reverence for nature, this sense of wonder and appreciation for life, this sense of being intimately connected with both our natural and social environments, that Makiguchi longed to communicate to his students and fellow beings. The development of such awareness and appreciation upon the part of human beings was, he believed, of crucial importance both for nature's sake and for the development of persons of moral character.[2]

Makiguchi tells us in the foreword of the book that the desire and compulsion to share these insights with his fellows became so strong that "they occupied my whole being. I could not think of anything else. I could not even work to make a living."[3]

As the passages referred to above suggest, Makiguchi was convinced that the development of a sense of interdependence and interrelatedness with the natural world, of which he perceived humans a part, is a central aspect of what it means to be a human being. Not only is this holistic orientation *A Geography of Human Life*'s most pervasive theme, it became the central theme of Makiguchi's life. Consider the following, for example:

> . . . being aware of the rich variety of phenomena that influence my life, I cannot help thinking of the way the whole earth operates. I look around and, although my eyes can reach only a few kilometers in any direction, my heart and mind are filled with excitement and wonder and curiosity about the earth and about the relationship between the earth and our lives on the earth. I begin to realize that if we would seek deeper understanding of this relationship, we must prepare ourselves to make observations and inquiries into several different aspects of the planet, such as its topography, dimensions, movements, and structure. (Makiguchi 1971, 86)

Such was Makiguchi's invitation to young people in particular, and to all his contemporaries in general, to join him in a journey to explore the wonders of the earth and life born of the earth. *A Geography of Human Life* is something like a ship's log or diary of that journey. But it was also intended as a handbook or travel guide for others who are motivated to take the journey themselves.

Before embarking on this journey of discovery, Makiguchi explained that the method of inquiry to be used was that of participant observation. But what was to be the scope of that observation? Here, again, we can let him speak for himself:

> I arrived at a conviction that the natural beginning point of understanding the world we live in and our relationship to it is that community of persons, land,

and culture, which gave us birth; that community, in fact, which gave us our very lives and started us on the path toward becoming the persons we are. In other words, that community which has given us our rootedness as human beings. The importance of this rootedness and personal identity given us by our native cultural community, our homeland, can scarcely be overemphasized. (Makiguchi 1971, 29–30)

If we think seriously about it, we can see that every aspect of this universe can be observed in this small area of our homeland. And because our homeland is the place where we live, where we walk, where we see and hear and gain impressions, it is possible for us to observe all these things directly. Thus, it is possible for us to explain the general nature of complex phenomena anywhere in the world through use of examples which we can find in abundance even in the most remote village or hamlet.

Let me stress my basic position again; every aspect of the entire universe can be found in the small, limited area of our home community. But we have to be sensitive to these untold riches all around us and we must learn how to be effective observers. (Makiguchi 1971, 38)

Makiguchi writes that with this wealth of information and examples all around us:

> . . . it is astounding to realize how quick are most people, and teachers in particular, to neglect this basic and profound observation and just stick to books, using all their energy in memorizing, forgetting what they have read, so starting to read again, forgetting, reading, forgetting, reading . . . and on and on. (Makiguchi 1971, 39)

He suggests that it might help in understanding the principle with which he is concerned to consider the famous people whom we look up to and who have made great contributions to human culture. Invariably, we find that these great geniuses of human history—Dante, John Louis Agassiz, Peter the Great, and many others—arrived at the discoveries for which we remember them in very simple surroundings and through the power of their own observations.

At this point, Makiguchi comes to one of his deepest convictions. When we consider such persons of genius, he says, we tend to believe that their great accomplishments were possible entirely because of their innate natural talents. "But," we think, "I can't be like that. It's impossible." Thus we tend to see a wide difference between these great people of history and "ordinary people like us." To this Makiguchi responds,

I am convinced . . . that in the beginning of life there is very little difference between people; every person has inborn natural talents and potential. Then, why do these differences come about? I believe it depends greatly upon whether or not a person learns to see and grasp the true nature of phenomena with penetrating insight and understanding. We have seen in the cases I have cited above that these "geniuses" developed this power of penetrating vision to a high degree simply through direct observation of the marvels of nature and the world around them.

The natural world inspires us, fosters our wisdom, and family, friends, neighbors and community groups nurture us in so many ways. This immediate, direct experience which we can have with the natural and social environments of our communities fosters compassion, good will, friendship, kindness, sincerity, and humble hearts. (Makiguchi 1971, 40–41)

Thus, one of Makiguchi's enduring themes is that at birth every person possesses potential for greatness and goodness. But it was one of the tragedies of contemporary life in his day, he observed, that in most people this inborn potential remained dormant and undeveloped. Most people "see" only on a surface level. They never develop the capacity for direct and intimate communication with natural phenomena. They tend to become a slave to books. Unfortunately, with such surface understanding, even after reading thousands of books, they remain ignorant of the really important insights and understandings they need for living fully and creatively. Their lives become stunted and their potential greatness lies unchallenged and unrealized.

Can anything be more important, then, than discovering how to plan educational experiences that will enable every person to develop the deeper understanding of life and nature that is so important for living a fulfilling and rewarding life? Both *A Geography of Human Life* and *A Theory of Value-Creating Pedagogy*[4] three decades later sought to clarify and provide answers to that question. While he did not deny the importance and the place of books and other secondhand materials in human learning, he maintained that children can achieve the full potential of their humanness only through direct, active communication with their immediate environment.

From this brief overview of Makiguchi's writings, the two related concerns that preoccupied him become clear: the developing of persons of moral character and the developing of social institutions capable of nurturing persons of character. He saw that the two must go together. In other words, good institutions can only be created by persons of good moral character, but good institutions are a prerequisite for a society of persons of character to develop.

Makiguchi offered his vision of a good society, which could nurture good, happy persons, as a model for the development of an industrial system in his country. At the time he was writing *A Geography of Human Life*, the American version of the Western model of industrialism was sweeping the earth. The contrast between that type of industrialism and the type that Makiguchi proposed is sharp and clear. It is especially clear in the respective views of the two models toward nature. A basic tenet of the American model, what Alvin Toffler (1981, 99) labels "indust reality," is that "nature is an object waiting to be exploited." For Makiguchi, on the other hand, to be human meant to live in harmony with the earth. To live as a human being meant to love and understand and appreciate the earth. "[I]t is through our spiritual interaction with the earth that the characteristics which we think of as truly human are ignited and nurtured within us" (Makiguchi 1971, 47–48). Makiguchi envisioned an industrial society developing in his country upon a basis of interdependence and interconnectedness between human beings and the earth. It was to the realization of such a society that he directed his life and his work.

Education as Means to Personal and Social Transformation

Education, then, is a key factor in the development both of healthy, happy individuals and of good societies. Education is of central importance because for both conditions to be present, the growth of persons of good moral character is indispensable. This, in turn, according to Makiguchi, depends on whether those persons develop a realization of their interdependence and interconnectedness with the natural and social phenomena in their environment. Such realization and awareness can develop in a person's life only through direct, firsthand experience upon the part of each person with that phenomena. What is needed, therefore, are educational structures and teacher guides capable of enabling every child and youth to have this kind and quality of learning experience.

Six general propositions are stated or implicitly assumed in *A Geography of Human Life:*

- The earth is perceived as a unity and all phenomena on the earth, including human beings, are perceived as interconnected and interdependent.
- Education must be associated with a specific place, a "community," a localized environment, which students can experience directly.

- Curriculum consists of the natural and social systems within that environment. Books and other secondhand material are used *in support* of the direct, personal experiencing of phenomena by the learner, but never in place of direct experience.
- Direct-experience learning implies and requires that learning take place in the midst of the phenomena, natural and social, which constitute the curriculum. Classrooms are for planning, reflecting on, comparing perceptions of phenomena experienced with fellow learners and with books and other secondhand material. Makiguchi in later writings (Bethel 1989, 154 160) systematized this element in a proposal for a "half-day school system."
- Learning cannot be imposed, but must grow out of each learner's own curiosity, questions, and explorations stemming from personal interests and motivation. Expressed another way, learning must be a process of elicitation, of drawing out, and not, as in the education of Makiguchi's day, and still today for the most part, by inculcation or putting in.
- Guidance of the learner in this community-based learning interaction occurs under the guidance of parents, educators (teacher-guides), and other adults in their varied community roles and specialties.[5]

During recent decades, evidence accumulating from many sources points to the wisdom and the relevancy for education and society of the educational principles and policies that Makiguchi proposed: the moral growth of individuals, interconnectedness with nature and with other individuals, education as a dialogue with a place through direct interaction with natural phenomena, the indispensability of community and "human scale" social structures within which this kind of education can be carried on and the nurture of persons of moral character occur.

Ron Miller and David Orr, two of the most articulate contemporary advocates of educational and social transformation, have written extensively about the need for educational and social policies similar to those proposed in *A Geography of Human Life* and Makiguchi's other writings. The essence of their views is expressed by Miller (1993, 5) in a review of Orr's *Ecological Literacy:*

> Education in a post-industrial society, argues Orr, will need to extend beyond the classical liberal arts of the modern age. "Ecological literacy" is a morally and experientially engaged way of knowing, involving a sense of wonder and respect for life and the realization that all human activities have consequences for the larger ecosystem. Orr maintains that ecological literacy cannot be

achieved by adding "environmental education" to our standardized compartmentalized curriculum, but entails radical educational as well as economic, political and cultural transformation. He asserts that "a great deal of what passes for knowledge is little more than abstraction piled on top of abstraction, disconnected from tangible experience, real problems, and the places where we live and work." Agreeing with Thoreau, Whitehead, and Dewey, Orr argues that an ecological education would immerse the learner in the natural world and the local community; it would engage the learner in conversation, in dialogue with the surrounding environment. Ecological literacy involves the whole body and feelings, not only the intellect; it cultivates a sense of place, not a rootless abstract intelligence; and it is most concerned with wholeness, connection, and relationship, rather than fragmenting knowledge into discrete specialties.

Elsewhere, Orr has stressed the importance of wonder in the learning experience of children. Referring to an observation by Rachel Carson in her book, *The Sense of Wonder,* that *feeling* is more important in learning than *knowing,* he writes:

> Feelings . . . begin early in life in the exploration of nature, generally with the companionship of an adult. The sense of wonder is rooted in the trust that the world is, on balance, a friendly place full of interesting life "beyond the boundaries of human existence." Wonder cannot be taught. . . it can only be felt and those early feelings must be encouraged, supported, legitimized by a caring and knowledgeable adult. My hunch is that the sense of wonder is fragile; once crushed it rarely blossoms again but is replaced by varying shades of cynicism and disappointment in the world. (Orr 1993, 33)

Orr, writing in the closing days of the 20th century, holds that we must develop this kind of education and approach to nature in order for human civilization to survive on the earth. A similar note is sounded by Catherine Burton, cofounder of the EarthBank Association:

> Where is the focal point of human activity in this emerging planetary awareness? It would appear that person and planet find each other in those naturally occurring ecological domains—called bioregions—that are like cells of the planetary skin. These bioregions transcend arbitrary political boundaries, reconnecting human beings with the biosphere. . . .To know our bioregion is to know and connect with our home planet. It is to breathe with the earth and to know ourselves as part of the sacred web of life. To know this place—where its water comes from, its trees, its wildlife, its food, its energy, its wisdom and its spirit is to know ourselves as whole. (Burton 1984, 37).

It was precisely these spiritual insights and realities that so obsessed Makiguchi at the beginning of the century and that he sought, in *A Geography of Human Life,* to share with his countrymen.

Contemporary Significance

It will be clear from what has been said above that Makiguchi's work does not add significantly to current educational insights or to our understandings as to what good education entails. The educational ideas and proposals Makiguchi expressed are, for the most part, being expressed and operationalized by increasing numbers of contemporary educators. The emphasis on holism in education that has emerged in Japan and the United States within the past decade is one example. At the same time, few contemporary educators have gone as far as Makiguchi in emphasizing the importance for education of direct learning within the learner's natural and social environments. Moreover, his proposal for organizing all levels of education as a journey into the natural systems of the learner's community, within the context of the discipline of a "new" geography, affords potentially useful insights and ideas and may, perhaps, be a useful and usable model for some learners and educators.

To emphasize Makiguchi's central concern again, direct learning of natural systems within the learner's community is crucial because growth of moral character, attitudes of appreciation and wonder toward the natural and social systems that sustain one's life, and a sense of responsibility toward those systems are indispensable for individual happiness and social health, and these outcomes can be nurtured in no other way. He charged that the indirect, secondhand learning system that had developed in his country was the height of folly. Primarily a product of implantation from Western cultures, that system of education confined learners to classrooms and forced them to go through a meaningless routine of "memorizing and forgetting, memorizing, forgetting, and on and on." Furthermore, it severed the learners' ties with the natural systems making up their environment. Makiguchi contended that long continuation of such a superficial system of learning would lead to unhappiness for individuals, serious problems for society, and destruction of the environment. The sense of urgency that he felt and that led him to publish *A Geography of Human Life* stemmed from his convictions about the dangers of this then predominant form of education in his country.

Beyond its implications for geography and education, Makiguchi's work raises intriguing questions about the beginnings and development of contemporary societies. Was the type of industrialism that originated in the West and has come to dominate all the cultures of the earth inevitable? Or could there have developed industrial societies with a different face? There has been a tendency upon the part of the world's people, particularly within the industrially advanced countries, to view the rise of industrial societies as an inevitable outcome of impersonal social, economic, technological, and political forces. Christopher Evans (1979, ix) has written, for example, that "once the process of the Revolution was fully under way, its dynamic growth was remorseless, and no power, no man or combination of men, could set it back against its course." Makiguchi's works suggest the possibility, on the contrary, that industrialism in Japan could have taken other forms and developed in other directions.

A Geography of Human Life was Makiguchi's attempt to respond to realities in Japan as he saw them. While he admired and approved many aspects of Western industrial culture, he counseled against wholesale adoption of the Western model and offered his countrymen a vision of a uniquely Japanese industrial society that would draw on the strengths and assets of Japan's geographical situation and cultural heritage.[6] While Makiguchi probably did not foresee the full extent of our modern dilemma or comprehend the potential for moral and spiritual bankruptcy to which our Western, scientistic industrialism has led, I suggest that he sensed its dangers intuitively and committed himself to work for industrial development in his own society that would not sacrifice the "enchanted world" that he loved.

How different the world might be today *if* the Japanese had, in fact, developed such a brand of industrial society, based on Makiguchi's perception of the environment and of education, and *if* that Japanese model had spread over the earth instead of the American-fashioned Western model! As we look back over the history of the 20th century from our vantage point at its end, we recognize and accept the fact that the people of Japan during the century's early decades rejected Makiguchi's vision as well as most of his admonitions. Just as Americans during the early years in the development of the industrial system in the United States rejected alternative models of industrial development that were available to them,[7] the Japanese rejected the alternative proposed by Makiguchi. Japanese society followed, with only slight variation, the American model of industrialism, based on unrestricted exploitation of the natural environment as well as of less technologically advanced human populations. We are now being forced to recognize the many negative consequences of the choices that were made during the formative stages of these two industrial giants.

This recognition, and the clearer historical understanding that it fosters, can also bring to our awareness the realization that we, too, are living in the formative stages of a new cultural epoch. Persons who seek now to lay the groundwork for a better and more humane 21st century, in education, in business, in all of society's social institutions, can find in Makiguchi's life and writings insights worthy of consideration and a wealth of ideas and practical methods to aid them in their efforts.

Let me conclude with these words from Henryk Skolimowski, a modern-day counterpart of Makiguchi:

> The rise of the ecological movement is a protest against the destruction of natural habitats and against the reduction of the diversity of life around us. But it is also a protest against the aridity and the soullessness of the mechanical modes of modern living. Whereas the existentialists of the first part of the twentieth century somehow succumbed to the idea of the meaninglessness of life in a meaningless universe, and in a sense wallowed in the existential miasma of nothingness—we, the ecologically conscious people of the second part of the century, insist that a life of meaninglessness is not our destiny.
>
> The most important task of our times is not to contain violence, aggression and terrorism—these are, in fact, the ill-conceived offspring of the meaningless universe. The main task is to regain our destiny as humans.
>
> As long as we create in our thought the universe which is bleak, cold and ruthlessly mechanistic, and which has no other purpose than to serve us through our dexterous manipulation, this view of the universe, and our consciousness that goes with it, will spill over to affect the whole of society. The violence we render to other humans is only an extension and a consequence of the violence we do to nature, to the universe and to our minds—treating them instrumentally, irreverently and dis-gracefully.
>
> The nature of the universe is a net of Indra, interwoven, in a variety of exquisite ways. We need to possess enough exquisiteness in our minds in order to decipher the exquisiteness of our relationships with the universe. Otherwise, we end up in a meaningless, cold universe.
>
> To the sensitive mind the universe is a beautiful place. To the coarse mind the universe is an obnoxious place. As we are so we think; as we think so we make our universe; as we shape our universe so it shapes us. (Skolimowski 1997, 27)

Here we have a modern expression of the cosmic realities that Makiguchi so yearned for his compatriots to understand and appreciate. It is meaningful for us to realize that he expressed them so clearly 100 years ago, but that his contemporaries chose to ignore and violate them. And it is meaningful for us to realize the consequences—in pain, in suffering, in destructiveness—of their violation, and ours.

Our efforts today to create a more humane 21st century will depend largely on the extent to which we are able to bring our individual and corporate lives into harmony with these cosmic realities that Makiguchi, and the seers of all ages, have sought to make real to us. We who now stand on the threshold of a new century, with that awareness, have an opportunity to create a better world than the torn and devastated world of the 20th century. The new century offers us an opportunity to regain our destiny as humans.

Notes

1. It is instructive to compare the view of nature held by Makiguchi with that of Western peoples prior to the Scientific Revolution. Note, for example, the following observation by Morris Berman:

   The view of nature which predominated in the West down to the eve of the Scientific Revolution was that of an enchanted world. Rocks, trees, rivers, and clouds were all seen as wondrous, alive, and human beings felt at home in this environment. The cosmos, in short, was a place of *belonging.* A member of this cosmos was not an alienated observer of it but a direct participant in its life. His personal destiny was bound up with its destiny, and this relationship gave meaning to his life. (Berman 1981, 16)

   According to Berman, this intimate view of nature and of the cosmos as a place of belonging were sacrificed as Western peoples came under the domination of the modern ethics and the exploitive view of nature spawned by the Scientific Revolution of the 16th and 17th centuries. Makiguchi sought to forestall this development in his own culture.

2. In this connection, David Korten (1993, 19–23) observes that the social and ecological crises we face at the close of the 20th century can be traced to the long historical processes by which the human species has become increasingly alienated from community and nature. The prevailing "economics of alienation," he writes, must be replaced with an "economics of community." See also Alfred North Whitehead's observation (1929, 1967, 51) that "First-hand knowledge is the ultimate basis of intellectual life. To a large extent book-learning conveys second-hand information."

3. We may better understand the depth of Makiguchi's conviction and his obsession with the need to share his ideas by noting Berman's conclusions as to the significance of modern Western culture's world view:

   The logical end point of this world view is a feeling of total reification: everything is an object, alien, not-me; and I am ultimately an object too, an alienated "thing" in a world of other, equally meaningless things. This world is not of my own making; the cosmos cares nothing for me, and I do not really feel a sense of belonging to it.

> What I feel, in fact, is a sickness in the soul.
> Translated into every day life, what does this disenchantment mean? It means that the modern landscape has become a scenario of "mass administration and blatant violence" . . . Jobs are stupefying, relationships vapid and transient, the arena of politics absurd. In the collapse of traditional values, we have hysterical evangelical revivals, mass conversions to the Church of the Reverend Moon, and a general retreat into oblivion provided by drugs, television, and tranquilizers. (Berman 1981, 17)

> While Makiguchi certainly could not have perceived the full extent of the disastrous consequences of the path Western societies had chosen to follow, what he did understand was enough to create within him a burning desire to help his own country avoid the dangers and pitfalls of the Western model.

4. *A Theory of Value-Creating Pedagogy* was Makiguchi's major work on education. It has been translated and was published by Iowa State University Press in 1989 under the title *Education for Creative Living: The Ideas and Proposals of Tsunesaburo Makiguchi.*

5. Makiguchi's views on the role of educators and other adults in the teaching-learning process, implicit in *The Geography of Human Life*, are more explicitly expressed and developed in his later writings.

6. Note how similar are the concerns and hopes expressed by Imran Khan, a Pakistani cultural and spiritual leader, in regard to present-day Pakistan and Pakistan's Islamic culture:

> Most of the elites living in the Third World, because of the technological and material advancement of the West, seem to think that is the only way forward. In other words, progress means Westernization. In that process they lose the most important thing: their own spiritual values . . . there are things in the West which are very commendable, which we should follow. But . . . there are also things which are disastrous for us. (Khan 1997, 9)

7. In this regard, Ron Miller (1990, 24) observes that "American society's response to industrialism was a cultural choice. Perhaps the development of industrial technology was inevitable, and perhaps the promise of cheaper, more diverse goods and regular wages was irresistible. But the social organization of industrialism could have taken other forms."

CHAPTER 12

Teaching Nonviolence to the States

Chaiwat Satha-Anand

There are at least two problems with the topic of this essay besides the problematic nature of both nonviolence and the state. First, based upon the theory of power à la Gandhi and Sharp, nonviolence ordinarily has an oppositional role vis-à-vis the state since it seeks to undermine state power in pursuit of freedom and justice. Second, due to the nature of the state as the embodiment of violence, can nonviolence be taught to the state? Equally important, perhaps, is the question: even if it can, *should* the state be taught nonviolence?

This chapter is an attempt to argue that there is a dire need to "teach" nonviolence to states in today's world. I will begin by pointing out reasons why states need to be taught nonviolence. Then I will discuss basic theoretical problems curtailing the possibilities of linking states to nonviolence: the antistate inclination of nonviolence and the violent nature of the state. I will examine my experience in trying to "teach" nonviolence to the security agency in Thailand. I will briefly analyze the moral dilemmas involved in teaching nonviolence to the states and, finally, will advance a critical note on the significance of "teaching."

Justifications: Why Should States Be Taught Nonviolence?

The most direct and seemingly rhetorical answer to the question of why states should be taught nonviolence is: Because the state *is* violent. But rhetoric aside, there is some truth in this answer. From Beijing to Bangkok, from Rangoon to Jakarta, one can hear stories of state-sponsored violence killing people. The saddest thing about these tales is that they can be told and retold. The plot of these tales is much the same: people without guns demanding freedom or justice in the streets met soldiers with guns in official uniforms authorized by the state to restore order. Sometimes they were ordered not to shoot. But then a shot was heard, a stone thrown, and bloodbath began. The day after began with body counts, missing sons and daughters, deep individual wounds, at times mixed with hatred, which later constitute collective traumas that are difficult to heal. Without healing, the cycle of violence could begin anew.

Although it is difficult to ascertain whether in a political confrontation it is the state that starts the acts of violence, it is highly likely that state agents would be the first to use violence.[1] Soldiers and policemen are trained to perform their tasks with violence. In Asia, they are normally armed, many with guns. In a confrontational situation, fed with frustration and anger, sometimes fueled with fiery speeches from the other side, those with guns may be more prone to aggression and use what they already possess (Berkowitz and Le Page 1970, 132–142).[2] It may therefore be suggested that there are more factors conducive to the use of violence from the state's side, which would contribute to the possibility of state agents using violence first in a conflict situation. If such is the case, to bring about social transformation toward the possibilities of peace and justice only through educating the people's side with theories, strategies, and practices of nonviolence may not decrease the likelihood of a situation of violence, where nonviolent protesters are met with cruel suppression at the hands of the states. The state needs to be educated with nonviolence as well if such a situation of violence is to be avoided.

Another reason why the state side needs to be taught nonviolence is its atrocious record. The late peace researcher William Eckhardt compared his estimate of 10.7 million civilian deaths in civil wars from 1945 to 1990 with Harff and Gurr's account of 12.3 million deaths resulting from "organized killing by a government or its agents of a people" during the same period. It was stupefying to find that the states, through their agents, kill more of their own civilians during "peacetime," occasionally shading into the immediate aftermath of civil wars, than they do in time of civil war (Eckhardt 1992, 52–53). Using Rummel's figure of 83.4 million deaths by governments, 84 percent of these killings took place in China and the former USSR, together with Harff and Gurr's estimate, which he suggested may be closer to the facts, Eckhardt arrived at the estimate of fewer than 48 million deaths at the hands of the states (Eckhardt 1992, 53). In the last half of this century, the states have killed at least 12 million, if the low estimate is used, or 83 million, if the high figure is used. I would contend here that it doesn't matter that much which estimate is more nearly correct because these figures conclusively prove two things. First, states do kill people. Second, these figures of several million are not mere numbers. They represent millions of human beings, with families and feelings, who have perished at the hands of states. It is therefore extremely important that nonviolence be taught to the state if such use of violence is to be avoided. But teaching nonviolence to the state is difficult. If nonviolence is to be taught to the state, these difficulties need to be construed and overcome.

Difficulties: Why Is It Difficult to Teach Nonviolence to the State?

It is difficult to teach nonviolence to the state because those representing state power do not think that they need to be taught the subject while those working in the fields of nonviolence seldom want to have anything to do with the state. But this answer is at once question-begging and revealing. First, several crucial questions can be immediately raised: What or who is the state? Second, which state is being discussed—liberal states or authoritarian ones? Will a capitalist state be more susceptible to nonviolence teaching than a semifeudal, semicapitalist state? Who are "those working in the fields of nonviolence"? would a Tolstoyan nonviolent activist want to teach the state, or would a nonviolent strategist such as Gene Sharp and his colleagues qualify better to do so? But then, can't a Gandhi be also considered a political strategist (Sharp 1979)? These are complex questions and beyond the scope of this essay. Here I would maintain that it is primarily the theoretical natures of both the state and nonviolence that make it difficult to teach nonviolence to the states anywhere in the world.

Nonviolence: Resisting the State

The idea of nonviolent action is based on the consent theory of power. The key question in Gene Sharp's magnum opus, *The Politics of Nonviolent Action*, is why do people obey? Arguing that obedience is the other side of power and people are the ultimate source of power, he maintains that the powerfuls are dependent on the cooperation of those who are ruled. If people refuse to cooperate using 198 methods of nonviolent action, which are divided into three classes: protest and persuasion, noncooperation, and direct intervention, power will eventually weaken or disintegrate (Sharp 1973).[3] The consent theory of power proposed by Sharp has been criticized on three major grounds. First, there are situations where the powerfuls do not depend on the people. Second, it fails to adequately take into consideration cultural facts that would influence the degree to which people would disobey. Third, the theory does not pay enough attention to social structures. As a result, a scholar recently proposed a modified consent theory of power that suggests that to undermine power, it is important to organize corporate resistance "by those constituencies on which it actually depends" (Burrowes 1996, 96).

It could be said that a nonviolence theory is conceptualized as a program to undermine power, especially state power. A history of human nonviolent action is a history of mistrust of state power, challenges and struggles against it. The major characters who inspire this history such as Gandhi, Tolstoy, and Thoreau are individuals with strong anarchistic inclinations. Gandhi, for example, said: "That state is perfect and non-violent where the people are governed the least. The nearest approach to purest anarchy would be a democracy based on non-violence" (Gandhi 1948, 292). Influenced also by Gandhi's thoughts and Thoreau's civil disobedience, among other things, an antistate inclination seems to be prevalent among those "in the fields of nonviolence."

It is therefore not accidental that examples of nonviolent action normally cited in nonviolence literature are cases of struggles against state power. Recent examples of nonviolent struggles cited in a textbook on nonviolence include the cases of Badsha Khan or the Frontier Gandhi, the Druze in the Golan, Cesar Chavez's nonviolent labor movement leadership, and the 1986 nonviolent revolution in the Philippines (Holmes 1990). More recently, Galtung highlighted 10 cases of successful nonviolent action where direct violence was averted and major structural violence undermined. They include: Gandhi's *swaraj;* the Berlin Jews' liberation in 1943; the civil rights campaign of Martin Luther King, Jr., in the United States; the anti-Vietnam war movement; the Plaza de Mayo mothers against the military in Argentina; people's power in the Philippines; children's power in South Africa; the *intifada* in Palestine; the democracy movement in Beijing; and the Solidarinose/DDR movements in Eastern Europe (Galtung 1996, 117–118). It is rare that nonviolence academics show interest in nonviolent actions used by the state. When they do, it is in the area of interstate relations that they advocate nonviolent actions, appropriately termed "civilian-based defense" as an alternative to military defense against foreign aggressors (Sharp 1990). Normally, those who study as well as advocate nonviolence tend to empathize with the people who struggle against the state, perhaps, with good reason when the nature of the state is considered.

The State: Resisting Nonviolence

The notion of the state is so highly problematic that a scholar suggests that the modern state is "an amorphous complex of agencies with ill defined boundaries performing a great variety of not very distinctive functions" (Schmitter 1985, 33). Inspired by Benedict Anderson's influential *Imagined Communities*, I have argued elsewhere that the power of the state lies in its abstract quality and artificiality as much as its concrete attributes and its functions (Chaiwat 1988, 27–41). Among other things, it is charged with the task of maintaining existing social orders. This task is usually in direct clash with nonviolent protagonists who carry out nonviolent actions such as peaceful demonstrations or sit-ins in order to call attention to their grievances and sufferings, which, in turn, could delegitimize the existing political order, so that social change can eventually take place. Those who carry out nonviolent actions are usually viewed by state agents as disruptive and need to be disciplined or even punished.

Moreover, the state is able to maintain social order because it is a monopoly of authoritatively binding rule-making, backed up by a monopoly of the means of physical violence (Mann 1988, 4). Although the state does have other means of enforcement and influence it can deploy, which in fact it normally uses, its occasional use of violence or the threat of using violence induces fear among the people. Fear strengthens obedience to state authority and enhances the effectiveness of its other means of social control. I would argue that this is perhaps a most important reason why the Weberian understanding of the state as an entity based on the monopoly of violence is generally agreed upon by modern state theorists (Giddens 1987, 18–19; Strange 1996, 5; Hay 1996, 3–19).[4] As an institution based upon physical violence, it is natural that state agencies and agents such as the police and the military would find it hard to accept the existence of nonviolent actions. In fact, organized nonviolent protests are sometimes classified by the state as riots aimed at creating disorders, backed by ill-intentioned parties and a challenge to its violence-backed authority. It is therefore difficult to teach nonviolence to the state. But difficulty is not impossibility. Despite all its abstract and concrete attributes as well as its violence-oriented tasks, the abstract state is represented by people who work for it. Some people can learn, and therefore teaching them is not totally impossible.

Experiences: What Are the Conditions that Provide a Possibility for Teaching Nonviolence to the Thai Security Agency?

Two years ago I attended a seminar at Chulalongkorn University in Bangkok where a deputy secretary general of the Thai National Security Council (NSC) was speaking about the present crisis in Thai society. He characterized it as a crisis of trust between the Thai people and the Thai state. In my view, it is quite unusual to find such a diagnosis of the situation from a high-ranking Thai security official. Believing that a dangerous crisis is imminent, the National Security Council, with the Thai prime minister as chairperson, is charged with peacefully courting social change in Thai society. From private conversations and public discussions, they have heard four main things. First, conflicts are natural in human society. Second, conflict and violence are two different things; conflict in Thai society need not be solved by violence. Third, judging from violent suppression of peaceful demonstrators in October 1973 and May 1992, as well as the massacre at Thammasat University in October 1976, Thai society is not an exception in terms of political violence. And fourth, there are nonviolent alternatives. As a result of this acquaintance and many other contributing factors, some officials within the NSC began to show interest in nonviolence. Numerous workshops on nonviolence are held all over the country attended by security officials, both military and civilians. At present, "nonviolent conflict resolutions" as they call it, is included as a part of several advanced study programs for high-ranking Thai officials. "Nonviolent conflict resolutions" also has a place in the 8th National Economic and Social Development Plan, prepared by the Thai National Economic and Social Development Board, which will be used to chart the country's next five-year course from 1997 to 2001. In addition, the new constitution of Thailand, which is being drafted and will be submitted for approval by the Thai Parliament in September 1997, does specify in Article 65 that it is the right of every Thai citizen to "nonviolently" resist a coup d'état should one ever take place again in the future (Constitution Drafting Assembly 1997, 13). The National Security Council has also commissioned me to write a small book on nonviolence to be circulated and used among security-related policymaking agencies. The book is tentatively titled *State and Nonviolence.*

What has recently happened in Thai society concerning nonviolence is unprecedented and borders on being a miracle. But miracle it is not. At least two crucial factors—the present crisis and the successful past—are instrumental in giving rise to such favorable conditions for the ideas of nonviolence.

First, the deteriorating ecological conditions in Thai society, such as deforestation and polluted water supplies in rural areas, are responsible for numerous conflicts involving local people and state agencies and agents. A group of researchers studied environment-related conflicts in Northeastern Thailand and found that there are 932 conflict spots in the Northeast alone, half of which are land-related conflicts. Some have already turned violent, and some are potentially violent (Wongsa and Suwit 1996, 33). Another scholar studied demonstrations in Thai society in 1994 and 1995. He found that there were 1,493 demonstrations in those two years, 40 percent of which were environment-related conflicts (Prapas 1996). Despite a successful family-planning program, it is inevitable that there are more people today than in the past while land and other natural resources are limited. Some people found themselves becoming encroachers on land their communities have been on for the past century. State agencies have turned into conservationists and have engaged in conflicts with villagers. Such conflict situations are dangerously prevalent and need to be dealt with peacefully lest they turn violent, as some already have. The sheer number of potential conflict spots in the Northeast alone seems sufficient to warrant the Thai state's finding a new and promising alternative in dealing with imminent conflicts.

Second, past success in coping with Communist insurgency provide the Thai state with confidence in peaceful means of solving conflicts. For more than two decades, the Thai state used force and psychological warfare against Communist insurgency. After the massacre of students and demonstrators at Thammasat University on October 6, 1976, a large group of students fled the city for the jungle to join forces with the Communist Party of Thailand. The fight turned more violent. Then in 1980, the Prime Minister's Office issued the now-famous order 66/23 changing the government's strategy from using force to political means. Those who earlier fought the state were no longer called "Communist insurgents" but "Thai National Development Participants." They are allowed to "return" to their normal lives through an open-armed policy. With conducive international conditions, the demise of the Communist Party of Thailand quickly took place. I would argue that the fresh memory of the recent success of the Prime Ministerial Order 66/23 enables the Thai state to be moderately enthusiastic about peaceful means in conflict situations. It was the state's initiative and it was a shining success. As the lack of confidence is oftentimes a source of violence, the state's confidence provides fertile soil for hope that nonviolence can be taught to the state because they might feel they had done it once, they can do it again by trying nonviolent alternatives for the future of Thai society.

Dilemma: Is It Right to Teach Nonviolence to the State?

Trained in the nonviolent tradition with an antistate inclination, I can't help but feel the tension of moral dilemma involved in teaching nonviolence to the state. The question that follows me in my dreams is what will happen to the people when the state learns more about nonviolence? If nonviolent actions are effective weapons as claimed, will teaching the state about it amount to enhancing the sphere of state power?

A more difficult fact to live with is that in addition to direct violence at the hands of the states, there are also structural violence, hunger, and preventable diseases resulting from states' policies. From 1945 to 1990, there were 795 million surplus deaths from the curse of structural violence, or more than 90 percent of all deaths caused by states during this period (Eckhardt 1992, 54).

To live with such a moral dilemma, it is important to examine two issues. First, the objective of teaching nonviolence to the state should be clarified. I teach the Thai security agencies to recognize nonviolent actions, to identify them as such, and to understand the communicative quality of nonviolent actions. Once they recognize nonviolent actions, it is likely that their responses would be less violent despite the state's violent nature. If they could identify people's peaceful collective actions as nonviolent, they may be able to use nonviolent language to characterize or describe them. In a way, this is a process of questioning the normality of violence where nonviolent discourse could enter into a discursive battle with violent discourse (Chaiwat 1991). An understanding of the communicative quality of nonviolent actions would help the state see that these actions are indeed attempts to communicate in the public sphere, that there are structural problems such as the lack of freedom resulting from uneven distribution of power or poverty resulting from uneven distribution of wealth.

Second, the relationship between direct and structural violence needs to be carefully assessed. If direct violence is sometimes caused by structural violence, will changes in the amount of direct violence have any consequence on the level of structural violence? If the answer is negative, it would mean that the relationship between these two types of violence is unidirectional. But if the answer is positive, then the relationship is reciprocal. What about the relationship between a reduction of direct violence, should the state become more nonviolent, on cultural violence? Perhaps, this theoretical question would require further research. But I would speculate that some kinds of dynamic and reciprocal relationship do exist among these three types of violence, the concepts advanced by Galtung (Galtung 1996), given the nature and complexities of the phenomenon of violence.

By Way of Conclusion: A Note on Teaching

I have attempted to point out that nonviolence should be taught to the state. Justifications for engaging in this teaching are suggested, difficulties analyzed, experiences examined, and moral dilemma explored. What is now left to be discussed is the notion of teaching itself. There are two main features of teaching that should be crystallized. First, teaching is political. Some scholars maintain that teaching could very well be seen as a subversive activity (Postman and Weingartner 1971). Athens knew this well and therefore the city put Socrates, a great teacher, to death for endangering the foundation of the state with his teaching.

Second, teaching does not mean giving something to the one being taught. In fact, a good teacher is someone who is able to bring forth the potential of his or her students. To try to bring out a given state's potential for nonviolence reflects three basic assumptions: within the abstraction of the state, as in all concrete classrooms, there are human beings; within these human beings are potentials for learning; and despite structural conditions, people can be transformed. It goes without saying that these three assumptions are important not only to teaching in general but also to nonviolence and peaceful social transformations for a better world.

Notes

1. In a comprehensive, though brief, study of American labor violence, Taft and Ross found that trade-unions violence was reactive because strikers would "virtually always" try to avoid violence and use peaceful means while the employers may not, in which case company guards, the police, or even the National Guard would be brought in (Taft and

Ross 1979, 187–241). They also assert that "The most virulent form of industrial violence occurred in situations in which efforts were made to destroy a functioning union or to deny a union recognition" (Taft and Ross 1979, 188).

2. See a recent and more comprehensive treatment of the anatomy of violence, especially killing, in Grossman 1995, 139–192.

3. See a critically insightful appraisal of Sharp's theory in Martin 1989, 213–222.

4. An interesting aspect of Hay's formulation is in trying to advance an understanding of "stateness" in two dimensions: moments of stateness, which include the state as nation, the state as territory, and the state as institutions, and levels of stateness from abstract "category" to concrete "state structure" (Hay 1996, 3–19).

References

Abat, F. V. 1997. "The Continuing Search for Enduring Peace." *Philippine Graphics*, March 17.

Abueva, Jose V., et al. 1992. *Ending the Armed Conflict: Peace Negotiations in the Philippines*. State of the Nation Reports. Quezon City: UP Center for Investigative and Development Studies.

Acharya, Amitav. 1995. "A Regional Security Community in Southeast Asia." *The Journal of Strategic Studies* 18, No. 3182.

Ahmed, Ishtiaq. 1996. "Options in Afghanistan." *The Nation*, November 5.

———. 1994. *New Global Realities and Alternatives for Asian Peoples; Three-Year Plan, 1994–1997*. Hong Kong: ARENA.

Asian Development Bank. 1997. *Annual Development Outlook*. Manila: Asian Development Bank.

Baker, James A. III. 1991–92. "America in Asia: Emerging Architecture for a Pacific Community." *Foreign Affairs* 70, No. 1:1–18.

Ball, Desmond. 1993 "Strategic Culture in the Asia-Pacific Region." *Security Studies* 13, No. 1:44–74.

———. 1993–94. "Arms and Affluence: Military Acquisitions in the Asia-Pacific Region." *International Security* 18, No. 3:78–112.

———. 1994. "A New Era in Confidence-Building: The Second-Track Process in the Asia-Pacific Region." *Security Dialogue* 25, No. 2:160.

———. 1994. "CSCAP: Its Future Place in the Regional Security Architecture." Paper presented at the 8th Asia Pacific Roundtable, June 5–8, Kuala Lumpur.

Banuazizi, Ali, and Myron Weiner, ed. 1986. *The State, Religion, and Ethnic Politics: Afghanistan, Iran and Pakistan*. Syracuse, NY: Syracuse University Press.

Barnes, Edward. 1996. "Friends of the Taliban." *Time*, November 4.

Bello, Walden. 1998. "East Asia on the Brink of Depression." *Pacific Reviews: Peace, Security and Global Change* 10, No. 2:95–110.

Berkowitz, Leonard, and Anthony Le Page. 1970. "Weapons as Aggression Eliciting Stimuli." In *The Dynamics of Aggression*, edited by Edwin I. Megargee and Jack E. Hokanson, 132–142. New York: Harper & Row.

Berman, Morris. 1981. *The Reenchantment of the World*. Ithaca: Cornell University Press.

Bethel, Dayle M. 1989. *Education for Creative Living: The Ideas and Proposals of Tsunesaburo Makiguchi*. Ames: Iowa State University Press.

Boulding, Elise. 1993. *The Roots of Peace in Conflict*. Lecture series of the Quaker Fellowship, Pennsylvania.

Bourdieu, Pierre. 1977. *Outline of a Theory of Practice*. Cambridge: Cambridge University Press.

Brass, Paul R. 1991. *Ethnicity and Nationalism: Theory and Comparison*. New Delhi: Sage Publications India.

Brown, Michael E. 1993. "Causes and Implications of Ethnic Conflict." In *Ethnic Conflict and International Security*, edited by Michael Brown, chap. 1. Princeton: Princeton University Press.

Brzezinski, Zbigniew. 1993. *Out of Control: Global Turmoil on the Eve of the 21st Century.* Macmillan.

Burns, John. 1995. "Beyond Afghan battle lines, Taliban sparks war of words." *The Sydney Morning Herald*, October 17.

Burrowes, Robert J. 1996. *The Strategy of Nonviolent Defense: A Gandhian Approach*. Albany: State University of New York Press.

Burton, Catherine. 1984. "New Options: Governance in the Planetary Age." *Context* 7:37.

Camilleri, Joseph A. 1993. "The Asia-Pacific in the Post-Hegemonic World." In *Pacific Cooperation: Building Economic and Security Regimes in the Asia-Pacific Region*, edited by Andrew Mack and John Raventill. Boulder, CO: Westview Press.

Chaiwat Satha-Anand. 1988. "Of Imagination and the State." In *Ethnic Conflict in Buddhist Societies: Sri Lanka, Thailand and Burma*, edited by K. M. de Silva et al., 27–41. London and Boulder, CO: Pinter Publishers and Westview Press.

———. 1991. "From Violent to Nonviolent Discourse." In *Peace Culture and Society: Transnational Research and Dialogue*, edited by Elise Boulding et al., 24–32. Boulder, CO: Westview Press.

Chen Luzhi. 1996. "Theory and Mechanism Problems of Asia-Pacific Economic Development." *World Economics and Politics* No. 11.

China Quarterly. 1993. No. 136, Special Issue. December.

Club of Rome. 1991. *The First Global Revolution*. New York: Simon and Schuster.

Constitution Drafting Assembly. 1997. Constitution of Thailand (Draft). Bangkok: Constitution Drafting Assembly. (In Thai)

Cox, Robert W. 1987. *Production, Power and World Order: Social Forces in the Making of History.* New York: Columbia University Press.

Cox, Robert W., with Timothy J. Sinclair. 1996. *Approaches to World Order.* Cambridge: Cambridge University Press.

De Jesus, Melinda Q. 1996. "Media's Role in the Creation of a Culture of Peace." In *Peace and Tolerance: Values Education through History*, by Lourdes R. Qusumbing and Felice P. Sta. Maria. Manila: UNESCO National Commission of the Philippines.

Deutsch, Karl, et al. 1957. *Political Community and the North Atlantic Area.* Princeton: Princeton University Press.

Drysdale, Peter. 1988. *International Economic Pluralism.* Sydney: Allen &

Eckhardt, William. 1992. "Death by Courtesy of Governments, 1945–1990." *Peace Research* 24, no. 2 (May):51–56.

Encarnation, Denis. 1994. "The Regional Evolution of Japanese Multinationals in East Asia: A Comparative Study." MIT Japan Program and Pacific Basin Research Program, Kennedy School, Harvard University, 1 November.

Evans, Christopher. 1979. *The Micro Millennium.* New York: Washington Square Press.

Evans, Paul. 1995. "The Prospects for Multilateral Security Co-operation in the Asia/Pacific Region." *The Journal of Strategic Studies* 18, No. 3:202–217.

Evans, Paul H., and Desmond Ball. 1994. *The Council for Security and Cooperation in the Asia Pacific Region (CSCAP* Annexes 1 and 2): CSCAP Pro-tem Committee.

Evans, Paul M. 1994. "Building Security: The Council for Security Cooperation in the Asia Pacific (CSCAP)." *Pacific Review* 7, No. 2:132–136.

———. 1995. *On Humane Governance: Towards a New Global Politics.* University Park: Pennsylvania State University Press.

———. 1997. Paper prepared for the forum, Alternative Security Systems in Asia-Pacific, Bangkok.

Friedberg, Aron. 1993–94. "Ripe for Rivalry: Prospects for Peace in a Multipolar Asia." *International Security* 18, No. 317.

Fukuyama, Francis. 1992. *The End of History and the Last Man.* London: Hamish Hamilton.

Galtung, Johan. 1996. *Peace by Peaceful Means: Peace and Conflict, Development and Civilization.* Oslo and London: PRIO and Sage.

Gandhi, M. K. 1948. *Non-Violence in Peace and War,* Vol. 1. Ahmedabad: Navajivan.

Ganesan, N. 1994. "Taking Stock of Post–Cold War Developments in ASEAN." *Security Dialogue* 25, No. 4 (December).

Garcia, Ed, and Carolina G. Hernandez, ed. 1988. *Waging Peace in the Philippines.* Quezon City: Ateneo Center for Policy and Development Affairs.

Ghaus, Abdul Samad. 1988. *The Fall of Afghanistan: An Insider's Account.* New York: Pergamon-Brassey's.

Giddens, Anthony. 1987. *The Nation-State and Violence: Volume Two of A Contemporary Critique of Historical Materialism.* Berkeley: University of California Press.

———. 1994. *Beyond Left and Right: The Future of Radical Politics.* Cambridge: Polity Press.

Grossman, Dave. 1995. *On Killing: The Psychological Cost of Learning to Kill in War and Society.* Boston: Little, Brown.

Guibernau, Montserrat. 1996. *Nationalisms: The Nation-State and Nationalism in the Twentieth Century.* London: Polity Press.

Gunaratna, Rohan. 1997. "Illicit Transfer of Conventional Weapons—The Role of State and Non State Actors." Paper prepared for Third Intersessional Workshop of the Panel of Governmental Experts on Small Arms, United Nations, Nepal, May.

Hammond, Thomas T. 1984. *Red Flag Over Afghanistan.* Boulder, CO: Westview Press.

Haqshenas, S. N. 1984. *Dasayis was junayat-i Rus dar Afghanistan: Az Amir Dost Mohammad Khan ta Babrak* (Conspiracies and Crimes of Russia in Afghanistan: From Dost Mohammad to Babrak). Tehran: Komiteh-i Farhangi Dafta-Markazi Jamiat-i Islami Afghanistan.

Harris, Stuart. 1996. "The Regional Role of 'Track Two' Diplomacy." In *The Role of Security and Economic Co-operation Structures in the Asia Pacific Region,* edited by Hadi Soesastro and Anthony Bergin, 143–154. Jakarta: Centre for Strategic and International Studies.

Hassan, Mohammed Jawhar. 1995. "The Concept of Comprehensive Security." Paper presented at the second meeting of the CSCAP Working Group on Concepts of Comprehensive Security and Cooperative Security, Kuala Lumpur, August 27–29.

Hay, Colin. 1996. *Re-stating Social and Political Change.* Buckingham-Philadelphia: Open University Press.

Hayes, Peter, and Lyube Zarsky. 1993. *Regional Cooperation and Environmental Issues in Northeast Asia.* La Jolla, California: IGCC Study Commission for the Northeast Asian Cooperation Dialogue, October 8–9.

Hellman, Donald C. 1995. "APEC and the Political Economy of the Asia-Pacific: New Myths, Old Realities." *Analysis* 6, No. 1:35–38.

Higgott, R. 1995. "Cooperation in the Asia-Pacific: APEC and the New Institutionalism." *Pacific Economic Papers 199* (September).

Holmes, Robert L., ed. 1990. *Nonviolence in Theory and Practice.* Belmont, CA: Wadsworth Publishing Company.

Hu, Weixing. 1996. "China and Asian Regionalism: Challenge and Policy Choice." *Journal of Contemporary China* 5, No. 11:45–46.

Huntington, Samuel P. 1993. "The Clash of Civilizations?" *Foreign Affairs* 72, No. 2:22–49.

Hurrell, Andrew. 1995. "Regionalism in Theoretical Perspective." In *Regionalism in World Politics: Regional Organization and International Order,* edited by Louise Fawcett and Andrew Hurrell. Oxford: Oxford.

Jackson, Robert. 1990. *Quasi-States: Sovereignty, International Relations, and the Third World.* Cambridge: Cambridge University Press.

Jennings, John. 1996. "The *Taliban* and Foggy Bottom." *The Washington Times,* October.

Jordon, Amos A., and Jane Khanna. 1995. "Economic Interdependence and Challenges to the Nation-State: The Emergence of Natural Economic Territories in the Asia-Pacific." *Journal of International Affairs* 48 (winter):433–462.

Katzenstein, Peter. 1996 "Regionalism in Comparative Perspective." *Cooperation and Conflict* 31, No. 2123–159.

Kausikan, B. 1993. "Asia's Different Standard." *Foreign Policy* 29:24–41.

Kennedy, Paul. 1993. *Preparing for the 21st Century.* New York: Vintage Books.

Khan, Imran. 1997. "Politics in Pakistan." *Resurgence* 180 (January/February):8–11.

Khan, Riaz Mohammad. 1991. *Untying the Afghan Knot: Negotiating Soviet Withdrawal.* Durham, NC: Duke University Press.

King, Charles. 1997. *Ending Civil Wars.* London: International Institute of Strategic Studies.

Korten, David C. 1990. *Getting to the 21st Century.* West Hartford, Conn.:Kumarian Press.

———. 1993. "Coming Back to Life." *Context* 36:18–23.

Krugman, Paul. 1994. "The Myth of the Miracle." *Foreign Affairs* 73:6.

Langdon, Frank, and Brian L. Job. 1997. "APEC Beyond Economics: The Politics of APEC." In *Economic Cooperation and Integration: East Asian Experiences,* edited by Kwan S. Kim and Robert J. Rienner. Notre Dame, IN: Kellogg Institute for International Studies, University of Notre Dame.

Lintner, Bertil. 1996. "The Drug Trade in Southeast Asia." *Jane's Intelligence Review,* Special Report No 5.

Leifer, Michael. 1995. "ASEAN as a Model of a Security Community?" In *ASEAN in a Changed Regional and International Political Economy,* edited by Hadi Soesastro, 129–142. Jakarta: Centre for Strategic and International Studies.

Looney, Robertt E., and P. C. Frederiksen. 1990. "The Economic Determinants of Military Expenditure in Selected East Asian Countries." *Contemporary Southeast Asia,* 11, No. 4:265–277.

Machado, it G. 1996. "Japanese Foreign Direct Investment in Asia." In *Foreign Direct Investment in a Changing Global Political Economy,* edited by Steve Chan, 39–66. London: Macmillan.

Mahbubani, Kishore. 1995. "The Pacific Way." *Foreign Affairs* 74, No. 1:100–111.

Makiguchi, Tsunesaburo. 1903, 1908, 1971. *Jinsei Chirigaku* (A Geography of Human Life). Tokyo: Seikyo Press.

————. 1930, 1972. *A Theory of Value-Creating Pedagogy.* Tokyo: Dai Nihon Publishing Company.

Mann, Michael. 1988. *States, War and Capitalism.* Oxford: Blackwell.

Manning, Robert A., and Paula Stern. 1994 "The Myth of the Pacific Community." *Foreign Affairs* 73, No. 6:85.

Martin, Brian. 1989. "Gene Sharp's Theory of Power." *Journal of Peace Research* 26, No. 2:213–222.

Mehrotra, O. N. 1997. "Troubled CIS." In *Taliban and the Afghan Turmoil: The Role of USA, Pakistan, Iran and China*, edited by Sreedhar et al., 105–118. New Delhi: Himalayan Books.

Mercado, E. 1995. In *International Forum on the Culture of Peace.* Manila: UNESCO and Government of the Republic of the Philippines.

Miller, Ron. 1990. *What are Schools For?* Brandon, VT: Holistic Education Press.

————. 1993. *Great Ideas in Education.* Brandon, VT: Holistic Education Press.

Nakayama, Taro. 1992. "Statement by Foreign Minister Taro Nakayama to the General Session of the ASEAN Post-Ministerial Conference, Kuala Lumpur, July 22, 1992." *Diplomatic Bluebook 1991*, 463–471. Tokyo: Ministry of Foreign Affairs.

National Unification Commission, Republic of the Philippines. 1993. "Report to President Fidel V. Ramos on the Pursuit of a Comprehensive Peace Process."

Nunez, Rosalita Tolibas. 1997. *Roots of Conflict.* Makati, Philippines: Asian Institute of Management.

Ohmae, Kenichi. 1995. *The End of the Nation State.* Harper Collins Publishers.

————. 1993 "The Dangers of Education." In *The Renewal of Meaning in Education*, edited by Ron Miller. Brandon, VT: Holistic Education Press.

Payne, Anthony, and Andrew Gamble, ed. 1996. *Regionalism and World Order.* New York: St. Martin's Press.

Postman, Neil, and Charles Weingartner. 1971. *Teaching as a Subversive Activity.* New York: Delta Book.

Prapas Pintobtaeng. 1996. "Demonstrations and Environment-Related People's Movement." Unpublished manuscript. (In Thai)

Rafferty, Kevin. 1996. *Economy, The Far East and Australasia.* London: Europa Publications.

Ramos, Fidel V. 1996. *Break Not the Peace: The Story of GRP-MNLF Peace Negotiations, 1992–1996.* Manila: Friends of Steady Eddie.

Rashid, Ahmed. 1995. "Afghanistan: Apocalypse Now." *The Herald*, October.

————. 1997a. "Poppy harvest is blooming under the Taliban's rule." *Daily Telegraph*, 3 April.

————. 1997b. "'Power play', and 'Pipe dreams.'" *Far Eastern Economic Review* 160, No. 15 (10 April):22–28.

————. 1998. "Pakistan and the *Taliban*." In *Fundamentalism Reborn? Afghanistan and the Taliban*, edited by William Maley, 72–89. London: Hurst and Company.

Report Cooperative Prosperity in Asia. 1995. The 4th Malaysian Economic and Cultural Seminar Symposium for Thinking of the EAEC, Feb./Mar. 1995, No. 385.

Rex, John. 1995. "Ethnic Identity and the Nation State: The Political Sociology of Multi-Cultural Societies." *Social Identities* 1, No. 1:21–34.

————. 1964. *Administration in Developing Countries: The Theory of Prismatic Society.* Boston: Houghton Mifflin.

————. 1969. "The Structures of Government and Administrative Reform." In *Political and Administrative Development*, edited by Ralph Braibanti and Associates, 220–324. Durham, NC: Duke University Press.

————. 1994. "Ethnonationalism, Industrialism and the Modern State." *Third World Quarterly* 15, No. 4:583–611.

————. 1997a. "Coping with Modernity: Constitutional Implications." MOST Policy Paper. Paris: UNESCO.

————. 1997b. "The Para-Modern Context of Ethnic Nationalism." In *Of Fears and Foes: Complex Interactive Dimensions of Insecurity*, edited by Jose Ciprut.

————. 1997c. "Presidentialism Versus Parliamentarism: Implications for Representativeness and Legitimacy." *International Political Science Review* 18, No. 3:253–279.

Rosenau, James N. 1990. *Turbulence in World Politics: A Theory of Change and Continuity.* London: Wheatsheaf.

Roy, Olivier. 1986. *Islam and Resistance in Afghanistan*. Cambridge: Cambridge University Press.

Rubin, Barnett. 1995a. *The Fragmentation of Afghanistan: State Formation & Collapse in the International System.* New Haven, CT: Yale University Press.

————. 1995b. *The Search for Peace in Afghanistan: From Buffer State to Failed State.* New Haven, CT: Yale University Press.

————. 1980. *The Rise and Fall of the Shah.* Princeton: Princeton University Press.

————. 1996. "The UN and Afghanistan: A Case of Failed Peacemaking Intervention?" *International Peacekeeping* 3, No. 1:22–24.

————. 1998. "The Rabbani Government, 1992–1996." In *Fundamentalism Reborn? Afghanistan and the Taliban*, edited by William Maley, 29–42. London: Hurst and Company.

Saikal, Amin, and William Maley. 1991. *Regime Change in Afghanistan: Foreign Intervention and the Politics of Legitimacy.* Boulder, CO: Westview Press.

Saravanamuttu, Johan. 1984. "ASEAN Security for the 1980s: The Case for a Revitalized ZOPFAN." *Contemporary Southeast Asia* 6, No. 2 (September).

―――. 1992. "The State, Ethnicity and the Middle Class Factor: Addressing Nonviolent, Democratic Change." In *Internal Conflict and Governance*, edited by Kumar Rupesinghe. London: Macmillan.

Schmitter, P. 1985. "Neo-corporatism and the State." In *The Political Economy of Corporatism*, edited by W. Grant, 32–62. London: Macmillan.

Second International Forum on the Culture of Peace (The Manila Forum). 1995. Final Report. November 26–30. Manila: UNESCO and the Office of the Presidential Adviser on the Peace Process (OPAPP).

Segal, Gerald. 1993 *Rethinking the Pacific*. Oxford: Oxford University Press.

Serrano, Isagani R. 1994. *Civil Society in the Asia Pacific Region*. Washington, DC: CIVICUS.

Sharp, Gene. 1973. *The Politics of Nonviolent Action*. Boston: Porter Sargent.

―――. 1979. *Gandhi as a Political Strategist: With Essays on Ethics and Politics*. Boston: Porter Sargent.

―――. 1990. *Civilian-Based Defense: A Post Military Weapons System*. Princeton, New Jersey: Princeton University Press.

Shaw, Martin. 1994. "Civil Society and Global Politics: Beyond a Social Movements Approach." *Millennium* 23:647–667.

SIPRI Yearbook. 1991. World Armaments and Disarmament. Oxford: Oxford University Press.

―――.1992. New York: Oxford University Press.

―――. 1996. Armaments, Disarmament and International Security. New York: Oxford University Press.

Skolimowski, Henryk. 1997. "The Song of Evolution." *Resurgence* 180 (January/February):27.

Smith, Anthony. 1993. "The Ethnic Sources of Nationalism." In *Ethnic Conflict and International Security*, edited by Michael Brown, chap. 2. Princeton: Princeton University Press.

Sreedhar. 1997. "Taliban Arrives." In *Taliban and the Afghan Turmoil: The Role of USA, Pakistan, Iran and China*, edited by Sreedhar et al., 37–38. New Delhi: Himalayan Books.

Sreedhar et al., ed. 1997. *Taliban and the Afghan Turmoil: The Role of USA, Pakistan, Iran and China*. New Delhi: Himalayan Books.

Stern, Rob. 1996. *Japan and the New World Order: Global Investments, Trade and Finance*. London: Macmillan.

Strange, Susan. 1996. *The Retreat of the State: The Diffusion of Power in the World Economy*. Cambridge: Cambridge University Press.

Taft, Philip, and Philip Ross. 1979. "American Labor Violence: Its Causes, Character and Outcome." In *Violence in America: Historical and Comparative Perspectives*, edited by Hugh Davis Graham and Ted Robert Gurr, 187–241. Beverly Hills: Sage.

Tai To, Lee. 1995. "ASEAN and the South China Sea Conflict." *Pacific Review* 8, No. 3:531–543.

Talisayon, Serafin. 1996. "Values in Our Quest for Freedom and Their Application for Future Development." In *Peace and Tolerance: Values Education through History,* edited by , Lourdes R. Quisumbing and Felice P. Sta. Maria. Manila: UNESCO National Commission of the Philippines.

Tapper, Richard, ed. 1983. *The Conflict of Tribe and State in Iran and Afghanistan.* London: Croom Helm.

Thant, Myo, Ming Tang, and Hiroshi Kakazu, ed. 1995. *Growth Triangles in Asia: A New Approach to Regional Economic Cooperation.* Hong Kong: Published for the Asian Development Bank by Oxford University Press.

Thomas, Christopher. 1997. "Taliban rout ends Islamabad's dream." *The Australian*, 4 June.

Toffler, Alvin. 1981. *The Third Wave.* New York: Bantam Books.

Tsang, Donald. 1998. "Bonds Can Free Asia's Economy." *The Wall Street Journal*, July 22, A14.

U.P. Center for Integrative and Development Studies. 1997. The SPCD, A Response to the Controversy. Program on Peace Conflict Resolution and Human Rights and the Mindanao Studies Program.

Valencia, Mark. 1995. "China and the South China Sea Disputes." *Adelphi Paper* 298. Oxford: Oxford University Press.

Wanandi, Yusuf. 1994. "The Future of ARF and CSAP in the Regional Security Architecture." Paper presented at the 8th Asia Pacific Roundtable, June 5–8, Kuala Lumpur.

Weiner, Myron. 1996. "Bad Neighbours, Bad Neighbourhoods, An Inquiry into the Causes of Refugee Flows." *International Security* 21, No. 1:5–42.

Whitehead, Alfred North. 1929, 1967. *The Aims of Education.* New York: Macmillan.

Willets, Peter. 1993. *Transnational Actors and Changing World Order.* Occasional paper Series No. 17. Yokohama: International Peace Research Institute Meigaku (PRIME).

Wolf, Martin. 1998. "Ins and Outs of Capital Flows." *Financial Times,* July 16, p. 15.

Wongsa Khamdee and Suwit Laohasiriwong. 1996. *Synthesis of Experiences and Documentary Research on Conflict Management in Thailand.* Khon Khaen: Institute for Dispute Resolution. (In Thai)

Woods, Lawrence. 1993. *Asia-Pacific Diplomacy: Non-Governmental Organisations and International Relations.* Vancouver: University of British Columbia Press.

Yousaf, Mohammed, and Mark Adkin. 1992. *The Bear Trap: Afghanistan's Untold Story.* London: Mark Cooper.

Zakaria, F. 1994. "Culture is Destiny—A Conversation with Lee Kuan Yew." *Foreign Affairs* 73, No. 2:102–126.

INDEX

DATE DUE

JAN ~~? 2002~~

APR ~~9 2004~~

APR ~~2006~~

APR 1 4 2008

Printed
in USA

HIGHSMITH #45230